Teachers Matter

Professional Learning

Series Editors: Ivor Goodson and Andy Hargreaves

The work of teachers has changed significantly in recent years and now, more than ever, there is a pressing need for high quality professional development. This timely new series examines the actual and possible forms of professional learning, professional knowledge, professional development and professional standards that are beginning to emerge and be debated at the beginning of the twenty-first century. The series will be important reading for teachers, teacher educators, staff developers and policy makers throughout the English-speaking world.

Published and forthcoming titles:

Elizabeth Campbell: *The Ethical Teacher*
Martin Coles and Geoff Southworth: *Developing Leadership*
Ivor Goodson: *Professional Knowledge, Professional Lives*
Andy Hargreaves: *Teaching in the Knowledge Society*
Alma Harris: *Improving Schools through Teacher Leadership*
Garry Hoban: *Teacher Learning for Educational Change*
Bob Lingard, Debra Hayes, Martin Mills and Pam Christie: *Leading Learning*
Judyth Sachs: *The Activist Teaching Profession*

Teachers Matter
Connecting work, lives and effectiveness

Christopher Day, Pam Sammons, Gordon Stobart, Alison Kington and Qing Gu

 Open University Press

Open University Press
McGraw-Hill Education
McGraw-Hill House
Shoppenhangers Road
Maidenhead
Berkshire
England
SL6 2QL

email: enquiries@openup.co.uk
world wide web: www.openup.co.uk

and Two Penn Plaza, New York, NY 10121–2289, USA

First published 2007

A catalogue record of this book is available from the British Library

ISBN–10 0335 220 045 (pb) 0335 220 053 (hb)
ISBN–13 978 0335 220 045 (pb) 978 0335 220 052 (hb)

Library of Congress Cataloging-in-Publication Data
CIP data applied for

Typeset by RefineCatch Limited, Bungay, Suffolk
Printed in Poland by OZGraf S.A.
www.polskabook.pl

The **McGraw·Hill** Companies

Contents

List of figures and tables

Tables

Series editors' preface

Teaching today is increasingly complex work, requiring the highest standards of professional practice to perform it well (Hargreaves and Goodson 1996). It is the core profession, the key agent of change in today's knowledge society. Teachers are the midwives of that knowledge society. Without them, or their competence, the future will be malformed and stillborn. In the United States, George W. Bush's educational slogan has been to leave no child behind. What is clear today in general, and in this book in particular, is that leaving no child behind means leaving no teacher or leader behind either. Yet, teaching too is also in crisis, staring tragedy in the face. There is a demographic exodus occurring in the profession as many teachers in the ageing cohort of the Boomer generation are retiring early because of stress, burnout or disillusionment with the impact of years of mandated reform on their lives and work. After a decade of relentless reform in a climate of shaming and blaming teachers for perpetuating poor standards, the attractiveness of teaching as a profession has faded fast among potential new recruits.

Teaching has to compete much harder against other professions for high caliber candidates than it did in the last period of mass recruitment – when able women were led to feel that only nursing and secretarial work were viable options. Teaching may not yet have reverted to being an occupation for 'unmarriageable women and unsaleable men' as Willard Waller described it in 1932, but many American inner cities now run their school systems on high numbers of uncertified teachers. The teacher recruitment crisis in England has led some schools to move to a four-day week; more and more schools are run on the increasingly casualized labour of temporary teachers from overseas, or endless supply teachers whose quality busy administrators do not always have time to monitor (Townsend 2001). Meanwhile in the Canadian province of Ontario, in 2001, hard-nosed and hard-headed reform strategies led in a single year to a decrease in applications to teacher education programmes in faculties of education by 20–25 per cent, and a drop in a whole grade level of accepted applicants.

Amid all this despair and danger though, there remains great hope and some reasons for optimism about a future of learning that is tied in its vision to an empowering, imaginative and inclusive vision for teaching as well. The educational standards movement is showing visible signs of over-reaching itself as people are starting to complain about teacher shortages in schools, and the loss of creativity and inspiration in classrooms (Hargreaves *et al.* 2001). There is growing international support for the resumption of more humane middle years philosophies in the early years of secondary school that put priority on community and engagement, alongside curriculum content and academic achievement. School districts in the United States are increasingly seeing that high quality professional development for teachers is absolutely indispensable to bringing about deep changes in student achievement (Fullan 2001). In England and Wales, policy documents and White Papers are similarly advocating for more 'earned autonomy', and schools and teachers are performing well (e.g. DfES 2001). Governments almost everywhere are beginning to speak more positively about teachers and teaching – bestowing honour and respect where blame and contempt had prevailed in the recent past.

The time has rarely been more opportune or more pressing to think more deeply about what professional learning, professional knowledge and professional status should look like for the new generation of teachers who will shape the next three decades of public education. Should professional learning accompany increased autonomy for teachers, or should its provision be linked to the evidence of demonstrated improvements in pupil achievement results? Do successful schools do better when the professional learning is self-guided, discretionary and intellectually challenging, while failing schools or schools in trouble benefit from required training in the skills that evidence shows can raise classroom achievement quickly? And does accommodating professional learning to the needs of different schools and their staffs constitute administrative sensitivity and flexibility (Hopkins *et al.* 1997), or a kind of professional development apartheid (Hargreaves, forthcoming)? These are the kinds of questions and issues which this series on professional learning sets out to address (M. J Coles and G. Southworth 2005, pp. xi–xii).

A central value position in all of the books in this series has turned on the critical question addressed in this book of *Teachers Matter*. There are of course a huge range of reasons why teachers matter but Day *et al.* put it very succinctly in their first chapter. Teachers matter because 'no educational reform has achieved success without teachers committing themselves to it: No school has improved without the commitment of teachers: And although some students learn despite their teachers, most learn because of them. . .'

This statement should provide enormous pause for thought to all those reformers pursuing the centralized agendas that have aimed to reform schooling. These reforms have often proceeded without collaboration with the teaching force and at times, almost willfully, in spite of teachers' belief systems and vocational purposes. The book *Teachers Matter* seeks to put teachers right back into the centre of the equation and in this act of moral re-centring hopes to reinvigorate an educational enterprise which at the moment seems to be too often unfocused and unfulfilling for the teaching force.

The project which is reported in this book took place between 2001 and 2005 and hence we have a very contemporary updating of VITAE (Variations in Teachers' Work, Lives and their Effects on Pupils). The authors quote Fielding, a commentator whose moral concern for schooling has been well evidenced over many decades, he says: 'The high performing school is an organization in which the person is used for the sake of the functional: staff are valued; the community is valued but selectively according to their power and influence and primarily the instrumental purposes within the context of the market place.' This, he says means that the personal is used for the functional and that 'Students are included or excluded, valued or not, primarily on whether they contribute to the organization and performance of the school.' Given this increasingly functionalist interpretation of teacher performance it was vital that the central government implementing such new initiatives should look at the effect on the teacher's life and work. It is to the credit of the Department for Education and Science that the VITAE project was initiated at a time when new central government policies on continuing professional development were being implemented. In March 2001 the first National Strategy for Teacher's CPD was launched and soon after the VITAE project began work.

One of the most impressive sections of this comprehensive book is the review of the literature in chapter two on studying teachers' work and lives. This is an extremely professional summary of the work in this area and adds a great deal to our synoptic understanding of this emerging field of study.

The research methods employed in the VITAE project – what the authors call a synergistic approach – is detailed very helpfully in chapter three. In this chapter they show how an initial audit of local authorities identified the range of representative schools which were later case studied and also they detail the initial teacher questionnaire survey which allowed for a degree of strategic and thematic focusing to take place in the research work. The essence of the research though is the case studies that were undertaken and these provide wonderful insights and illuminations to the study of how teachers' life and work, school context and reform initiative interact in complex and indeterminate ways. The subtlety of the approach to the teacher's life cycle and the treatment of the emotional intensity of teaching are both well achieved. This is important work that extends the work on the teacher's lifecycle pioneered by Michael Huberman and taken up by Pat Sikes and Lynda Measor. The research here extends a great deal our understanding of the teacher's lifecycle and the emotions of teaching. If there is a heartland to the VITAE project, it is in this area, for we begin to understand the way in which the teacher's commitment and vocational purpose are intimately interlinked in the hinterland between life and work.

As we work our way through the book the evidence in this field of the teacher's personal and professional domain and the evidence on school context builds up a remarkable picture of the complexity of schooling and any reform process which aims to change the nature of schooling. We move through this data with exemplary commentaries by the authors who in a light-handed but subtle way point to the implications of their data for both existing and future policy making. The work is both incisive but restrained and understanding in the way that it draws its ultimate conclusions. This is nowhere clearer than in the final conclusion where they say:

> 'Effective teaching is physically and emotionally demanding. What is required by policy-makers, LAs and school leaders in particular, is a better understanding of how teachers manage the complex interaction of a range of professional, personal and situated mediating factors and other influencing factors (i.e. teachers' professional life phases and identities) to sustain their commitment, resilience and effectiveness over time.'

Sensitivity to these issues is imperative and in some cases overdue if the issues of teacher retention and indeed teacher recruitment are to be dealt with successfully. Too often insensitivity to these issues has led to a paradox of performativity. Namely that the reforms which aim to increase teacher performativity by defining criteria and accountability structures have actually led to a process where creative teachers are driven out. Hence in trying to increase the competence of teaching insensitive and over bureaucratized reform procedures have actually ended up driving out the creative vanguard of the teaching profession. In rooting out the incompetent teacher they have ended up driving out the most highly competent teachers. This sort of paradox can be found at work where insensitive performativity structures have been implemented in a variety of countries. A reflective reading of *Teachers Matter* would I think allow more carefully calibrated reform initiatives to emerge.

There is much to ponder in this book for policy makers, but also for all of us interested in the complex conundrum of schooling. It is as we know no easy task to increase the performance of schooling and many different approaches have been tried over the decades. The one truth, which this book so elegantly epitomizes, is that when reforms ignore the teacher's sense of vocational and public purpose the reforms without exception falter and ultimately fail. This above all is the lesson of *Teachers Matter* and the testimonies in this book add great weight to this argument.

Ivor Goodson and Andrew Hargreaves

References

Coles, M.J. and Southworth, G. (2005) *Developing Leadership: Creating the Schools of Tomorrow*, with a preface by A. Hargreaves and I. Goodson (Open University Press: Maidenhead).

DfES (Department for Education and Skills) (2001) *Achieving Success* (London: HMSO).

Fullan, M. (2001) *Leading in a Culture of Change* (San Francisco: Jossey-Bass/ Wiley).

Hargreaves, A. (2003) *Teaching in the Knowledge Society* (New York: Teachers College Press).

Hargreaves, A. and Goodson, I. (1996) Teachers' professional lives: aspirations and actualities, in I. Goodson and A. Hargreaves (eds), *Teachers' Professional Lives* (New York: Falmer Press).

Hargreaves, A., Earl, L., Moore, S. and Manning, S. (2001) *Learning to Change: Beyond Teaching Subjects and Standards* (San Francisco: Jossey-Bass/Wiley).

Hopkins, D., Harris, A. and Jackson, D. (1997) Understanding the schools capacity for development: growth states and strategies, *School Leadership and Management*, 17(3): 401–11.

Townsend, J. (2001) It's bad – trust me, I teach there, *Sunday Times*, 2 December.

Waller, W. (1932) *The Sociology of Teaching* (New York: Russell & Russell).

List of contributors

Christopher Day (co-ordinating author) is Professor of Education in the Teacher and Leadership Research Centre, School of Education, University of Nottingham, Co-ordinating Director of the VITAE project, a Board Member of the International Council for the Education of Teachers (ICET) and Adjunct Professor of the Chinese University of Hong Kong. Recent publications include: *Developing Teachers and Teaching: the Challenges of Lifelong Learning* (1999), Falmer; *International Handbook of CPD* (Editor with J. Sachs, 2004); *A Passion for Teaching* (2004) Routledge; and *Successful School Principalship: International Perspectives* (2007). He is editor of *Teachers and Teaching: Theory and Practice*, coeditor of the *Educational Action Research International Journal* and a member of the Advisory Board for a number of international journals.

Pam Sammons is Professor in Education in the Teacher and Leadership Research Centre, School of Education at the University of Nottingham. She is Codirector of the VITAE project (DfES funded). Pam joined the School of Education in 2004; previously she was a Professor at the Institute of Education, University of London and Co-ordinating Director of the International School Effectiveness and Improvement Centre (1999–2004). Pam has led many research studies involving both primary and secondary schools; she also has interests in the evaluation of policy initiatives. Publications include: *School Effectiveness: Coming of Age in the twenty-first Century* (1999), Swets & Zeitlinger; *Improvement through Inspection: an Evaluation of the Impact of Ofsted's Work* (with Matthews, London Ofsted/Institute of Education. HMI 2244, 2004); England: a Country Report (in Hans Dobert, Eckhard Klieme and Wendeline Sroka (eds) *Conditions of School*

Performance in Seven Countries – a Quest for Understanding the International Variation of PISA Results, Waxmann, 2004).

Gordon Stobart is Reader in Education at the Institute of Education, University of London. He is Codirector of the VITAE project and recently evaluated the Key Stage 3 Strategy Pilot (DfES funded). He is a member of the Assessment Reform Group, which campaigns for more use of formative assessment in teaching and learning, and editor of the journal *Assessment in Education: Principals, Practice and Policy*. He previously worked as a secondary school teacher and as an educational psychologist before moving into educational research. Publications include: *Assessment: a Teacher's Guide to the Issues* (3rd edition, 1997).

Alison Kington is a Senior Research Fellow in the School of Education, University of Nottingham. She is a Principal Research Officer on the VITAE project. Alison has previously been involved in, and led, a range of research projects at the National Foundation for Educational Research (NFER) and the Roehampton Institute where her research has been predominantly in the areas of classroom relationships and interaction, the professional development of teachers, and the use of new technologies to enhance teaching and learning. Prior to that she worked as a primary school teacher.

Qing Gu is a Research Fellow in the School of Education, University of Nottingham. She is a Research Officer on the VITAE project. She was Assistant Lecturer in the School of Foreign Studies of Anhui University, China, where she was also a member of a three-year Department for International Development (DFID) teacher education project. She has researched and published in language education, teacher education and comparative education in both national and international journals. Her current research interests are teacher professional development and intercultural education.

Acknowledgements

We would like to thank first the teachers, headteachers and students who participated in the VITAE research project which forms a basis for this book. We wish to thank also those in the Department for Education and Skills (DfES) who were responsible for creating the opportunity for the research to be carried out. There are relatively few longitudinal government funded national educational studies in England which seek to understand more closely the complex contexts in which policies are implemented. There are many individuals, also, who made valuable direct and indirect contributions to our thinking, and we have acknowledged them in our report of the research. However, we wish to acknowledge again the unstinting support of Hayley McCalla, who patiently incorporated the many major and minor amendments to the text and whose commitment, resilience and effectiveness was an example to us all.

one

Why teachers matter: policy agendas and social trends

Introduction

Teachers matter. They matter to the education and achievement of their students and, more and more, to their personal and social well-being. No educational reform has achieved success without teachers committing themselves to it; no school has improved without the commitment of teachers; and although some students learn despite their teachers, most learn because of them – not just because of what and how they teach, but, because of who they are as people.

> when you go back to a list of qualities that made your best teachers so effective, you probably noticed that so much of what made them significant in your life was not what they did, but who they were as human beings . . .
>
> (Zehm and Kottler 1993: 2)

A recent OECD report (2005), like most research on school effectiveness and improvement, identifies the crucial role of the teacher to the social and economic well-being of society. Ask most parents and they will tell you that it is the teacher who matters most in the education of their children.

So the rhetoric is clear. Teachers matter. Usually, the conversation then turns to what kinds of teachers we need, and, while lip service will be given to the need for teachers who care and who 'make a difference' to the education of the whole student, it soon focuses upon 'standards', 'competencies' and skills required of today's knowledge workers. Moreover, in today's results driven environment, it is those aspects of teaching and learning which can be most easily quantified, benchmarked and used as comparators which define how well teachers are perceived to do their work.

What marks teachers out as good, or better than good, is not only their content knowledge and pedagogical skills. It is their commitment to their teaching, their students and their learning and achievement. Yet, although it is widely acknowledged that commitment and resilience are indispensable to high quality teaching, we do not know much about how these are sustained, or not sustained, in times of change.

The VITAE project

The VITAE research project (Variations in Teachers' Work, Lives and their Effects on Pupils) was commissioned by the Department for Education and Skills (DfES) in order to explore variations in teachers' lives, work and effectiveness in different phases of their careers. It was conducted between 2001 and 2005 and involved a nationally representative sample of 300 primary (Key Stage 1 and 2) and secondary (Key Stage 3 English and mathematics) teachers working in 100 schools across seven local authorities (LAs). The schools themselves were selected to be representative in terms of levels of social disadvantage and attainment. The research examined influences upon and between teachers' professional and personal lives, identities, the school contexts in which they worked and their effectiveness.

So far as we know VITAE is the most comprehensive, large-scale and extensive study of teachers' work and lives and the first to explore associations between these and effectiveness over time. The findings have much to offer in considering issues of teacher preparation, quality and standards, teacher retention, and in relation to these, the factors that enable (or do not enable) teachers to build and sustain their sense of identity, commitment, resilience and effectiveness.

In conceiving and conducting the research, we recognized that definitions of effectiveness lie both in teachers' perceptions of their own effectiveness, and their impact on pupils' progress and attainments. The data thus provided the possibility of examining both relative effectiveness (one teacher's effectiveness in relation to another who has similar experience and works in similar organizational contexts), i.e. how their 'performance' in terms of pupil progress and attainment compares and why; and relational effectiveness (how one teacher is and how (s)he performs in relation to his/her past history). It was, therefore, able to focus upon two key policy agendas. One relates to recruitment and retention, and the other to the 'standards' agenda. As the chapters in this book will show, the data suggest that there are associations between the two.

The aim of VITAE was to assess variations over time in teacher effectiveness, between different teachers and for particular teachers, and to identify factors that contributed to variations. Key questions were:

1 Does teacher effectiveness vary from one year to another, in terms of different pupil outcomes, and do teachers necessarily become more effective over time?
2 What are the roles of biography and identity?
3 How do school and/or department leadership influence teachers' practice and their effectiveness? What particular kinds of influence does continuing professional development (CPD) have on teachers' effectiveness?
4 Are teachers equally effective for different pupil groups or is there differential effectiveness relating (for example) to gender or socio-economic status?
5 Do the factors which influence effectiveness vary for teachers working in different school cultures, contexts, or for different kinds of outcomes?
6 Do factors influencing teachers' effectiveness vary across different sectors (primary and secondary) and different age groups (Key Stage 1, 2 and 3)?

National reform policies and their effects

Teaching is no longer, if it ever was, an activity which takes place behind closed doors. It is subject to central control and direction, is answerable to multiple agencies and has to respond to the expectations and needs of a rapidly changing society. For these reasons, if we are to understand variations in teachers' work, lives and effectiveness, it is important to sketch the broad policy and social contexts, as well as the particular school contexts which influence them.

This part of the chapter takes a selective look at the central government policies, and social challenges in England, which directly impacted on the working lives of the teachers in the project. We do not attempt a comprehensive account. Other studies provide this in more detail (Docking 1999, 2000; Fielding 2001; Galton and McBeath 2002; Lawton 2005). Rather, we indicate the range of initiatives which teachers had to manage, between 2001 and 2005 – the course of the project. The most immediate of these were the consequence of policy interventions from a government which has made education a priority in its attempts to raise standards through improving schools, teaching and learning. Many of these have been based on 'informed prescription'. These policy interventions have taken place in the wider context of a changing society in which some social, and generational, divisions are widening. There has been considerable discussion and criticism of the impact of market-based reforms in England (Gewirtz *et al.* 1995; Thrupp 2003):

> Despite all the reforms, all the changes and initiatives, the same issues that vexed Callaghan and his advisors are still troubling our schools. There are still concerns about the achievement of a significant minority of young people, about the state of the exam system, about whether standards are being eroded over time, about the quality of practice in our classrooms.
>
> (Revell 2005: 3)

While this observation appears to illustrate the apparent failure of successive reforms to meet the educational needs of society, it might be seen also to suggest that there are continuing changes in the social and economic fabric of society itself, which at the very least make the success of any reform problematic. If reforms themselves continue to focus only upon raising standards of achievement, without taking into account the changing conditions in which teachers teach and students live and learn, then they are unlikely to succeed.

Successive and persisting government policy reforms have for two decades dominated the contemporary realities of teachers. They have changed what it means to train and be educated for teaching and, once qualified, be a teacher, as the focus of control has shifted from the individual to the system managers and as contract has replaced covenant (Bernstein 1996). These initiatives, and the changing conditions in which teachers teach and students live and learn, have combined to place strong 'performativity' and increased workload pressures upon teachers. For example, in England the three terms of Labour government have already seen eight separate Education Acts and hundreds of separate initiatives (Chitty 2004; Walford 2005).

While much of the direct central intervention into what goes on in schools can be traced back to previous Conservative governments, it has continued undiminished under Labour administrations (Lawton 2005). From 1988 onwards, successive governments introduced a range of measures designed to raise education standards system-wide (particularly in literacy and numeracy, and overall public examination results). Key features included for the first time a national curriculum (focusing on a common entitlement for all, with an emphasis on the core subjects of English, mathematics and science) and national assessment at Key Stages associated with different phases and age groups aligned to that curriculum. In addition, regular inspection of schools (on a 4–6-year cycle until 2005 when a shorter but more frequent system with a greater emphasis on self-evaluation was introduced) was instituted from 1993 onwards with the creation of the Office for Standards in Education (Ofsted) using a published common Framework to monitor and evaluate the quality of provision and education standards on a regular basis. Ofsted's self-selected aim was to promote 'improvement through inspection'. The new phenomenon of public inspection, identification of 'failing' schools (later termed those requiring special measures) or those with serious weaknesses, was seen as very stressful by many teachers, particularly during the first cycle of inspections (1993–1998), because of the potential stigma of being publicly labelled as 'failing'.

Schools received national and local guidance material and support from LAs in relation to inspection (including detailed advice on School Development Planning and post-inspection Action Planning), and on the national curriculum and assessment procedures. In addition, teachers were provided with considerable in-service education and professional development opportunities, especially in the core curriculum subjects (English, mathematics and science) and in relation to teacher assessment and feedback.

Open enrolment and parental 'choice' were heralded as ways to increase education providers' responsiveness to the consumer and encourage competition between providers.[1] The Conservative governments, of the period 1988–1996, sought to drive up standards by applying market forces to education, promoting choice and diversity and increasing accountability. National performance tables naming schools' and LAs'[2] results were published annually from 1992 onwards and received much media coverage, being compiled into ranked 'league tables' by newspapers. National inspection led to the public identification of schools with 'poor' performance. These were targeted for intervention and followed up after inspection. If schools did not improve within a specified period, the sanction of closure or 'fresh start' was available.

Action planning, target setting and the monitoring of performance, especially students' attainment levels and progress, and the quality of teaching, remain important features of the English school system. They are intended to serve both an accountability function and to enhance quality by providing pressure for improvement. The introduction of delegated funding under Local Management of Schools from 1990 likewise proved a significant policy shift. Schools were given greater autonomy and many welcomed their increased financial flexibility. The period 1988 to 1997, therefore, involved both decentralization of funding and weakening of the role of local education authorities, and centralization with the triple strands of national curriculum, assessment and inspection.

Considerable consistency in many aspects of education policy was evident after the election of a New Labour government in 1997. Education was identified as a key policy lever to enhance life chances for disadvantaged groups. Key aspects of Conservative policy (national curriculum and assessment, national inspection, local management of schools, publication of schools' results) were retained, although more support and guidance was provided for schools to promote improvement and there was an increased emphasis on equity, and on using education to combat social exclusion.

More performance data were provided and target setting and benchmarking using national assessment and examination data were encouraged. More recently, contextual value added indicators have been further developed to explore pupil progress and are now included in national tables of schools' results. A National Literacy Strategy (NLS) followed by a National Numeracy Strategy (NNS) was introduced in 1998 and 1999 respectively, with primary schools expected to teach daily literacy and numeracy lessons, and from 2001 the Key Stage 3 strategy focused on raising attainment in the lower secondary years (11–14) in English, mathematics, science and information and communications technology (ICT).

The Labour government committed itself to increase education spending in real terms year on year, although significant increases to schools were not implemented until 1999 onwards. Early years education and care also received a considerable emphasis and there has been a significant expansion of pre-school places. Class sizes were reduced to a maximum of 30 students for Key Stage 1 (ages rising 5-years to 7-years plus). Initiatives included better pay, the introduction of new career routes for 'advanced or expert' teachers, more classroom assistants, professional development and school improvement funds. More resources for continuing professional development (CPD) were made available to schools and, a major capital building programme to upgrade school buildings and infrastructure was instituted.

The education policy reforms during the 1988–1997 period thus reduced the power and functions of LAs but gave greater autonomy to schools and powers to their governing bodies, while increasing their accountability for educational standards. Although the Conservative Government's introduction of grant maintained status of schools (outside LA control) and plans to increase the number of selective grammar schools were removed, a policy of increasing diversity of provision in terms of school type has been pursued further since 1997 (for example, through the introduction of Specialist and Beacon schools and more recently City Academies). The establishment of more faith schools has received official encouragement. LAs were given responsibilities for school improvement but remained subject to inspection by Ofsted and could be privatized if standards were judged to be poor.

From the 1988 Education Act onwards, what went on in classrooms moved from a *laissez-faire*, locally devised, curriculum to centrally regulated curriculum and assessment systems (Stobart and Stoll 2005). England is now unusual in the extent to which both content and approaches to teaching are centrally spelled out and then assessed through national tests. During the same period there has been increasing fiscal deregulation of schools and marginalizing of local authorities. Ball (2001) has pointed out that some of these continuities were part of global trends, particularly the principles of:

1 Choice and competition.
2 Autonomy and performativity.
3 Centralization and prescription (Ball 2001: 46).

The Labour Government's rationale for these was based on what Michael Barber (2001), then head of the School and Effectiveness Unit at the Department for Education and Science (DfES), called 'informed prescription' which, it was claimed, was based on evidence and good practice – though this basis of such claims was not always made explicit (Stobart and Stoll 2005). This followed the eras of 'uninformed professionalism' and 'uninformed prescription' – which, it is claimed, ended with the election of the Labour Government. The use and validity of these interpretations has been challenged (Dainton 2005) and they have been described as a: '... distorted and politically partisan an account of recent educational history as one is likely to find' (Alexander 2004: 13). Nevertheless, they have stuck. The VITAE project was initiated by DfES in anticipation of the next stage – when informed prescription would give way to 'informed professionalism' in which, the rhetoric suggested, teachers would have more say in their professional development and practice.

Goodson and Numan (2002) have observed that like Britain, Sweden and New Zealand have also witnessed an era of the standards movement and similar 'development patterns of political and administration control over teachers'. The same applies to Australia, the USA and many other countries worldwide. Hargreaves has noted that teachers' work is becoming increasingly intensified, with teachers expected to respond to greater pressures and comply with multiplying innovations under conditions that are at best stable and at worst deteriorating (1995, 2000, 2003). It is little wonder that teaching in the twenty-first century is rated as one of the most stressful professions (Kyriacou 2000; PriceWaterhouseCoopers 2001; Nash 2005). Fielding (2006) argues that in the 'high performance' model of schooling which now dominates the policy landscape in England, 'the personal is used for the functional: students are included or excluded, valued or not, primarily on whether they contribute to organizational performance of the school'. The same may be said of teachers. He continues:

> The high performing school is an organization in which the personal is used for the sake of the functional: staff are valued; the community is valued, but selectively according to their power and influence and primarily for instrumental purposes within the context of the marketplace.
>
> (Fielding 2006)

Performativity agendas, coupled with the continuing monitoring of the efficiency with which teachers are expected to implement externally generated initiatives, have had five consequences. They have:

1   Implicitly encouraged teachers to comply uncritically (e.g. teach to the test so that teaching becomes more a technical activity and thus, more susceptible to control).
2   Challenged teachers' substantive identities.
3   Reduced the time teachers have to connect with, care for and attend to the needs of individual students.
4   Threatened teachers' sense of agency and resilience.
5   Challenged teachers' capacities to maintain motivation, efficacy and thus, commitment.

More recently, reforms have also:

1   Provided additional time and resource to enable teachers to manage their teaching and engage in continuing professional development (workforce reform agenda).
2   Ensured that teachers are rewarded for leadership responsibilities which are directly connected to teaching and learning review (TLR).
3   Continued to demand more of teachers (e.g. the Every Child Matters agenda).

To date, however, there is little independent evidence which suggests that levels of morale and commitment have been raised. Indeed, there can be no doubts that reforms – particularly those which are poorly managed – at least temporarily disturb the relative stability of teachers' work and, in some cases, their beliefs, practices and self-efficacy, and that in general they challenge existing notions of professionalism (Goodson and Hargreaves 1996; Helsby 1999; Sachs 2003; Bottery 2005).

Much research related to the effects of centralized reform efforts has been produced by those who are critical of the reforms themselves, has tended to be small scale, and has focused upon particular groups of teachers for whom reform is difficult and perhaps unacceptable. Jeffrey and Woods (1996) conducted research on teachers under stress in what they called a 'low trust' society in England; and Kelchtermans (2005) has written of teachers' vulnerability. Similar research has been conducted in Australia by Dinham and Scott (1996, 2000); in Canada by Burke and Greenglass (1993, 1995); in America by Blasé (1986) and Farber (1991); and in England by Nias (1999).

Essentially, research of the kind exemplified above presents potentially depressing portraits of the effects of reform upon teachers, perhaps because of the researchers' own values and perhaps because of their focus, important though it may be. Self-reports by teachers, in response to surveys at least in

part, mirror these (*Guardian* 2003). While such research has been challenged by school effectiveness and improvement studies, neither the former
nor the latter have been able to take a broad and deep longitudinal perspective. Although the reality is that most teachers do adapt or at least survive,
and do not leave the profession, little is known about variations in their lives
and work in changing times, and how these affect their effectiveness. Such
knowledge would not only be useful to teachers themselves, but also to
school leaders and everyone with a stake in quality education.

VITAE teachers' responses

Central policies impact on many areas of teachers' work and teachers vary in
their attitudes towards them. The key policies in place, or implemented,
during the VITAE project will be discussed in relation to curriculum and
pedagogy; accountability and assessment; schools and pupils; and conditions
for professional development.

In a nationally representative survey conducted in the first phase of our
research, 'DfES policy and initiatives' were rated as having the most negative
impact on teaching, along with Ofsted and the media portrayal of the
teaching profession. Negativity, about these external factors, tended to be
greatest for teachers with 16–30 years experience, who may have had
experience of earlier less directive policy contexts. Teachers with 0–7 years
experience were much less likely to identify policy as a negative issue, especially those in primary schools. Such generational differences (Goodson
et al. 2006) will be explored in some detail in later chapters.

Assessment and accountability

The importance of the National Curriculum test results, and examination
results in secondary schools, continues to permeate the culture of most
schools as they seek to get the best results possible. The accountability pressures come from local and national targets, media coverage of 'league tables'
and the use of results as the basis for Ofsted's Performance and Assessment
(PANDA) reports. The provision of central funding for 'booster classes',
intended for pupils on the key level boundaries, also reinforces this message.
Limited progress in reaching government targets has resulted in further
efforts and resources to boost performance.

VITAE project teachers were particularly aware of these accountability
pressures because they taught classes in key years (Years 2, 6 and English
and mathematics in Year 9). Some reported that disappointing test results
had a negative impact on their feelings of self-efficacy, though good results

sometimes gave a boost. There were some modifications to National Curriculum tests during the project, with Key Stage 3 English being the most substantial, but these did not involve major changes to teaching.

School accountability makes National Curriculum assessments a key indicator of effectiveness for teachers. This was especially the case for Year 6 teachers, since good Key Stage 2 results were seen as vital to a school's position and reputation. Our Year 6 teachers were very aware of their responsibilities and the pressure to get good results. From our early teacher surveys there was a strong sense that the need for 'paper evidence' related to assessment and, more general 'accountability' information was one of the most negative aspects of teachers' work.

The emphasis on performance management, target setting and accountability as levers for improvement has been strongly criticized by some educators who are worried that teachers' creativity and professionalism has been undermined, and there are regular calls to abolish school league tables and reduce or limit national assessment, especially at Key Stage 1 (for 7-year-olds). There are also concerns that the emphasis on the core curriculum subjects, assessed at the various Key Stages, has endangered the provision of a broadly balanced curriculum, especially at the primary level, and made school less 'fun' for students and teachers. It has been suggested that the time devoted to music, physical education and art/drama has been eroded in English primary schools in particular, though reliable statistics to demonstrate this are not available. Research on primary schools in the 1970s and 1980s does not lend much support to the view that the majority of children then experienced a broader or more balanced curriculum (indeed many criticisms of the 'narrow elementary' curriculum in many primary schools, before the introduction of a national curriculum were made).

Teacher recruitment, retention and morale are also areas where concerns have been raised, with a perceived erosion of teachers' professional responsibilities and autonomy, and increased workloads (especially in relation to new initiatives in education, and to pupil assessment, monitoring, target setting and recording). These are seen as factors that can create excessive stress and lead to the exit from schools of a significant number of qualified teachers, within the first five years after training. Ofsted inspection is often cited as an additional burden and source of anxiety for teachers. While, overall, there are currently more teachers in post in English schools than previously, and recruitment to initial teacher education courses is strong, the recruitment of teachers to weaker schools and those serving disadvantaged communities, however, can be difficult, especially for shortage subjects (such as science and mathematics). The high costs of living in some cities, particularly London, are seen as a deterrent to teachers working in some areas of high challenge. Initiatives to improve access to affordable housing and reward teachers working in challenging circumstances may be important to help improve the supply of teachers, and thus the quality of education in urban areas in the longer term.

Curriculum and pedagogy

The main policy impact, on primary teachers during the project, came from the National Literacy Strategy (NLS), launched in 1998, and the National Numeracy Strategy (NNS), which followed a year later. Judged by its Canadian evaluators as 'the most ambitious large-scale reform initiative in the world' (Earl *et al.* 2001: 11) it specified in detail both the English and mathematics curriculum and was strongly directive in its guidance to teachers about how it should be 'delivered' – including time allocations, for example 'the literacy hour'. By the start of the VITAE project this had become an accepted part of a primary teacher's work.

The evaluators had cautioned in their final report that 'after four years, many see NLS and NNS as needing to be re-energized: that the early momentum and excitement have lessened and a new booster would be helpful' (Earl *et al.* 2003: 9). Coupled with criticism about the way the curriculum and teaching were being narrowed by the emphasis on English and mathematics test results and, that learning was increasingly less enjoyable (Galton and McBeath 2002), this re-energizing was promoted by *Excellence and Enjoyment* (DfES 2003). This renewal policy was launched in autumn 2006. While the Primary Strategy it introduced, encouraged a broader view of the curriculum, and more imaginative approaches to teaching and learning in general in primary schools, for VITAE teachers with Year 6 classes (pupils aged 10–11 in their last year of primary school), the focus remained on preparing for national tests, 'the SATS', and a recognition that the curriculum had to be restricted in order to do this. For teachers of Year 2 classes (pupils aged 6–7), there was a shift later in the project away from national tests to supported teacher assessment in which tests play a subsidiary role.

The perception by policy-makers that the primary strategies had been successful, led them to turn their attention to Key Stage 3 (ages 11–14). The Key Stage 3 Strategy mathematics and English strands were rapidly introduced in 2001 after a short pilot phase. Several other stands were then added over the next two years. The English and mathematics strands were extensions of the NLS and NNS, and these involved changes to the content of English and mathematics curricula. While the detailed Frameworks for mathematics, based on NNS, were largely welcomed, the English Framework, with its perceived emphasis on word and sentence level literacy (rather than on literature), represented an unwelcome change for many English teachers (Stoll *et al.* 2003). This then evolved into the National Secondary Strategy for 11–14. This has placed more emphasis on its use as a whole school improvement strategy, which 'provides a platform for professional development across the school through its emphasis on teaching and learning' (DfES 2005).

Both the Primary and Secondary Strategies had pedagogical implications for teachers. These included, for example, whole class teaching, personalized learning, paying more attention to student learning styles, Assessment for Learning and rigorous target setting. The pace of change and the volume of initiatives, featured in the VITAE survey responses, were often commented upon in the interviews:

> There never seems to be enough time to become fully conversant with new 'policies' and so I always have the feeling of never getting to grips with or completing a task properly.
>
> (primary teacher 2002)

> I think new ideas are good and essential, but unfortunately the government springs from one trend to another without forward planning.
>
> (primary teacher 2002)

Schools and pupils

The 2002 Education Act consolidated many of the structural changes, as well as encouraging the development of extended schooling, which involves schools in providing more flexible services for their local communities. These include extended child care arrangements, as well as offering learning opportunities for adults.

A more widespread policy impact was that of the inclusion agenda. In 1998 the Green Paper, *Excellence for All Children*, discussed the provision for children with special educational needs. A Social Exclusion Unit was set up in the Cabinet Office and, the subsequent Special Educational Needs and Disability Act 2001, ensured that all schools would teach the broad range of students. The requirement for a more inclusive approach, to pupils with special educational needs and/or behaviour problems, was seen as problematic by those teachers who, as a consequence, had such children in their classes. This was particularly the case if there were attendant behaviour problems which made teaching more difficult. A significant number of the VITAE teachers attributed variations in their classroom effectiveness, to the presence of one or more 'disturbed' children in a particular class. There was a strong sense that these children should not have been in the class and that it had disrupted learning for the others.

Concerns with inclusion were further reflected in The Children Act 2004 which was part of the Every Child Matters reform programme, which also included a new requirement for local authorities to promote the educational achievement of 'looked after' children (for example those in local authority care). The vision is one of universal services to which every child has access, and which involve educational professionals working closely with health and social service professionals to provide an integrated, multidisciplinary service. The five Every Child Matters outcomes are:

- Be healthy
- Stay safe
- Enjoy and achieve
- Make a positive contribution
- Achieve economic well-being.

Again, there are major implications for the way teachers see their work. These outcomes are substantially different from the narrower results driven agenda with which many teachers are currently working.

Conditions for professional development

The VITAE project was initiated by DfES at a time when new central government policies on CPD were being implemented. In March 2001 the first national strategy for teachers' CPD was launched. The thrust of this was to increase schools' capacities for effective professional development by building stronger CPD infrastructures in school, as well as informing schools of those CPD practices. It was accompanied by central CPD funding going directly to schools through 'Education Formula Spending'. There was a particular emphasis on the professional development of teachers in their first five years of teaching, as well as an Induction Support Programme for Newly Qualified Teachers. While the funding was devolved, there nevertheless remained a good deal of central guidance. For instance, the Teachers' Standards Framework sets out the standards of practice expected at particular career stages, and suggests supporting developmental activity. So while CPD was made a school-based activity, there was still considerable direction from the centre.

Examples of this can be seen in the centrally devised, but locally delivered, training accompanying major initiatives, such as NLS, NNS and the Key Stage 3 Strategy, which directly impacted on teachers' classroom practices. This has typically been in the form of a 'cascade' model, in which scripted training is regionally disseminated to LA consultants, who are centrally funded, who in turn provide training for teachers in schools, and work alongside them in schools (Stoll *et al.* 2003).

Teachers in the VITAE survey were most negative about the lack of time and opportunity to learn with colleagues and to reflect on practice. The implementation of the National Workforce Agreement (2003), based on the Workforce Remodelling Policy (DfES 2002) has the potential to address some of these issues. The reform stemmed from the PriceWaterhouseCoopers study of teachers' workload (2001) which found that two-thirds of teachers' time was spent on activities other than teaching. As a consequence, the Workforce Agreement was intended to reduce the number of administrative tasks for which teachers are responsible (e.g. collecting dinner money); limit time spent covering for absent colleagues; and guarantee planning, preparation and assessment time.

These changes were beginning to impact positively on some primary teachers by the end of the project. The increased provision of teaching assistants was generally welcomed, though with some reservations about the additional preparation this required and how they were allocated to classes. There was limited application in secondary schools, which mainly used teaching assistants in lower ability classes. While there were some initial grumbles about what teachers were not encouraged to do (e.g. wall displays), there was a welcome for the freeing up of time during the working day and the opportunities this gave for planning, marking and discussion. During the period of the fieldwork there was little evidence, however, of the reduction of routine administrative tasks or workload. Thus, the improved work–life balance, a key feature of the policy, had not yet been realized.

School policies

In England, every school must develop, cost, implement and evaluate school wide SIPs (School Improvement Plans). Included in these are every aspect of the schools' own aspirations for their work; and these are coupled with those of central government and local authority. It is not surprising, then, that policies developed by the schools themselves were seen by VITAE teachers as having an important, and generally positive, impact on teachers' effectiveness. These were often linked to the quality of leadership support teachers received. In secondary schools this was often, also, focused on department level leadership.

Both primary and secondary teachers felt school policies on pupil behaviour had most impact on their teaching in the classroom. For primary teachers, policies on learning support were also very important, as were curriculum policies. For secondary teachers, of whom two-thirds thought pupil behaviour policies were 'highly important', learning support policies were slightly less important than curriculum and banding/setting policies, policies which had been centrally encouraged.

Social trends and challenges

While some of these education policies reflected broader social changes, for example the shift to market forces and the focus on performance, there were other social pressures which cut across these. We now discuss five of these which are indicative of the social challenges which continue to influence teachers' work.

The challenge of disruption

Reports over the last ten years have repeatedly drawn attention to deterioration in student behaviour in classrooms. In 1996, Parsons estimated that over 11,000 pupils from secondary and 1800 from primary schools were excluded, and that this represented a 45 per cent increase between 1993–4 and 1995–6 in primary and an 18 per cent increase in secondary schools (Parsons 1996). Although physical aggression was relatively rare, most teachers have reported verbal abuse and aggression, and the morale-eroding effect of everyday 'low level' disruption of learning, in the form of talking out of turn, avoiding work or preventing other pupils from working – all of these requiring teachers' attention. For example, in 1997, 80 per cent of teachers reported that school violence was a serious threat to morale and, 40 per cent, that schools were 'no longer safe places to work' (NUT 2001; NASUWT 2002; Revell 2005). Myers (2004) also provides evidence of 'teacher bullying' in schools. In 2004, Ofsted reported that half of all secondary school lessons are being disrupted (Ofsted 2004). The Chief Inspector of Schools reported in February 2005, that 9 per cent of secondary schools suffered from 'persistent and unsatisfactory behaviour' – a rise of 50 per cent since 2000 (Source Ofsted); and the national Teacher Support Network (http://www.teachersupport.info) states that 98 per cent of its respondents report verbal abuse and nearly 50 per cent report violence.

In 2001, the Special Educational Needs and Disability Act ensured that all schools would teach the broad range of students. Some of these students have severe emotional and behavioural difficulties and this, according to Ofsted's observations, 'continues to be the hardest test of the inclusion framework' (Ofsted 2004). Furthermore, 'the focus of the teachers' planning was on how the pupils with special educational needs (SEN) could be kept engaged, rather than on what the pupils needed to learn next' (Ofsted 2004).

There are an increasing number of young people who find school to be an uncomfortable learning environment. We cannot write these people off and say they got it wrong. Young people can often be disaffected from school rather than from learning (Munroe 1997).

The challenge of workload

Teachers' workloads have also changed. As government policies have demanded increasing management, monitoring and assessment of teaching and learning, so the number of leadership and management responsibilities have increased. New and extended pastoral and behaviour management systems in secondary schools, for example, have created the need for more staff to participate in leadership roles outside their classrooms, as has encouragement for more collaborative team working and distributed leadership in primary schools. Almost everyone, it seems, now has a leadership responsibility. Inevitably, in a climate of persisting transparency and accountability, bureaucracy has increased and despite the 're-modelling' agenda with the opportunities it presents for increased planning time for teachers, it seems unlikely that workload will decrease significantly in time or, more important, intensity. Indeed, it is now acknowledged that teachers' work is more intensive than in many other occupations. In 2001, primary teachers were working an additional 3–4 hours and secondary teachers an additional 2 hours per week over those worked in 1993 (DfES and PWC 2001). In 2005, accounts by the overwhelming majority of the 300 teachers who participated in the VITAE project suggested that working in the evenings, weekends and holidays was still a regular feature of their work lives (Day *et al.* 2006c), and perceived as necessary simply 'to keep up with the job'.

The challenge of low trust

Arguably, the current organizational climate in schools is based upon distrust of teachers' ability to teach well without being subject to annual public assessment, evaluation and monitoring, and inspection of their work through a series of regulatory devices. Such a climate challenges notions of professional integrity, and promotes the development of what Whitty (2002) has called a 'low trust relationship' between society and its teachers. This is further evidenced through the media, which is generally critical of teachers' work, and through policy groups such as Politeia, which suggested that 'You do not need to be Wittgenstein to teach in a primary school, and its better if you're not' (Lawlor 2004). Michael Barber acknowledged that there was some justification for the teaching profession's sense of, 'anxiety about change, sensitivity to criticism and a sense of being overburdened' (Barber 2001: 32) and coined the term 'earned autonomy' (2001: 38) – earned that is, through improved performance which itself was defined as that which meets government targets related to pupils' performance in national tests.

The challenge of pupils who worry

A recent survey of 40,000 children aged 10–15 years (Schools Health Education Unit (SHE), Exeter, *Young People in 2004*), found that more than one third of girls aged 10 and 11 were afraid of being bullied in school, and one quarter of primary pupils surveyed claimed to have been bullied often or daily in the previous month:

... the proportion of young people who report being afraid to go to school because of bullying has been absolutely flat since we started these surveys (1986). It is disappointing.

(SHE 2004)

A further indication of felt uncertainties by pupils of their own personal and social contexts was their concern about weight (60 per cent of 14–15-year-old girls and over 50 per cent of 12- and 13-year-olds); drugs (up to 60 per cent of older pupils claimed to know someone who took them and 25 per cent claimed to have tried cannabis); painkillers (50 per cent of older girls and 33 per cent of boys reported taking at least one in the previous week); weapons (25 per cent of older boys and 18 per cent of girls stated that their friends carried weapons for protection when they went out); and alcohol (one in ten primary and 25 per cent of boys claimed to have drunk alcohol in the previous week, as did 25 per cent of 13-year-olds and 45 per cent of pupils in Year 10).

Even if these reports are exaggerated, the emerging picture of pupils in schools is one of uncertainty and insecurity; and it is these insecurities which teachers must take into account in their everyday attempts to engage their pupils in learning.

The challenge of changing values

In a report which formed part of the international Schooling for Tomorrow project (OECD 2004), the English Group summarized the results of five national seminars involving a range of senior officers from national training and development organizations, headteachers of schools facing challenging circumstances, school students and senior policy-makers. It found that 'there is a feeling that the location of values has shifted away from family and religion to peer groups and media'; and school leaders reported 'a continuing and growing preoccupation with material wealth' (OECD 2004: 10). The consequences, they suggest, are that:

School remains the only shared space among growing inequality and segregation and, strikingly, disadvantage endures despite the rhetoric of constant change . . . school for many children offers a unique common experience of stability.

(OECD 2004: 11)

When Fukuyama writes about the 'ligatures binding [individuals] in webs of social obligation [being] . . . greatly loosened' (1999: 47), this has implications for the social functions of schools and, therefore, for teachers, in school environments that are socially disadvantaged and with pupils 'whose parents have failed to provide . . . [them] . . . with adequate social capital and are not managing to keep up' (Fukuyama 1999: 259). This is compounded in places where there are diminished opportunities for high quality education caused by problems of staff recruitment, lack of appropriately qualified specialist teachers in key areas, retention, and issues of quality, which, it seems, are becoming permanent features in the landscape of some schools in many countries.

Conclusion

This chapter has sketched the context within which the VITAE teachers, on whom we report in detail over the following chapters, worked. They were at the centre of a complex web of policy, social expectations and local demands. The policy context was one of multiple central and local directives, which directly impacted on what went on in the classroom and on their autonomy. The volume of initiatives and legislation over the last ten years alone meant that they were constantly having to respond to new initiatives, some of which were welcome, many of which were not. The perception of more experienced teachers, who may have previously worked under less constraining conditions, was that the relative loss of autonomy impacted negatively on their work. This was particularly the case for the curriculum and its assessment. At the same time there were strong social influences at work, many of which generated and continue to generate challenges for teachers. Issues of pupil behaviour and social attitude were a particular concern for many, along with the heavy workload demands which their changing professional and social roles placed on them.

These policy and social challenges do not affect all schools and teachers equally. However, together with the challenges of changing child and youth cultures, of a rapidly developing technological world and of increasing professional demands, they are common to all. They provide the 'background noise' for the local contexts in which teachers live and work.

two

Studying teachers' work and lives: research contexts

Introduction

This chapter is in three parts. The first two provide a critical overview of selected literature which informed the research. The third part focuses upon what was known, prior to VITAE, about variations in the development of teachers' effectiveness. From the outset, VITAE brought together research in two areas: mainly quantitative research on teacher (and school) effectiveness on the one hand, and mainly qualitative research on teachers' work and lives on the other. Each of these has, in the majority of cases, been associated with 'paradigm-specific' methods of data collection and analysis. Despite many studies (Mortimore and Watkins 1999; Muijs and Reynolds 2005) and syntheses of research (Brophy and Good 1986; Walberg 1986; Wittrock 1986) on these areas individually, no major research study had examined the interplay between primary and secondary teachers' perceived and relative effectiveness, and their work lives in schools in different socio-economic contexts over an extended period of time. In this part of the chapter, we will explore issues relating to schools, classrooms and pupils from the perspective of the teacher and school effectiveness research. The largely qualitative studies of teachers' beliefs, conditions of work and lives place teachers at the centre of debates on quality and standards. We will explore these in Part 2 of this chapter in order to bring together what is known about influences which affect teachers' work, lives and effectiveness.

School and teacher effectiveness: looking broadly

School and teacher effectiveness research have been characterized by their specific attempts to measure differences between schools, departments or teachers in their impact on pupils' educational outcomes, taking into account differences in the prior attainments and other characteristics of their pupil intakes (Mortimore *et al.* 1988). In this research a more 'effective' school or teacher is defined as one where pupil progress, or other educational outcome are better than that predicted on the basis of intake. In England, Reynolds (1995) was influential in suggesting that the 'touchstone' criterion, for evaluating different educational policies or practices should be their impact on pupil learning outcomes. The choice of these outcome (more accurately, output) measures is of particular importance in thinking about teacher quality, since they have become the criteria by which policy-makers and others judge their effectiveness. Yet this focus on a narrow range of outputs (which takes no account of pupil and teacher background, motivation or individual/collective efficacy, or the effects of social, cultural, economic and organizational contexts in which they work on these) can provide at best only partial indicators of academic effectiveness; and leaves unmeasured other important features, such as social, affective and behavioural aspects.

Campbell (2003) and Kyriakides' (2004) review of research, develops the case for a model of teacher effectiveness in which a broader view of differential effectiveness is incorporated. They identified five problems with existing concepts of teacher effectiveness: undue influence of available techniques upon the concept; emphasis on school (ignoring the role of teacher) effectiveness; tenuous relationship to teacher improvement; narrowness of operational definitions in research; and the development of generic, rather than differentiated, models. As it has continued to develop, and as conceptual and practical associations have been made with school improvement literature, models of educational effectiveness which attempt to demonstrate the nature and direction of links between particular school and classroom processes, and pupil outcomes have been developed. The framework of input-process-output has been commonly adopted, and in recent years the importance of context has also been widely recognized (Teddlie 1994; Sharp and Croxford 2003). The levels involved comprise the individual pupil, the classroom, the school and the school environment (the latter covers matters such as the national or local context).

Sammons' (1996) work in particular demonstrates a more holistic approach, and includes case studies as well as quantitative measures. Effectiveness is seen as a relative and sometimes politically contested term which is outcome, context and time specific. Sammons argues that, in addition to cognitive measures, social and affective outcomes should be studied and that attention should also be given to the equity implications (whether schools or teachers are equally effective for different pupil groups, for example according to gender, ethnicity or socio-economic status (SES)). This area of enquiry is commonly referred to as differential effectiveness. She goes on to suggest that studies of effectiveness should consider three important questions:

1   Effective in promoting **which** student outcomes (cognitive and social affective)?
2   Effective over **what** time period (variations over time including stability of effects, or trends of improvement or decline)?
3   Effective for **whom** (the equity dimension – are effects different for some student groups)?

Thus, although school effectiveness research (SER) continues, by and large, to rely upon data from large samples in order to apply statistical techniques which are significant, it does, nevertheless, acknowledge that schools are best studied as organizations which are made up of nested layers – pupils within classrooms, departments within schools. The most pervasive view on cross-level influences in nested (i.e. multilevel) models of school effectiveness, is that so-called 'higher-level' conditions (e.g. aspects concerning school leadership, policy and organization) in some way facilitate conditions at so-called 'lower-levels' (the quality of teaching and learning in classrooms) which, in turn, have a direct impact on pupils' academic outcomes (Hill and Rowe 1996; Goldstein 1997).

The impact of school context

Studies relating to school and teacher effectiveness are increasingly concerned to explore the impact of context, whether this is at the national or local level. The SES context of a school may also influence teacher, student and community expectations and behaviours. The 10-year Louisiana School Effectiveness study explored low SES context effective schools in comparison with high SES effective schools and identified some differences in approach and teaching strategies (Teddlie and Stringfield 1993). A recent study of 18 high achieving low SES primary schools in Wales (James *et al.* 2006) similarly illustrates the importance of context. Likewise, Reynolds (1995) draws attention to Borich's (1996) analysis of teacher factors that may be necessary to obtain high achievement gains in low versus high SES contexts. Pupils' prior achievement levels are related to SES context, and thus pupils' in schools in low SES areas, on average, are likely to have lower attainment than those in high SES contexts.

Low SES context teacher behaviours:

- Generating a warm and supportive affect by letting children know help is available
- Getting a response, any response, before moving on to new material
- Presenting material in small bits, with a chance to practise before moving on
- Showing how bits fit together before moving on
- Emphasizing knowledge and applications before abstractions, putting the concrete first
- Generating strong structure and well planned transitions
- The use of individual differentiated material
- The use of the experiences of pupils.

High SES context teacher behaviours:

- Requiring extended reasoning
- Posing questions that require associations and generalizations
- Giving difficult material
- The use of projects that require independent judgement, difficult problem-solving and the use of original information
- Encouraging learners to take responsibility for their own learning
- Very rich verbalizing.

In the Netherlands, Luyten (1995) and Luyten and Snijders (1996) have sought to explore this issue, while Hill and Rowe (1996) have conducted analyses in Australia, which seek to separate school and class level or teacher effects. These analyses point to considerable differences in effectiveness between teachers within schools in the primary sector. At the secondary level, the question of variations in teacher effects over time in different SES contexts has not been directly addressed in SER studies, although departmental differences in terms of subject performance have received attention (Harris *et al.* 1996; Sammons *et al.* 1997a). The VITAE study was designed in part to address the potential impact of SES in both primary and secondary phases of schooling, seeking to explore connections between different school contexts and teachers' effectiveness.

A further perspective on school context has been addressed by Muijs *et al.* (2004) who provide a review of the research evidence surrounding schools in difficult and challenging circumstances. Themes emerging from the literature include: a focus on teaching and learning, leadership, creating an information-rich environment, creating a positive school culture, building a learning community, continuing professional development, involving parents, external support and resources. Chapman and Harris (2004) also outline the contemporary research evidence concerning school improvement in challenging contexts. Drawing upon findings from recent studies in the UK, funded by the Department for Education and Skills (DfES) and the

National College for School Leadership (NCSL), their work describes some of the improvement strategies that have been successful in raising achievement in schools in challenging contexts. They argue that school improvement interventions must offer differential strategies for change that fit the particular developmental stage of the school and conclude by suggesting that more fine-grained and differentiated approaches to school improvement are needed that offer more flexibility and choice, particularly for those schools facing difficult or challenging circumstances.

Teachers' classroom activity and pupil learning

While teaching is a behaviour which can be observed, learning is not. It can only be inferred indirectly by attempts to measure and monitor its results in some way, often by seeking to measure change in particular outcomes over a given time period. Moreover, the relationships between teaching and learning may well vary for different learners. As Sammons has observed:

> . . . even when pupils share the same teachers and classroom environment, their classroom experiences and thus their opportunities for learning can often differ (due to different curriculum coverage, expectations, pupil grouping methods etc).
>
> (Sammons 1998: 57)

A large number of sources already synthesize the research on effective teaching (Light and Smith 1971; Bloom 1976; Glass 1977; Gage 1978; Brophy and Good 1986; Walberg 1986; Wittrock 1986). In addition to the extensive research on teaching behaviour, much has been written about effective teaching skills (Perrott 1982; Wragg 1984; Calderhead 1986; Clark and Peterson 1986). These studies note how teachers' effectiveness in the classroom seems to depend on how well teachers modify and change their strategies as lessons proceed.

The Hay McBer (2000) report, *Research into Teacher Effectiveness*, stressed the teacher's role in creating a positive classroom climate. Classroom climate was defined by measuring the collective perceptions of pupils regarding those dimensions of the classroom environment that had a direct impact on their capacity and motivation to learn. The report identified three factors which are particularly significant to maximizing pupils' learning opportunities: lack of disruption; encouragement to engage; and high expectations. Despite criticisms on methodological and theoretical grounds, it should be noted that the main conclusions of the Hay McBer study are in accord with much previous literature in the field of teacher effectiveness.

Conversely, Stoll and Fink (1996) reviewed studies concerning the characteristics of ineffective schools and highlight four aspects: lack of vision; unfocused leadership; dysfunctional staff relationships; ineffective classroom practices.

Fraser's (1989) overview of research syntheses on school and teaching effectiveness with a particular focus on curriculum and classroom environment variables, though limited to quantitative, empirical studies, concludes that no single factor is sufficient (or has an impact on student learning by itself) but rather that combinations of factors must be optimized for improved learning as measured by cognitive gains.

Effectiveness across different curriculum subjects

Relatively few studies have explored whether teachers are equally effective in different areas of the curriculum, and in terms of different types of outcomes (cognitive and social/affective). There is evidence at the primary level that effects differ in reading, mathematics and science (Sammons and Smees 1998) and this suggests that teachers are likely to vary in their success in teaching these different areas.

Much research on teacher effectiveness has concentrated on mathematics and reading performance and was conducted with younger age groups (primary rather than secondary). From his syntheses of reviews, which covered studies in different curriculum areas (mainly reading, mathematics and science), Fraser (1989) concluded that effects are similar in primary, junior high and high school studies and that the findings are fairly robust in size and magnitude.

One school effectiveness study which has addressed the question of variations in GCSE (General Certificate of Secondary Education) subject results at the departmental level is the *Forging Links* study (Sammons *et al.* 1997b). This showed that there is greater stability in overall measures of examination performance than in subject results. It suggested that departmental effects can vary significantly over a three-year period of study, and that this may reflect variations in teacher effectiveness as well as changes in staff and departmental policy and practice. The study also found that common aspects of policy and practice were related to greater effectiveness as measured by overall GCSE performance and subject results. Although the *Forging Links* study did not measure individual teachers' behaviour directly owing to its retrospective research design, head of department ratings of selected aspects of teacher behaviour were collected. These pointed to quality of teaching, academic emphasis, high expectations of students, an absence of staff shortages, positive morale and low levels of staff absence as being related to academic effectiveness.

The limitations of school effectiveness research

The input-process-output model on which much of school effectiveness research is based has been criticized by those who research the nature of teaching and learning, and teachers and learners, as inadequate in explaining how and why internal and external conditions influence, and the relative extent of their impact. Although external social, policy, school and classroom level factors are important, they do not in themselves fully account for either teacher effectiveness or student learning and achievement. Moreover, there is little research worldwide into the effectiveness of teachers' learning over the course of a career, how they build and maintain – or do not maintain – their effectiveness, and what are the positive and negative factors upon this.

Other approaches have used, for example, case study, narrative and action research within social and policy analyses of the wider contexts in which teaching, learning and achievement occur, in order to understand rather than reduce complexity. In turn, these have been criticized either for being ideologically driven or too fine-grained and small-scale to provide any authoritative conclusions. Yet collectively they present a recognizably powerful and vivid mosaic of the complexity of teachers' work and lives. The second part of the chapter explores the dynamic, unpredictable and non-linear qualities of teachers, and thus examines the factors which influence their perceived effectiveness.

Teachers' work and lives: looking deeply

Whereas the effective schools literature tends to place pupil learning outcomes at the centre of its agenda, there is a vast amount of literature which acknowledges and seeks to understand the roles, identities, beliefs, motivations and commitments of teachers. Such research is, arguably, central to understandings of influences upon teachers' capacities to affect pupils' learning and achievement. Influencing factors bearing on teachers' work can exert a positive or negative impact on their effectiveness and, therefore, on pupil learning. Understanding how the interrelationships among these influences work and how they exert their effects is, however, not easy. Ancess (1997), like Askew *et al.* (1997), acknowledged the crucial importance of teachers in the school effectiveness and improvement relationship, and concluded that there is 'a reciprocal influence among restructuring, teacher learning and practice, and student outcomes'.

Across many strands of educational research there is a developing awareness of the connection between teachers' private lives, the personal and biographical aspects of their careers, and how these intersect with and shape professional thoughts and actions (Day 1999; Goodson 2003). It has been increasingly clear from the literature on teachers' work, professional lives and development that expertise, capability, personal and professional biography, situational, emotional and psychological factors, as well as the complexity of the pupils whom they teach, and changes over time and circumstance, affect their effectiveness as teachers (Hargreaves 1999; Van Den Berg 2002):

> Teachers teach in the way they do not just because of the skills they have or have not learned. The ways they teach are also rooted in their backgrounds, their biographies, and so in the kinds of teachers they have become. Their careers – their hopes and dreams, their opportunities and aspirations, or the frustrations of these things – are also important for teachers' commitment, enthusiasm and morale. So too are relationships with their colleagues – either as supportive communities who work together in pursuit of common goals and continuous improvement, or as individuals working in isolation, with the insecurities that sometimes brings.
>
> (Hargreaves 1999a: 7)

Woods (2001, see also Woods *et al.* 1997) described how teachers adapted to restructuring in curriculum, pedagogy and assessment; to the 'new public management'; accountability; to new forms of school organization; to changes in teacher culture, professional development; and to the intensification of their work. He categorized influencing factors as arising at three levels: structural (macro), organizational (meso) and personal (micro) and argued that these are interrelated (see also Helsby 1999). As with the literature on school and teacher effectiveness, the review focused on three levels of influence: structural (e.g. external policy contexts and community), situational (school-specific issues) and personal (e.g. values and efficacy[3]).

Intensification of work

Hargreaves (1994) described job intensification as being a result of large-scale reform and redefinition of teacher role expectations. With complex and multidimensional change mandates being received by teachers at a fast rate, they experience additional stress due to the new set of demands placed on them by reform initiatives. Intensification leads to reduced time for relaxation and reskilling, can cause chronic and persistent work overload, can reduce quality of service, and separates the conceptualization from the execution of tasks. The introduction of new roles and responsibilities, an extended curriculum, new assessment tasks and the need for retraining (Campbell and Neill 1994) have all contributed to intensification and this has been sustained over a long period in England, as new initiatives by central government continue to demand change in schools. It is not surprising, therefore, that much research over the period reports on this phenomenon.

Over the past 20 years within the UK, research has documented massive work overload, a loss of spontaneity and reflective time, an increase in stress and a burgeoning of bureaucracy (Campbell *et al.* 1991; Osborn and Broadfoot 1992; Pollard *et al.* 1994). Some argue that the way teachers think and feel has also been exploited. For example, according to Campbell *et al.* (1991), teachers have been caught in the 'trap of conscientiousness', doing their best to meet the prescribed targets, but compromising the quality of learning and their own health in the process. Bartlett (2004) provides further, more recent examples of the intensification of work demands based on data collected in the United States. She suggests that teacher overwork is, in part, a result of the expansion of teacher work roles but that these alone do not adequately account for teachers' overwork. In a further study from the United States, Bushnell (2003) illustrates how educational reforms may subordinate elementary school teachers and reduce their opportunities for professionalism (see also Ingersoll 2003; Elliott 2004).

A recent study of secondary school teachers' workload (MacBeath *et al.* 2004), commissioned by the National Union of Teachers (NUT), found that time was considered more important to teachers than additional support when faced with increased paperwork and declining classroom behaviour:

> ... it is about changing the overall atmosphere for the better so that relationships between teachers and pupils are considerably improved, and teachers can feel relaxed and unstressed when they are teaching.
>
> (MacBeath *et al.* 2004: 48)

Restructuring of schooling and the impact on professionalism

In addition to teachers' work being intensified, it has also been dramatically restructured in a number of ways. For example, Louis and Miles (1991) examined changes to teachers' contracts, career ladders, control over curriculum, policy and resources, broadened roles in school management, professional development and opportunities for professional interaction in America. The intensification and restructuring of teachers' work will, to an extent, impact upon feelings of 'professionalism' (Englund 1996) among teachers (Campbell and Neill 1994; Ozga 1995; Helsby 1999) who have experienced a move from a culture of classroom autonomy and a focus on the individual and their expertise, to a culture of goals, standardized criteria, and accountability (Brennan 1996). In turn, this can have the effect of diminishing teachers' sense of agency (Hargreaves 2000) and control over, in particular, curriculum content, pedagogy and assessment (Helsby 1996; Talbert and McLaughlin 1996). According to some researchers (Ballet 2001), a process of 'de-professionalization' and 'de-skilling' will have taken place when the beliefs, attitudes and values that most teachers have acquired and developed during the course of their careers appear to be declining in importance. In addition, the manner in which schools deal with the changes being imposed influences the professional identities of teachers (Van Den Berg 2002). A considerable number of negative outcomes for teachers relate to policy developments which, it is claimed, have produced a perception of professional incompetence (Vandenberghe and Huberman 1999; Woods 1999).

Researchers, such as Hargreaves (1994, 1997), Little (1986), and Nias (1996), have reported that teachers feel a lack of professionalism and inadequate in their role owing to, among other factors, the monotony of daily classroom activities, changing attitudes of students who appear to be less respectful, less disciplined and less motivated, and confusing local, regional or national policies. In contrast, however, Osborn (1995) suggested that teachers were coming to terms with their restructured work and roles and were developing new professional skills. Similarly, in their observations of the rapid intensification of primary teachers' work, Campbell and Neill (1994) also claimed that this had not led to de-skilling and de-professionalization but to an enhanced professionalism, in terms of teachers' professional identity and their use of new skills. On a positive note, also, Cooper and McIntyre (1996) found the National Curriculum to be an effective stimulus to collaborative planning, shared professional learning and the development of teachers' professional craft knowledge.

However, the overall trend identified in much qualitative research in the 1990s (Woods 1993; Troman 1996; Helsby 1999) was in the direction of de-professionalization or, more accurately, 're-professionalization', with a new 'flexible' generation of teachers working towards the effective implementation of new policy initiatives (DfEE 1998). McNess *et al.* (2003) drew on the evidence from projects which examined the impact of policy on the lives of classroom teachers and the experience of their pupils. The Primary Assessment Curriculum and Experience (PACE) project of English primary teachers, reviewed their practice in the light of the successive waves of legislative change following the 1988 Education Reform Act, and the ENCOMPASS Project (Education and National Culture: a comparative study of attitudes to secondary schooling) was a cross-cultural study which investigated the attitudes of pupils to schooling and the impact of policy on the work of secondary teachers in England, France and Denmark. Evidence from both projects suggested that teachers in England were concerned that externally imposed educational change had not only increased their workload but also created a growing tension between the requirements of government and the needs of their pupils. A perceived demand for a delivery of 'performance', for both themselves and their pupils, had created a policy focus that emphasized the managerially 'effective', in the interests of accountability, while ignoring teachers' deeply rooted commitment to the affective aspects of teaching and learning. More recently, Elkins and Elliott (2004) outlined the ways in which successive UK governments have regulated and controlled the teaching profession since the 1980s.

Teachers involved in responding to demands for reforming and restructuring their schools are engaged in two major tasks: reinventing the school and reinventing or redefining themselves (Miller 1999). Both of these undertakings are complex, multi-faceted processes of socialization. How educational reform is interpreted and implemented is shaped by the school context (Datnow 2000); the kinds of socio-emotional (Warren-Little 1981) and material support teachers receive or are denied (Berman *et al.* 1977; Woods *et al.* 1997); teachers' beliefs about their own capacity/efficacy (Berman and McLaughlin 1977; Leithwood *et al.* 1999); and their sense of their own agency or ability to make a difference (Fullan 1993; Ghaith and Shaaban 1999; Smylie 1999).

McKinney *et al.* (1999) found that both school and professional development depend not only on individual teacher factors but also on the culture of the school. More than a decade ago, Nias (1996) suggested that a 'culture of care' was breaking down in the primary school. An example of Nias' concerns is exemplified in a study of one 'failing' school carried out by Troman and Woods (2001). They found that the teachers' experiences of shock, self-doubt and feelings of shame and inadequacy, undermined their confidence and devalued their expertise, transforming positive emotions into negative ones. As a consequence, they felt de-professionalized (see also Jeffrey and Woods 1996) and demoralized (Nias 1996). The school's experience of 'failure', during the time spent in 'special measures', had transformed the culture of caring, sharing and commitment to one of a more technical-rational character.

Classroom culture

Research over the years has consistently found that teaching of the highest technical competence counts for little if classmates are uncooperative or teachers unfair or uncaring (Fraser 1991; Walberg 1991). Rudduck *et al.* (1997) proposed that:

> Though educators rightfully emphasize achievement, they should also think of motivating their students and awakening a love of learning for its own sake. Affectionately remembered classes sustain interest

in learning in the workplace and over a lifetime ... well-organized classrooms foster responsibility, humaneness and mutual respect – the very social skills students need to participate productively in our civic society.

(Rudduck *et al.* 1997: 46)

Woods *et al.* (1997) argued that 'in general, in situations where teachers otherwise feel under pressure, the one thing that keeps them going is their relationship with pupils ... and dedication to the cause of their needs' (1997: 161; see also Lortie 1975, on the psychic rewards of teaching).

Other researchers have also emphasized the negative impact that some pupils can have on teachers. Freeman (1987), for example, notes that while teachers need to perform effectively, lack of pupil motivation and poor pupil behaviour can induce feelings of stress. Further, Kyriacou and Sutcliffe (1978) and Kyriacou and Roe (1988) demonstrated that pupils' poor attitude to work can be a major problem for teachers. Troman and Woods (2001), in their research, found that when teachers had restricted opportunities to form personal and educational relationships with their pupils owing to workload, class sizes and inclusion policies, they experienced stress and feelings of guilt (see also Hargreaves 1994). The VITAE study also found that these influenced teachers' perceptions of their own effectiveness.

School and neighbourhood characteristics

Many researchers have reported the importance of school ethos or climate in encouraging school and teacher effectiveness (Rutter *et al.* 1979; Galloway *et al.* 1982; Mortimore *et al.* 1988), and some years ago Pollard (1985), among others, showed how 'institutional bias' shapes staff and pupil/teacher relationships. Osborn *et al.* (1996) also found that schools in different types of catchment/socio-economic areas experience varying pressures as a result of the introduction of the National Curriculum. They concluded that teaching became difficult, and was less rewarding for teachers in inner city schools. Likewise, Woods *et al.* (1997) reported in their research that within disadvantaged inner city areas teachers found it difficult to adapt their teaching to take account of the individual needs of the children, whereas in middle-class areas 'teachers were more likely to see the National Curriculum enhancing their teaching qualities' (1997: 157). More recently, in his recent research concerning the impact of standards-based reform in eight secondary schools in Canada and the United States, Hargreaves (2003) demonstrated that the teachers in 'magnet' schools, teaching more advantaged students, were more likely to feel 'enhanced' by the reforms. In contrast, those teachers whose schools served poor districts, reported feeling that the emphasis on academic standards benefited neither the students nor themselves. However, other research has suggested that disadvantaged students in English schools have benefited from standards-based policies (Matthews and Sammons 2005).

Variations in the development of teachers' effectiveness

Despite all the school effectiveness research, and that which focuses upon conditions of work and teacher professionalism, there is as yet little empirically-based knowledge of the ways in which teacher effectiveness in the classroom grows and/or diminishes over the course of a career and in different contexts. Such studies, as exist in England, are relatively small-scale. Yet it is widely acknowledged (Schön 1987; Eraut 1994; McLaughlin and Talbert 2006) that lifelong learning is necessary for sustaining teacher morale, for career advancement and promotion, for a vibrant workforce, for managing change, and for improving skills, content knowledge or pedagogy. Internationally there have been a number of studies of teacher career development – in the USA (Lightfoot 1983; Fessler and Christensen 1992); England (Ball and Goodson 1985; Nias 1989; Bolam 1990); Australia (Ingvarson and Greenway 1984); Canada (Butt 1984) and Switzerland (Huberman 1993). These have been paralleled by research on the development of expertise (Dreyfus and Dreyfus 1986; Sternberg and Horvath 1995) and research on critical learning moments in teachers' lives (Watts 1981; Sikes *et al.* 1985; Denicolo and Pope 1990; Day 1993). In the USA, Fessler and Christensen's (1992) research is also useful because it conceptualizes teacher development as consisting of a dynamic interplay between career cycle, personal environment, organizational environment and the growth of expertise.

While these strands of influence, together with the psychological, affect teachers in all phases of development, only the research by Huberman (1993) has been longitudinal. The research draws on a large study of Swiss secondary teachers who experienced major reform in the 1960s and 1970s, and explores how teachers' professional experiences impact upon fatigue, stress, commitment, disengagement, learning and reflection. This work has become widely cited for its development of a non-linear empirically-based schematic model of a five phase teaching career cycle. One major contribution of Huberman's research was his identification that 'a large part of development is neither externally programmed nor personally engineered but rather discontinuous' (1993, 1995). The non-linear nature of development has been confirmed in studies by Feiman-Nemser (1990) and Korthagen and Wubbels (1995).

It is acknowledged that teacher learning requires time and commitment, if substantial rather than cosmetic changes in practice are to occur (Hargreaves and Fullan 1992; Eraut 1994; Guskey and Huberman 1995); and recent research (see Day 2000) has supported the idea of a synthesis of personal/ professional development and lifelong learning. Within this perspective, the literature identifies the primary role of high quality leadership in promoting sustained professional development through enquiry and reflection.

School leadership, effective teachers and teaching

Major categories of successful headteacher leadership practices have been identified in a series of recent reviews by Leithwood and his colleagues (Leithwood and Levin 2004; Leithwood and Jantzi 2005; Leithwood and Riehl 2005; Belchetz and Leithwood 2006). This work has developed a classification system that includes Setting Directions, Developing People, Redesigning the Organization and Managing the Instructional Program. It is suggested that these practices are common across contexts in their general form, but highly adaptable and contingent in their specific enactment (Day *et al.* 2000; Leithwood *et al.* 2006; Day and Leithwood 2007). It has been shown that these particular leadership practices, along with others, are most effective when they are widely distributed across the organization (Bell *et al.* 2003); and contemporary studies continue to explore the relationship between different forms of distributed leadership practice and pupil outcomes (Gronn 2000, 2002; Spillane *et al.* 2001; Harris 2004, 2005; Spillane 2006). This is especially relevant to schools in England, which have experienced a dramatic proliferation of leadership roles in English primary and secondary schools, due mainly to central government education policy of the past two decades. This has had the effect of transforming schools from relatively simple to highly complex organizations and has impacted on teachers' working conditions, and the demands placed upon them (Reid *et al.* 2004).

The most recent research, internationally, has acknowledged that leadership (a key factor in teachers' efficacy, commitment and effectiveness, and successful leadership) is both an intellectual and emotional practice (Blasé and Blasé 1999). Organizational improvement, then, relies upon transformational, direct and indirect qualities, influences and behaviours of the headteacher (Day *et al.* 2000; Mulford *et al.* 2005; Day and Leithwood 2007). It suggests, further, that the same leadership behaviours may have quite different effects on teachers, for example, depending upon an individual teacher's gender, age, amount of experience or levels of stress. Evans' research has demonstrated the negative impact on effectiveness of deteriorating relationships between headteachers and their staff (Evans *et al.* 1994). She focused on identifying and explaining the factors that affect job-related attitudes in teachers (Evans 1998), and revealed the complexity of three specific job-related attitudes: morale, job satisfaction and motivation. In relation to all three of these, leadership was found to have a negative impact in terms of the reality of expectations, the individual's perspective of themselves within the school, and their feelings of professionalism. Her study suggested that leadership influences teachers' morale, job satisfaction and motivation in an indirect way, through shaping the work context in terms of '. . . equity and justice, pedagogy or androgogy, organizational efficiency, interpersonal relations, collegiality and self-conception and self-image' (Evans 2001: 306).

Teachers' learning and development

The quality of leadership has been shown to play an important part, also, in enabling or discouraging the development of professional communities. Many studies have focused on the role of learning organizations in effective teaching. Marks and Louis (1999) identified five significant dimensions of organizational learning structure, shared commitment and collaborative activity, knowledge and skill, leadership, feedback and accountability. Learning communities have emerged within a growing volume of literature, particularly, though not exclusively, in North America, as holding much promise for teacher renewal and school improvement (Warren-Little 1993, 1999; Louis and Kruse 1995; Talbert 1995; Westheimer 1998; King and Newmann 1999; Witziers *et al.* 1999; Grossman *et al.* 2000; McLaughlin 2001; Stokes 2001; McLaughlin and Talbert 2006; Achinstein, in press). Warren-Little, one of the leading advocates of 'learning in teachers' communities of practice' argues that 'despite some caveats . . . research has steadily converged on claims that professional community is an important contributor to instructional improvement and school reform' (2001: 1).

The literature suggests that effective professional development is school-based, collaborative, progressive, and focused closely on pupils' learning (National Partnership for Excellence and Accountability in Teaching (NPEAT) 1998); and that it encompasses a wide range of concepts, including mentoring or interaction with colleagues (Sandholtz 2000), peer coaching (Lieberman 1996), critical friends (Day 1999), as well as a range of activities, such as observation, working on tasks together, sharing ideas or discussing the implementation of resources (Duncombe and Armour 2004). Day (2002) suggests that the models of teacher development adopted by policy-makers do not adequately address teachers' learning needs over a career, or contribute to enhancing motivation and commitment essential to raising standards in the classroom. In recent years, 'being the best' as a teacher has become less of a moral imperative based on a sense of integrity and trust, and more of a diktat from governments intent on imposing their performativity agendas on teachers in the name of raising standards. One consequence of the rise of the so-called school reform agenda is that there has been a demise of teacher renewal and the sustainability of commitment (Day *et al.* 2005; Hargreaves and Fink 2006).

Personal values and job satisfaction

It is increasingly evident from the literature that events and experiences in the personal lives of teachers are intimately linked to the performance of their professional roles (Ball and Goodson 1985; Goodson and Hargreaves 1996). Complications in personal lives can become bound up with problems at work (Woods *et al.* 1997). Commenting on Huberman's (1993) text on the personal and professional career trajectories, Hargreaves argues that:

> Teachers don't just have jobs. They have professional and personal lives as well. Although it seems trite to say this, many failed efforts in in-service training, teacher development and educational change more widely are precisely attributable to this neglect of the teacher as a person – to abstracting the teacher's skills from the teacher's self, the technical aspects of the teacher's work from the commitments embedded in the teacher's life. Understanding the teacher means under-standing the person the teacher is.
>
> (Hargreaves 1993: 8)

Woods *et al.* (1997: 152) also argue that 'teaching is a matter of values. People teach because they believe in something. They have an image of the "good society"'. Woods (1995) and Woods and Jeffrey (1996) have researched 'creative' primary school teachers who were characterized as having strong child centred principles (Sugrue 1997), committed to innovation and experienced ownership of curriculum and pedagogy; and Nias (1996) has shown the central important contribution of values to positive interpersonal relationships in the primary school.

In a study of primary teacher morale and job satisfaction, Evans (1992) found the situation specific variables of headteacher behaviour and staff relationships to be key factors influencing the teachers' satisfaction/dissatisfaction with teaching. Her study of teachers' working lives found their job satisfaction, motivation and morale to be strongly related to their professional identities. Her 'extended professionals' (Hoyle 1974) experienced high levels of job satisfaction in schools where leaders and management were also 'extended professionals'. Dissatisfaction and stress were experienced when leaders and colleagues were perceived to have a 'restricted' view of professionalism. Bogler's (2002) later study from Israel attempts to construct profiles of two types of teachers: those with a low level of job satisfaction and those with a high level of job satisfaction. The results suggest that teachers with a low level of satisfaction can be reliably distinguished from teachers with a high level of satisfaction by their occupational perceptions, principals' leadership styles, and a number of their demographic characteristics. Unsurprisingly, Hall *et al.* (1992) found that teachers who were planning on leaving the profession reported less job satisfaction and a more negative attitude towards teaching as a career. More recently, Smithers and Robinson (2003) investigated the factors affecting teachers' decisions to leave the profession. The study identified five main factors which were influential in teachers' decision to leave the profession: workload, new challenge, the school context, salary and personal circumstances (2003: 1).

Teacher efficacy

A key area of work in teacher development and its relationship to pupil achievement is the mediating factor of teacher self-efficacy (Ashton and Webb 1986; Rosenholtz 1989), the self-belief of teachers that they can exert a positive effect on their students' success. In 1976, the RAND organization published the findings of an evaluation of a range of reading 'programs and interventions' in the United States of America (Armor *et al.* 1976). The RAND researchers concluded that teacher efficacy (defined by the use of a two item scale) was strongly related to variations in reading achievement among minority students. Subsequent research in the RAND-Rotter tradition has sought to expand the number of items in efficacy assessment scales and focus on the nature of relationships between teacher' sense of efficacy and:

- Teachers' willingness to implement innovation
- Teachers' stress levels
- Teachers' willingness to stay in teaching.

In order to teach effectively, teachers must not only feel psychologically and emotionally 'comfortable', they must also have some sense of self-efficacy. They must feel their professional work is bringing about positive change in their pupils. They need to know that, for instance, they are making a difference in the lives of children they are teaching and that those children are learning. Rudow (1999) notes that teachers need to feel wanted and important, and require affirmation of this by those they live and work with.

Personal teaching efficacy has been found to be particularly related to the 'proportion of time the teachers spent in interactive instruction after training' (Smylie 1988 cited in Tschannen-Moran *et al.* 1998: 205), and improved teacher efficacy related to reduced stress among teachers (Parkay *et al.* 1988). Teachers leaving teaching have been 'found to have significantly lower teacher efficacy than teachers either in their first year or their fifth year of teaching' (Glickman and Tamashiro 1982 cited in Tschannen-Moran *et al.* 1998: 205).

Moore and Esselman (1992) observed that teachers with a greater sense of general teaching efficacy outperformed their peers in mathematics teaching, and Ross (1992) found that high levels of student achievement were associated with teachers having higher personal and general teaching efficacy. In addition to student achievement, teacher efficacy seems to impact on students' attitudes towards school, the subject matter taught and the teacher (Woolfolk *et al.* 1990). Meijer and Foster (1998) found that in their research 'high efficacy teachers were more likely to feel that a problem student was appropriately placed in the regular classroom' (Tschannen-Moran *et al.* 1998: 217).

Owing to the methods often adopted for research into the complexities of teachers' work and lives (e.g. in-depth interviews, diaries, narratives), previous studies have been able to consider the wealth of influences, such as efficacy, motivation, career and commitment. However, there are major limitations to much of the qualitative research on teachers' work and lives. This is because, unlike school and teacher effectiveness studies which often engage with large-scale samples via remote methods (e.g. questionnaire surveys, collection of pupil test scores), it is either too 'fine-grained' and small-scale to be generalizable or transferable, or it focuses on only one aspect while excluding others.

Conclusion

This chapter has provided a critical overview of selected literature from the wide range of research into teacher and school effectiveness and teachers' work and lives. The starting point was a recognition that research into teachers' effectiveness needs to relate to their cognitive and affective processes and that these are likely to be influenced by a range of factors, including personal and professional biography, school specific conditions (leadership, cultures), broad cultural and policy contexts, and psychological factors, classroom organization and teaching approaches used and the characteristics and backgrounds of the pupils whom they teach.

The chapter has illustrated how definitions of what constitutes 'effective' practice vary according to the research tradition adopted. The examination of the literature led directly to a clearer conceptual understanding of the dimensions of effectiveness. Thus, effectiveness is both perceived by teachers themselves and can be measured by pupil outcomes. While each dimension is important in its own right, it was thought possible that there might be a relationship between the two.

Perceived effectiveness (relational) – Effectiveness in this sense is defined as the extent to which teachers believe that they are able to do the job to the best of their ability. By 'relational', we mean that teachers might perceive themselves to be more or less effective in the classroom, in relation to their past performance and according to perceived variations in effectiveness (how one teacher perceives the present and how (s)he performs in relation to his/her past history). This includes teachers' perceptions of the effectiveness of their classroom relationships and pupil progress and achievement, and how their belief in their ability to be effective related to their self-efficacy, motivation and commitment. Effectiveness for each individual varies in different organizational contexts and professional and life phases; and this is influenced – positively and/or negatively – by pupils (attitudes and behaviour), colleagues, departmental and school leadership, external policy and personal circumstances. The investigation of teachers' perceptions of effectiveness led us to examine more closely the effects of these mediating factors on teachers' professional life phases and identities (Chapter 7) and the relationship of these to their commitment and resilience (Chapters 10 and 11).

Effectiveness in terms of pupil attainment and progress (relative) – By 'relative', we mean that teachers in similar schools and of similar age and experience, might be compared in relation to their effectiveness in terms of 'value added' pupil attainment scores. Effectiveness in this sense is measured by 'value added' pupil attainment data as defined by national tests at Key Stages 1, 2 and 3, as well as results of independent baseline tests adminis-tered at the beginning of the year to pupils at Key Stage 2 (Year 6) and 3 (Year 9). The cognitive results enabled us to look for relationships with i) pupil attitudes collected through annually administered surveys and ii) teachers' perceptions of effectiveness.

Based on this conceptual development, Chapter 3 describes the mixed methods approach chosen to explore the notions of relational and relative effectiveness.

three

The VITAE research: a synergistic approach

Introduction

This chapter discusses the ways in which qualitative and quantitative approaches were combined within an integrated, synergistic design in order to provide a 'best fit' methodology for the research purposes of VITAE. The project was designed against a set of specifications in a competitive tender which defined its overarching aim as:

> . . . to assess variations over time in teacher effectiveness, between different teachers and for particular teachers, and to identify factors that contribute to variations. The Department wants to understand how teachers become more effective over time.
>
> (DfES 1999)

The specification demanded that, 'teacher effectiveness should be assessed in relation to outcomes'; that, 'robust and reliable quantitative data, and in-depth qualitative data from a representative sample of LAs/maintained schools' should be collected; and that the research should involve '. . . teachers at different stages in their career' (DfES 1999). The rationale of the study, set out in the original specification, was that:

> Expertise, capacity, personal and professional biography, situational and psychological factors, as well as the complexity of the pupils whom they teach and changes over time and circumstances affect teachers' effectiveness. Thus, any attempts to sustain initiatives aimed at raising standards in schools and classrooms and to retain high quality teaching are unlikely to succeed without a more comprehensive

understanding of teacher effectiveness, its complex configuration and its antecedents.

(DfES 1999: 6–7)

The review of literature (Chapter 2) confirmed our view that there had previously been no large-scale project which had attempted to combine qualitative and quantitative measures to provide a means of establishing, over time, associations between the lives and work of teachers and their perceived and measured (by value added pupil attainment scores) effectiveness.

Design of the study

The review of relevant literature provided an initial conceptual framework (Day *et al.* 2006b, 2006c) for the development of a research design (Figure 3.1). However, the concepts were kept sufficiently broad to allow an iterative process of progressive focusing as the research advanced (Hammersley and Atkinson 1983; Strauss and Corbin 1998).

Three key challenges faced us in designing a methodology appropriate to these questions:

1   How could we measure the effectiveness of teachers working within different school phases, contexts and at different points in their careers in terms of pupil attainment and progress?
2   How could we identify and assess variations in effectiveness between teachers at different career points over time?
3   How could we differentiate between, and assess the significance of, the key factors associated with variations in teachers' effectiveness?

Methodological synergy

The demands of the VITAE specifications led to the development of an integrated, mixed method approach involving the combination of a range of research techniques, including approaches traditionally associated with both 'positivist'/'quantitative' and 'interpretive'/'qualitative' paradigms. This was necessary in order to gather the range of information needed to address all of the complex and potentially interrelated issues and concerns, and to provide a detailed, holistic and methodologically robust, rigorous account of teachers' work, lives and effectiveness. As Shulman (1986) maintains, research programmes growing out of one particular perspective tend to '. . . illuminate some part of the field . . . while ignoring the rest' (1986: 4). So while teacher case studies were the prime focus of the study, these were

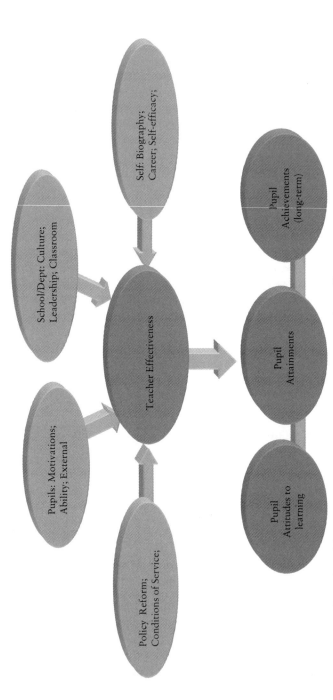

Figure 3.1 Initial model of factors contributing to variations in teacher effectiveness.

constructed using three main sources of evidence: interviews, teacher and pupil questionnaires and pupil assessment data[4]. This more complex combination of approaches provided greater mapping, analysis, interpretation and holistic understandings of the research area, than would have been gained if relying on a single paradigm or approach (Tashakkori and Teddlie 2003).

We, therefore, chose an approach less constrained by limiting theoretical perspectives and more focused on the conceptual, methodological and practical challenges of addressing particular, and in our view important, research questions (Bryman 1988: 183). Research methods were selected on the basis of fitness for purpose. While this approach has been described as methodological eclecticism by Hammersley (1996), the term 'eclecticism' is, in our view, misleading as it might suggest a lack of conceptual or theoretical clarity, which was not the case for VITAE. Rather, the research team adopted the term 'conceptual synergy' to describe the philosophical underpinnings being driven by our concern to emphasise fitness for purpose.

The VITAE project, then, sought first to develop a distinctive theoretical position, and then to translate this into the project design using (a) a combination of 'qualitative' and 'quantitative' approaches; and (b) a synergy of these approaches in relation to data collection, data analysis and data interpretation. A potential flaw of this approach was that the quantitative and qualitative elements of the research would be designed and conducted separately, and combined only at the stage of interpreting findings. VITAE, however, sought to integrate the various forms of data in an ongoing and interactive way (Tashakkori and Teddlie 1998; Cresswell 2003) by, for example, feeding the findings from an initial survey of teachers directly into the sampling, and design of instruments for the case study phase of research. These, in turn, fed into a re-analysis of the questionnaire data. Similarly, the results from the multilevel analyses of effectiveness were incorporated into teacher profiles, and then used as one of several important attributes for subsequent analyses of teacher identity, professional life phase and variations in effectiveness.

This iterative process of analysis, synthesis and integration enabled triangulation, complementarity and development (Greene *et al.* 1989: 259). Furthermore, new insights from the emerging empirical analyses, were able to interact with critical surveys of appropriate literature, to produce new theoretical developments which themselves added to understandings of variations in teachers' work, lives and effectiveness.

Phase 1

Audit of local authorities

Phase 1 (2001–2002) involved an audit of LAs in order to identify a group which, between them, could offer a range of representative schools. Seven LAs were selected to cover a range of areas (inner city, suburban metropolitan and rural), and different levels of ethnic diversity and socio-economic disadvantage.

Data for each LA comprised matched pupil level data files, linking Key Stages 1–3 national assessment data and Key Stages 2–3 national assessment data, enabling analyses of effectiveness patterns for schools across Key Stages 2 and 3 from 1999–2001. The data covered a range of high, medium and low SES schools in urban, suburban and rural areas and demonstrated a broadly representative sample of teachers' age and experience profiles.

Initial teacher questionnaire survey

During this phase (spring term 2002), a questionnaire was sent to all Year 2 and Year 6 teachers in all primary schools, and Year 9 mathematics and English teachers in all secondary schools, in the seven LAs selected, with the aim of providing a representative cross section of schools and pupils in terms of social economic status and pupil attainment. The survey was carried out for three main reasons:

1   To identify groups of teachers within a range of schools who were prepared, in principle, to take part in the main body of the research that would eventually involve a representative sample of some 300 teachers in 100 schools across 7 LAs.
2   To establish, in conjunction with the literature review, a 'baseline' of key conditions and factors, which teachers perceived currently to affect their ability to impact upon pupil learning and achievement. This baseline subsequently informed the more detailed analysis of the views of 300 teachers who took part in the three-year longitudinal study.
3   To initiate the development of an empirically based analytical framework for interpreting the factors affecting teacher effectiveness.

The questionnaire survey design was informed by the initial review of relevant literature and examination of a number of instruments used in a variety of earlier surveys, and was piloted with several groups of teachers prior to the main survey. A total of 1378 primary and 250 secondary schools were sent questionnaires. Returns from 1186 (810 primary and 376 secondary) teachers were received. The results have been summarized and reported in Chapter 4.

Phase 2

Case studies

Phase 2 (2002–2005) involved the selection of case study schools and teachers, and in-depth data collection for a duration of three years. The study employed a number of approaches to interviewing various participants (teachers, school leaders, pupils) involved in the research. Over the course of the project, the 300 participating teachers were involved in a total of six interviews (including semi-structured, hierarchically focused, narrative approach, and telephone interviews). Data collected via these methods, together with school level data, pupil focus group and questionnaire data, contextual (Year 2) and value added analyses of pupil attainment and progress across Year 6 (primary) and Year 9 (secondary), provided estimates of teachers' relative effectiveness for particular pupil outcomes (English and mathematics), and enabled the combination of context and cohort specific factors.

Schools, teachers and pupils

Phase 2 (2002–2005) involved the selection of case study schools and teachers. One of our initial research tasks was to ensure that the 100 schools and 300 teachers in the project were representative of the national picture, and drawn from seven LAs which between them represented geographical spread, urban/rural, school size and relative affluence. We were aware of the impact of socio-economic status (SES) factors on teachers and schools, and our sampling prioritized this. We 'over-sampled' schools with relative high levels of deprivation, in order to have a large enough sample from which to generalize. Tables 3.1 and 3.2 show how we sampled for both percentage

Table 3.1: Primary schools case study matrix (75 schools) – Banded performance at Key Stage 2 % (level 2 & above)

% Free School Meals	Top	Second	Third	Bottom	Total	Actual	National
	Attainment Quartile					Sample	
Up to 8%	8	13	2	0	23	31%	33%
more than 8% up to 20%	2	14	4	0	20	27%	29%
more than 20% up to 35%	0	3	6	6	15	20%	19%
more than 35%	0	1	8	8	17	23%	19%
Total					75		

Table 3.2: Secondary schools case study matrix (25 schools) – Banded performance at Key Stage 3 % (level 5 & above)

% Free School Meals	Top	Second	Third	Bottom	Total	Actual	National
	\ Attainment Quartile					Sample	
Up to 13%	3	5	3	0	11	40%	45%
More Than 13% to 35%	0	3	4	1	8	36%	36%
More than 35%	0	0	1	3	4	20%	14%
Grammar Schools	1	0	0	0	1	4%	5%
Total					25		

free school meals and for school achievement – with national test results classified into four groups (top to bottom quartiles).

The teachers

Within the 75 primary schools, we worked with 150 Year 2 and Year 6 teachers. This selection of teachers was to enable us to use national test results to study pupil progress and attainment as one measure of teacher effectiveness. We recognized that because of the emphasis placed on these results, these teachers might not be fully representative of those teaching in less pressured years. In the 25 secondary schools we recruited 150 Year 9 teachers of English and mathematics, again because this allowed their pupils' national test results to be analysed. The limited representativeness of these, in relation to teachers of other subjects, was recognized.

The teachers we selected within this school sample, broadly matched primary school national distributions in terms of gender (90 per cent female as against 88 per cent nationally). In secondary schools there were slightly more females (62 per cent against 55 per cent nationally), perhaps as a consequence of English being one of the two subjects.

In terms of years of service, our primary school sample had relatively more teachers with 20+ years of experience (32 per cent against 23 per cent nationally), while new teachers (0–4 years were relatively underrepresented (12 per cent against 33 per cent) (Figure 3.2). The explanation for this may be that these high stakes 'SAT-years' are given to more experienced teachers. The secondary sample was far closer to the national distribution (Figure 3.3). This sampling left us confident that we would be able to represent the experiences and perceptions of a nationally representative group of teachers in a representative group of schools.

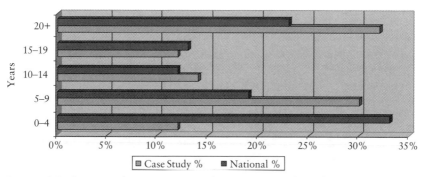

Figure 3.2 Case study primary teachers compared with national profile number of years in service.

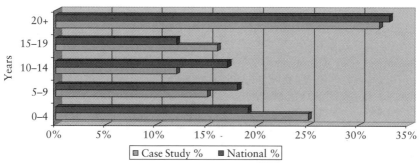

Figure 3.3 Case study secondary teachers compared with national profile number of years in service.

As part of the school selection criteria, consideration was taken of the numbers of pupils on the school roll, in order to provide, as far as possible, a representative number of small, medium and large schools. Figures 3.4 and 3.5 show that, on these criteria, our achieved sample matched fairly closely the national profile. However, we included a higher proportion of small and very large schools in our sample, in order to facilitate meaningful analysis in this area.

In addition to the profile of the school sample, the teacher sample was selected in order to ensure representation in the following categories: age, experience, gender, phase, subject specialism, length of service and career phase. The teachers were located in schools which represented a range of: geographical locations (urban, suburban, rural), SES (high to low disadvantage), pupil key stage attainment, and mobility of pupils.

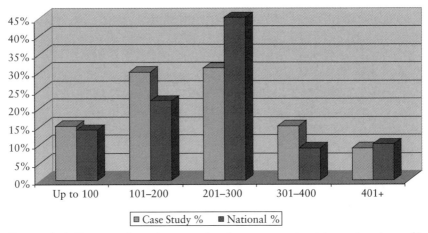

Figure 3.4 Case study primary schools compared with national profile number of pupils on roll.

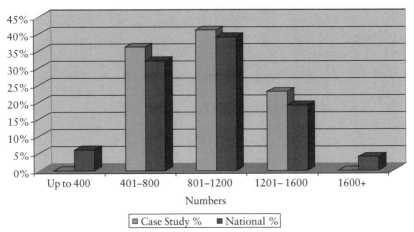

Figure 3.5 Case study secondary schools compared with national profile number of pupils on roll.

Methods of data collection

Data collection

Over the course of the project, the 300 participating teachers were involved in a total of six interviews, during the autumn and summer term, of each of the three years of fieldwork. The study employed a number of different approaches to interviewing depending on the purpose and focus of the interview, each chosen for its specific strengths in gathering particular types of data. Four of the six interviews with teachers were semi-structured in design (including one telephone interview). However, two of the interviews had alternative structures, relevant to the timing and focus of the interview, as new understandings were developed through concurrent strategies.

Each of the narrative approach interviews was tailored to the specific situations, contexts and concerns of individual teacher-participants, in order to focus on developments in their personal and professional lives at that time, and also to allow reflection on such developments. While the narrative itself was firmly located in the present, the process of reflection encouraged the interviewee to raise issues of change over time. Therefore, the narrative was directed towards a number of core areas, including key events, significant people (such as parents, siblings, partners, children, colleagues, etc.) and changes in personal and professional beliefs, values and practices which affected, and were affected by, classroom, school, and broader social and policy contexts.

Semi-structured interviews were used with school leaders, (headteachers, heads of department, Key Stage co-ordinators) to gain a further perspective on (a) the role leadership played in teachers' effectiveness, and (b) the effectiveness of participating teachers. The interview focused on questions relating to the context, priorities, and community involvement of the school. In addition, questions relating to the case study teachers – concerning their professional development needs and performance over the past school year were included.

Data collection with pupils

Prior attainment measures

Prior attainment measures, using standardized National Foundation for Educational Research (NFER) assessments of English and mathematics, designed to be compatible with the national curriculum, were used to provide data that would be subsequently linked to national assessment outcome measures, collected towards the end of the school year. No prior attainment data were collected for pupils in Year 2, thus although multilevel contextual models were used for these classes, to provide measures of attainment adjusted for pupil intake characteristics, it was not possible to assess their progress over the year using value added approaches which controlled for prior attainment as was done for Year 6 and 9.

Attainment outcome measures

Key Stage 2 and 3 results in English and mathematics, were linked to the results of pupils' baseline assessments in Years 6 and 9. For Year 2, Key Stage 1 results were used as outcome measures.

Pupil attitudinal survey

In addition to the use of pupils' cognitive outcomes in national curriculum tests, the research team recognized the importance of the social and affective outcomes of education. The information was gathered through an annual survey of pupil attitudes, which asked what the pupils thought of their schools and classrooms. This allowed us to relate these answers to the teachers' perceptions. We were also able to compare the responses over three years (different classes, same teacher) to see what was consistent and what was shifting in pupils' responses. As the VITAE project was about variation over time, it was valuable to know whether pupil attitudes to their teachers varied. We analysed the responses from over 10,000 pupils at several levels. At the most general level, we analysed the responses by year group for each of the three years. Within this we looked at sub-groups (e.g. by gender of pupils and by school factors, such as FSM levels).

Focus group interviews

Focus group interviews were employed with a sample of Years 2, 6 and 9 pupils (summer 2003, 2004 and 2005). Four to six children were selected in a total of 32 classes, representing pupils of approximately 10 per cent of the 300 case study teachers. The focus group agenda was based around issues raised by the pupil attitudinal survey, and allowed open discussion regarding pupils' views on school, learning, and their current class.

First stage data analysis

Data collected from teachers and school leaders

Each round of interviews was digitally recorded, saved on sound files and subsequently saved as anonymized files onto a PC. The first stage analysis on this data took place shortly after the interview was conducted, by the researcher who had conducted the interview. This resulted in a preliminary understanding of the responses given and the development of analytical codes. A second stage analysis was conducted in order to further interrogate the emerging findings and to establish what, if any, were the predominant themes.

Data collected from pupils

Data from multiple sources were collected to conduct the multilevel analyses and produce indicators of school or teacher relative effectiveness (residuals at the class level – see Goldstein 1995).

1   Baseline prior attainment data for individual pupils were collected from teachers by the VITAE project at the beginning of the 2002/2003 academic year for Years 6 and 9 pupils. The baseline assessments were part of the NFER-Nelson 'progress 5–14' series (NFER assessments 'progress in English/mathematics 10' and 'Progress in English/mathematics 13'). They provide raw and age standardized scores that adjust pupils' performance according to their age, and provide comparisons with a nationally representative sample.
2   Outcome data in the form of Key Stage 1, 2 and 3 attainment (levels and test scores) were provided by the DfES at the end of the academic year.
3   Pupil background information, such as age within the year group, ethnicity, special educational needs, English and an additional language (EAL), etc. was collected from the Pupil Level and School Context (PLASC) dataset, also provided by the DfES.
4   Some school level information was also collected from the PLASC dataset, such as proportion of pupils in the school entitled to free school meals.

Second stage analysis

At the second stage of analysis, patterns and connections between the separate datasets were emerging. Linking the results of qualitative and quantitative analysis techniques was accomplished by treating each dataset with the techniques usually used with that type of data – that is, qualitative techniques were used to analyse qualitative data (e.g. content and narrative analysis techniques), and quantitative techniques were used to analyse quantitative data (e.g. statistical techniques). In the case of VITAE, statistical analysis involved the multilevel modelling of school, teacher and pupil level characteristics in each of three years of the fieldwork, to enable classification of teachers in terms of relative (value added) effectiveness. Value added residual estimates, at the teacher level, and their associated confidence limits, were used to divide teachers into five groups ranging from significantly above expectation to significantly below expectation in each year and each subject. Interview and other qualitative data were analysed using NVivo (computer-assisted data analysis software).

Having obtained indicators interpreted in terms of teachers' relative effectiveness for different cohorts, these results were added to teachers' profiles. The initial data cut explored this aspect of effectiveness by comparing teacher profiles for the 'more effective' and 'less effective' groups, as identified by the multilevel analysis of relative effectiveness. The criteria for greater or lesser effectiveness included teachers with above or below expectation in either of the two main year cohorts.

Analytical synthesis and integration

The results of the independent analyses (discussed above) were combined at the interpretation stage of the research using NVivo, although each dataset remained analytically separate. NVivo provided a tool for the storage and synthesis of data collected, and a range of key attributes, based on prior analysis and classification of data (interviews, surveys, pupil progress measures etc.), were linked to the interview data at an individual teacher level. For example, attributes included the characteristics of the school in which the teacher worked (e.g. more or less disadvantaged context, based on the percentage of pupils eligible for free school meals (FSM) group); also high to low attainment in national assessment results (ranging from top to bottom quartile). Other attributes included teachers' years in teaching, posts of responsibility and gender. In the same way, value added indicators of academic effectiveness and measures based on pupils' views were also added to NVivo each year.

Further analysis was carried out which combined the separate datasets into one overall database, prior to various analytical techniques being applied. Thus, in applying a full range of appropriate analytical techniques to the data (regardless of the method of data collection), and yet preserving the integrity of the data (i.e. not convert data unnecessarily), VITAE employed an approach of analytical synthesis and integration.

Teacher profiles

Throughout the analytical process, individual profiles were constructed for teachers and updated after each round of data collection. These profiles were developed in order to preserve the individual teacher's story as the project progressed. Each profile included data from the interviews and questionnaire, and used scores from instruments to create these portraits of each teacher. These profiles were a key outcome of the mixed method strategy and combined qualitative and quantitative measures. They formed a foundation from which the team was able to explore various patterns and connections in the data.

Understanding teachers' work, lives and effectiveness

Validity and reliability

Validating interpretations of what is happening in a particular environment is considered a key advantage of mixed method research (Tashakkori and Teddlie 1998; Sammons *et al.* 2005). All research methods have limitations, but mixed method approaches enable biases inherent in any single method to 'neutralize or cancel the biases of other methods' (Cresswell 2003: 15). In order to enhance validity of data collected and reliability of the instruments used, three main strategies were adopted:

1 Reviews of relevant areas, such as CPD, teacher identity, commitment, and school and teacher effectiveness, were used to inform the development of instruments.
2 Piloting of each instrument with a group of 'similar' participants not in the main study – in the case of teacher interviews, one group of teachers participated in the piloting for each round of interviews in order to ensure continuity of questions between visits. In addition, other teachers were also involved who had not been included in the piloting of previous rounds to ensure content validity construct validity, and internal consistency. Where there were differences in an instrument relating to age, for example the pupil attitudinal survey, piloting was conducted with pupils from each age group to ensure suitability of the instrument.
3 Interviewer training – training was given, postpilot interview, to all members of the research team, in order to promote inter- and intra-judge reliability (Tashakkori and Teddlie 1998).

Conclusion

This chapter has discussed how VITAE created a mixed method design as a dynamic means for identifying and tracking variations in teachers' perceived and relative effectiveness over three consecutive years (Day *et al.* 2006b). The project used a wide range of conceptually synergistic methods to study the influence of teachers' personal and professional experiences, and to relate such information to measures of pupil outcomes, both cognitive and affective. The research provided detailed information about teachers' views and perspectives, and also obtained information from pupils regarding classroom climate and processes which influenced their educational outcomes. The use of a large number of case studies, and the development of teacher profiles, was part of the process of qualitizing quantitative evidence, quantitizing qualitative evidence, and integrating the two. The strengths of the mixed method strategy include the professional learning enabled through the iterative process of data collection, analysis, hypothesis generation and interpretation.

The study faced various challenges, including the inevitable time lag on cognitive outcome data (available and analysed to provide value added indicators a year behind interview data), the capacity of NVivo to handle the large amounts of data generated for 300 case study teachers, and the lack of complete datasets due to the voluntary nature of participation. This was especially true of the pupil attitude, and value added data that required teachers to administer special baseline tests and questionnaire surveys in each year of study. By the third year the response rate to these additional requests was lower than that of the repeat interviews.

The longitudinal nature of the VITAE research also posed some challenges in terms of project staffing and expertise, as well as maintaining the interest and participation of schools and teachers over an extended (4-year) period. The benefits did, however, outweigh the challenges. They included the development of relationships within the team, which was spread across institutions; the building of authentic rapport with participating teachers and schools; and the ability to track changes over several years. These were essential components for identifying and understanding variations in teachers' work and lives and gaining the holistic, multi-faceted view of the associations between these, and their effects on pupils which the following chapters represent.

four

The schools, their teachers and their pupils: expectations, experiences, perceptions

Introduction

This chapter looks at aspects of the motivations, influences and experiences expressed at the beginning of the VITAE project by schools and teachers involved in the study. It also provides an overview of pupils' attitudes to their schools and teachers. At the outset of the VITAE project, we invited all Year 2, Year 6 and Year 9 mathematics and English teachers from the seven LAs involved to complete a questionnaire. Teachers were asked what attracted them to teaching, about their current commitment motivation, levels of satisfaction and what factors affected their effectiveness in the classroom. There were 1200 respondents. The purpose was to create a representative picture of teacher attitudes, and to provide an initial base for identifying teachers and schools that could be invited to join the project. We then looked at the similarities and differences between the responses of 300 VITAE teachers, and the larger representative sample (Mujtaba 2005). The overall pattern of differences suggested that the VITAE teachers were, generally, slightly more positive and motivated about their work than the larger sample. They reported lower stress levels and were more likely to participate in CPD, as well as being more satisfied in various aspects of their current CPD.

Primary and secondary differences

One of the features of both the initial and VITAE teacher surveys were the differences in the concerns of primary and secondary teachers in relation to:

- **Satisfaction with workload:** Primary teachers reported more satisfaction with liaising with parents, behaviour management, working with colleagues and individual pupil needs. More secondary teachers reported that they were satisfied with the time for planning.
- **Pupil impact on teaching:** More primary teachers reported that pupil self-esteem, home–school relationships, and pupil mobility were highly important. Secondary teachers placed more emphasis on the social background of their pupils.
- **Factors outside the school that impact teaching:** Primary school teachers were more likely to rate media portrayal as highly important.
- **School policies that impact teaching:** Primary teachers were more likely to rate learning support and CPD as highly important. Secondary teachers were more likely to report pupil behaviour and banding/setting as highly important.
- **School leadership/teaching staff that impact on teaching:** Primary teachers were more likely to report staff morale, staff relationships, commitment of other teachers, effectiveness of other teachers, senior management team and governors involvement in the school, as highly important. Secondary teachers placed more emphasis on departmental support.
- **The professional health of teachers:** Primary teachers were more likely to report very high current motivation levels.
- **CPD:** Primary teachers were more likely to report that they either had taken part in further training or would like to take part in training over the next four years compared to secondary teachers.

What these differences signalled from the outset, was that generalizing about 'teachers' in a way that did not take account of the phase in which they work would be unproductive. The context of the primary school is different from the secondary, and so are many of the teachers' perceptions. The same point was true for the socio-economic status of the school. Teachers in deprived inner city schools were likely to face some very different demands from those working in more advantaged settings.

Additional responsibilities

The survey alerted us to another complexity in teachers' work: the frequency and demands of teachers' additional responsibilities. Our findings differed from earlier research studies in that most of our teachers (70 per cent) had school responsibilities outside of the classroom. In primary schools, this was the case for 90 per cent of the teachers. For many, this would be a co-ordinating role within a Key Stage or in a subject, or across subjects (e.g. ICT; literacy). Even more striking was how early in their teaching career, teachers had taken on additional responsibilities. Three-quarters of teachers with 4–7 years experience had such responsibilities.

This became an important factor in understanding the contexts in which VITAE teachers worked. Few were solely classroom teachers, and so there were often competing demands between the classroom and management responsibilities. These responsibilities were a positive recognition of their professional standing, so important for their identity and motivation. However, they also created further demands on their time and energy. For some teachers, therefore, promotion had brought less satisfaction because they felt their classroom teaching had suffered as a result.

The extent to which teachers had other responsibilities, and what these involved, also affected how we interpreted their responses to issues, such as workload, effectiveness, school management and their own sense of well-being. We found that competing school demands, coupled with increasing personal demands, were particularly intense for teachers with 8–15 years experience (see Chapter 5). This finding mirrors Sturman's (2002) study on 'The Quality of Working Life among Teachers' which found that the hours teachers worked, their roles and responsibilities all added to stress and impacted on the quality of their working life.

Teachers' perceptions of their effectiveness

Efficacy

Teachers were asked about their sense of efficacy and their belief in their ability to have a positive affect on pupils' progress. Table 4.1 summarizes their responses. The results suggest that the majority of teachers, at both primary and secondary levels, were at least 'fairly satisfied' about their ability to improve the attainment of their pupils, but that sizeable minorities were fairly dissatisfied with the opportunities they had to engage with pupils so that they were excited by learning and able to be creative in the classroom.

Teachers were also asked where, in the past three years, they had experienced the greatest increase in satisfaction and where they had experienced the most dissatisfaction. For primary teachers, the time given to whole class teaching (88 per cent), liaising with parents (83 per cent), to behaviour management (71 per cent) and to working with colleagues (71 per cent), were the areas in which they felt fairly satisfied – although relatively few responded that they were very satisfied. Primary teachers were much less satisfied about the time they had for marking/assessment/feedback than any other activity (nearly 66 per cent were fairly or very dissatisfied).

Secondary teachers were significantly more dissatisfied with the time

Table 4.1: Teacher efficacy ratings

	No. Responses		Very Satisfied (%)		Fairly Satisfied (%)		Fairly Dissatisfied (%)		Very Dissatisfied (%)	
	P*	S*	P	S	P	S	P	S	P	S
My ability to improve the attainment of my pupils	145	108	30.3	18.7	63.4	69.2	6.2	12.1	0.0	0.0
My confidence in myself that I can make a real difference to all/ most pupils' learning	146	108	37.9	25.2	55.9	64.5	5.5	8.4	0.7	1.9
The opportunities I have to engage with pupils so that they are excited about their learning	145	108	20.1	16.8	62.5	61.7	16.7	20.6	0.7	0.9
The extent to which I can be creative in my classroom	146	108	17.2	15.0	49.7	56.1	27.6	25.2	5.5	3.7

* P=Primary; S=Secondary

they had for behaviour management (43 per cent satisfied) and administrative tasks (59 per cent) than their primary counterparts. The time given to activities other than whole class teaching was the area of most satisfaction.

Pupil motivation and behaviour

When asked about the key factors which impacted upon teaching in the classroom, pupil motivation, behaviour and self-esteem were seen as critical (see Figure 4.1). Pupil motivation was seen as the most positive of all of the school and external factors for teachers, with between 8 and 30 years experience. However, while pupil motivation was a source of encouragement to many, pupil behaviour was consistently reported as having a negative impact, irrespective of the experience of the teachers – though it was most pronounced for teachers with 4–7 years experience. Secondary teachers in particular were likely to report a decline in pupil behaviour and the effect that had on their commitment. This does not mean that all teachers saw pupil behaviour as a negative. There were teachers, albeit primarily in the more advantaged primary schools, who reported pupil behaviour as a positive feature in their work.

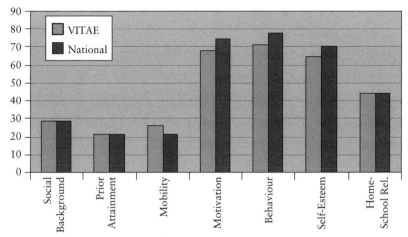

Figure 4.1 Teacher ratings of pupil factors (percentage rating as very important).

We therefore identified a situation for many teachers in which they reported good relationships with their pupils, were positive about their motivation, yet saw pupil behaviour as having a negative impact on their teaching.

External factors

When teachers were asked to rate the importance of 'external' factors in relation to their impact on the classroom, it was parent attitudes and media portrayals of the teaching profession which were most negatively rated, ahead of government and local authority policies and Ofsted. However, when we asked for open-ended comments on what impacted on their effectiveness, the responses of those who replied were overwhelmingly negative and focused on DfES policies and Ofsted. Teachers also identified more negative influences as coming from outside their schools than from within. Typical comments were:

> DfES and Ofsted have a negative impact on school and teaching . . . initiatives are imposed on top of school-based priorities.
> Ofsted is destructive and causes too much stress on staff and indirectly pupils.

One interpretation of these apparently paradoxical findings is that while many teachers did not want to acknowledge the direct impact of DfES and Ofsted on their work (with only 12 per cent and 8 per cent respectively rated as 'highly important' to teachers' impact in the classroom), nevertheless, they were seen as external threats to their autonomy and effectiveness. This was particularly so for teachers with 16–30 years experience who were consistently negative about both Ofsted and government policies. Teachers with 0–7 years experience, especially primary teachers, were much less likely to identify policy as a negative issue, though Ofsted was cited, after pupil behaviour, as having the most negative impact by those with 4–7 years experience. For newer teachers (0–3 years), it was media portrayal that concerned them most, followed by pupil behaviour and other teachers' expectations. The obvious interpretation of this is that newer teachers had not known any context other than a centrally determined curriculum, with accompanying directives on methods of teaching and learning, for example the National Literacy Strategy. For 16–30 year teachers there had been less regulated periods, which for some, seemed like a 'golden age'.

School policies, school leadership and relations with colleagues

When asked about the impact of school policies, it was behaviour policies which were seen as the most important. This was consistent with teachers, particularly newly qualified and secondary teachers who rated pupil behaviour as one of the most negative factors in their work (see Figure 4.2).

In relation to the ethos of the school, staff morale was seen as the most important factor, with over 60 per cent of teachers rating it as highly important. Great importance was attached to staff relationships and the commitment and effectiveness of others, which half the teachers rated as

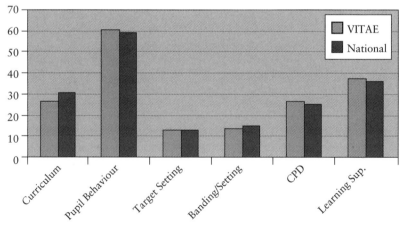

Figure 4.2 Teacher ratings of the impact of school policies on teacher effectiveness as highly important.

highly important. Forty per cent also gave this rating to management and departmental/key stage leadership.

Staff relationships were particularly important to newer teachers. These had the highest single positive impact (22 per cent) on teachers in their first three years, as well as those with 4–7 years experience. While it remained important for more experienced teachers, the positive role of the senior management team and departmental/key stage leadership was seen just as important. The quality of leadership was particularly important to teachers in the final phase of their career (31+ years experience).

The professional health of teachers

Responses about policies and pupils can be seen as reactions to external factors. We also explored the more personal factors that impacted on teachers' work, by asking a series of questions about their motivation, well-being, commitment and stress levels.

Motivation

Half gave 'working with children' as the reason for their motivation to become teachers, while almost a quarter gave their reasons as wanting to make a difference to children's lives. One in three secondary teachers had been drawn to teaching through their enthusiasm for their subject.

The teachers were then asked whether these reasons still motivated them. For 71 per cent of primary and 73 per cent of secondary teachers they still applied, with 12 and 18 per cent respectively feeling they no longer did. When asked about their current motivation level, half the VITAE primary and secondary teachers (50 per cent and 53 per cent respectively) reported high levels of motivation with a further one in five reporting very high levels (22 per cent and 20 per cent). A quarter of primary teachers reported only moderate motivation, and this dropped to 18 per cent of secondary teachers, with 8 per cent of them rating it as low, in contrast to only 2 per cent of primary teachers.

Changes in motivation

Given the levels of motivation reported at the start of the project and our interest in variations over time, we asked teachers about changes in their motivation over the previous three years. The pattern for the larger sample was one in which around half (48 per cent primary and 52 per cent secondary) reported a decrease in motivation, with only 16 per cent reporting increased motivation. The VITAE teachers responded more positively, with a quarter reporting increased motivation (27 per cent primary; 25 per cent secondary), while 38 per cent of primary and 30 per cent of secondary teachers reported a decrease. This is a lower proportion than that reported in the 2002 General Teaching Council survey of over 20,000 teachers, which found over half reported lower morale than when they started teaching. The key demotivating factors were workload, compounded by initiative overload and target driven cultures, and these resonate with our own findings.

While levels of motivation were reported as high for three-quarters of the VITAE sample at the start of the project, changes over time mean that motivation cannot be assumed to be in a 'steady state'. However positive they were, only a third of primary teachers thought that their motivation had stayed the same over three years. While the proportion was higher for secondary teachers (45 per cent), this was still less than half. Tracking these variations in motivation, and the impact on commitment, during the three years of fieldwork, was to become an important part of our research.

Teacher retention

Despite the decrease in motivation for a minority of teachers, only a small proportion (8 per cent) indicated they were likely to leave teaching. Teachers indicated that the most likely change would come through applying for a post in another school

Continuing professional development (CPD)

The further development of professional skills and knowledge, building and sustaining self-efficacy and commitment, can be seen as essential to improving teacher effectiveness. However, the success of this depends in part on the opportunities that are offered and the quality of these.

Three-quarters of the VITAE teachers were satisfied with the CPD opportunities they had, and the overall quality of the CPD in which they had participated. CPD in this context was perceived in terms of courses and training/INSET. However, this masked differences between teachers in relatively advantaged schools, who were significantly more positive about their opportunities, than those in schools with relatively high levels of eligibility for free school meals (FSM groups 3 and 4). In a policy context of CPD which is predominantly targeted at policy implementation, and effective management of this, there was a general satisfaction both with what was offered and its quality. Four out of five primary teachers and two-thirds of secondary teachers, in the survey, were satisfied with their CPD opportunities. Uptake varied in relation to experience and role. For example, new teachers sought more classroom knowledge (as did teachers approaching retirement), while mid-career teachers also opted for role effectiveness CPD (e.g. National Professional Qualifications for Headship (NPQH)).

There was much less satisfaction expressed by most teachers with the opportunities for more 'informal' CPD – learning with their colleagues and reflecting on their own teaching, for which they did not feel they had adequate time. Only 18 per cent of primary teachers and 28 per cent of secondary teachers were satisfied with the time available. When these views were analysed in relation to years of experience, new teachers (0–3 years) were more positive about the time for reflection and sharing of practice with colleagues, while those with over 31 years experience, who report the most hours worked per week of any professional life phases, were the most dissatisfied. These differences may be partly accounted for by schools allowing time for newly qualified teachers. Teachers in less advantaged schools (FSM 3 and 4) reported significantly more dissatisfaction with the time available for reflection than colleagues in other schools, again indicating greater pressures in these more disadvantaged contexts. VITAE teachers also reported experience of a very narrow range of CPD. Chapter 7 details this, and discusses CPD provision needs identified in relation to each of six professional life phases (see also Chapter 5).

It seemed that, for most teachers, particularly the more experienced, opportunities were lacking for the more informal forms of professional development, working with colleagues and reflecting on one's own practice.

Pupil attitudes to school

Central to teachers' attitudes to, and satisfaction with, their work are the pupils themselves. Teachers are motivated by their abilities to create and sustain positive and rewarding relationships with their pupils, so that they can make a difference to their lives. In this final part we explore the attitudes of the pupils towards their teachers and their schools. These attitudes further inform us about the contexts in which teachers work. We found through our interviews that virtually all of our teachers reported good relationships with their pupils – though pupil behaviour was sometimes seen as undermining these, particularly for new teachers and those with over 30 years experience.

Annual pupil attitude surveys provided a context in which to interpret teachers' perceptions and experiences. While many of the results of these might be expected, there were some surprises. Predictably, younger children were much more positive about school than older children and there were predictable gender effects, which lessened with age. The socio-economic effects were less predictable, with more FSM pupils being more strongly positive about their teachers than non-FSM pupils, while a minority of FSM pupils were more strongly negative. We look now at those analyses which provide insights into our understanding of the variations in teacher effectiveness both over time and between teachers.

Consistency over time

A feature of the pupil survey was that each year a different group of pupils were responding to questions about the same teacher and school. When the results of the surveys over the three years were compared, we found that Years 2, 6 and 9 pupils' responses to the survey remained largely consistent over the three consecutive years. The three different groups of Year 2 pupils remained positive and consistent in their responses over the three years, as did Year 6 pupils. Year 6 pupils became more positive about teacher clarity (e.g. 'My teacher is good at explaining what we are learning') and expectations ('Makes sure that I learn a lot in his/her lessons'), as well as teacher interest and fairness ('Is interested in me as a person/Treats me fairly'). Year 9 pupils showed a similar pattern of change around expectations and fairness. Where there was an increase in more negative responses, these were typically around pupil motivation (e.g. more disagreement with 'Most pupils at this school want to do well in tests' and exams and that 'Hard work is rewarded in this school').

The implication of these similar attitudes over time is that teachers were not dealing with widely fluctuating attitudes in the different groups of pupils they taught over successive years, though this does not mean that class behaviour and discipline were also constant from year to year. These attitudes were largely positive, especially those of younger pupils – again illustrating the differences in context between primary and secondary teaching.

Class level differences

While different pupils gave similar responses to the same teacher over the three years, responses were not the same from teacher to teacher. We compared the overall responses across the different classes, and found that pupils in Year 2, 6 and 9 classes differed significantly in their attitudes to their school and their classroom environment. Larger differences between classes were found for older children, which may be partly because of setting at Year 9, where the composition of classes is much more varied – so that a Year 9 teacher may be taking a top set one year and a lower set the next.

Year 2 pupils showed most consistency across classes. The largest differences between classes were found for reported noise levels in the class and whether they found school interesting. The items with the largest variations were:

The other children in my class are noisy in lessons.

I like my teacher.

School is interesting.

I like school.

In the most negative classrooms all of the pupils agreed with the 'are noisy' statement; whereas in the most positive classes, only one or two pupils agreed.

Year 6 pupils' responses indicated most variation over bullying, homework and in their perceptions of teacher attitudes. The largest variation in school factors was in relation to fears of bullying:

Some children are called names by other children.

Some children get bullied by other children.

At the classroom level it was items related to homework (e.g. 'Sets us homework every week; marks and returns the homework promptly') that showed the greatest variation.

Other items which showed large differences between classes related to teaching and learning and interpersonal issues. The teacher:

Makes the lessons interesting/Sets me my own targets for my learning.

Is there at the start of lessons.

Seems to like all the children/Is interested in me as a person.

Some extreme differences between classes were striking. In relation to homework, there were classes in which no pupils reported having homework set or marked every week, in contrast with those in which all of the pupils had homework set and marked. 'Agreement with the teacher makes lessons interesting' ranged between 32 and 100 per cent. This shows that the teacher makes a significance difference to the quality and enjoyment of classroom experiences for pupils.

Year 9 classes showed similar differences around homework, clarity and interest. Once again there were dramatic differences between classes. 'Agreement with the teacher makes the lesson interesting' ranged between 8 and 100 per cent, with 'The teacher seems to like all of the pupils' ranging between 18 and 100 per cent.

Conclusion

Through this survey work, we were able to look at the attitudes and experiences of the VITAE teachers as they joined the project and of their pupils throughout. The schools in which they worked were typical of state schools, though we deliberately over-represented schools in more disadvantaged circumstances (see Chapter 3). The teachers in the VITAE schools were similar in their attitudes to the larger nationally representative sample, though they tended to be slightly more positive in their responses and in their reporting of their motivation levels.

Far more noticeable were the differences in attitudes between the primary and secondary teachers in the project. The survey indicated some strong differences between primary and secondary work contexts, and that most teachers had additional responsibilities which impacted on their feelings of classroom effectiveness. It also signalled the importance to them of maintaining positive relationships with pupils. This had been part of their motivation for becoming teachers and was particularly important to them in sustaining their commitment. The pupil attitude surveys showed that this was reciprocated by generally positive attitudes towards teachers, though at the class level there were some considerable differences in how teachers were perceived by their pupils, indicating that some were much more successful than others in developing positive relationships and classroom climate; and also that there were variations in the extent of academic focus between classes taught by different teachers.

While there were few changes in pupils' attitudes over the 3-year period, there were pronounced differences in perceptions of their teacher's attitudes towards them, the expectations and demands placed on them and what went on in the classroom across different schools and in classes within the same school. Given the importance which teachers place on their relationships with their pupils, their pupils' perceptions of both the classroom climate and their teacher's attitudes towards them are important influencing factors. The teacher survey also indicated the importance of pupil behaviour and motivation to teachers' sense of efficacy, along with good staff relationships and effective leadership.

These factors were essentially school-based, with professional satisfaction based on pupil and staff relationships, including the quality of leadership. External factors, particularly government policies and Ofsted, were generally seen more negatively, especially by teachers who had been teaching longer. The fine-grained analysis, over three years, of how the VITAE teachers managed the complexities of their work and lives and how these contributed – positively and negatively – to their effectiveness in the classroom is developed in detail in the following chapters.

five

Teachers' professional life phases: a research informed view of career long effectiveness

Introduction

Our analysis of teachers' professional life phases, revealed that they are an important influence in teachers' work, lives and effectiveness; and that variations in teachers' perceived effectiveness can be understood by examining teachers, and groups of teachers, within and between particular phases of their professional lives. We identified key influences on teachers' work in different professional life phases, and the differential impact of these on teachers' commitment and perceived effectiveness. Understanding the impact of such interaction between the influences of teachers' professional life phases and identities, and the mediating factors in these: the situated (workplace), the professional (ideals and policies) and the personal (life experiences and events), was central to achieving an understanding of what causes variations in teachers' professional lives and effectiveness.

The VITAE work on the progression of teachers' professional lives, builds on Huberman's (1993) seminal study of the lives of Swiss secondary school teachers, which has been widely cited for its development of a non-linear empirically-based schematic model of a five-phase teaching career cycle. We found that teachers' work and lives spanned six professional life phases – 0–3, 4–7, 8–15, 16–23, 24–30 and 31+ years of teaching. The division of the six phases was grounded in our empirical data, collected and analysed over the three-year field work phase of VITAE, and informed by an extensive review of previous studies on teachers' careers and professional development. 'Professional life phase' refers to the number of years that a teacher has been teaching. Although years of experience generally relates closely to a teacher's age, some teachers have less experience than might be expected for their age, as a result of being late entrants to teaching or through taking a career break.

One major contribution of Huberman's research was his identification that 'a large part of development is neither externally programmed nor personally engineered but rather discontinuous' (1993: 195). Huberman found that 'professional career journeys are not adequately linear, predictable or identical – are often, in fact, unexplainable using the tools at our disposal' (1993: 264). In contrast, our research showed that despite individual and work context differences, it is possible to discern distinctive key influences, tensions, shared professional and personal concerns and 'effectiveness' pathways or trajectories relevant to most teachers in different phases of their careers. Our research also extends Huberman's study and provides additional, previously unresearched dimensions of teachers' professional lives, by examining teachers in both primary and secondary schools in a period of continuing national policy changes.

Teachers' professional lives: the research context

Prior to VITAE, empirically based knowledge of the ways in which teachers' commitment, resilience and perceived effectiveness in the profession, grows and/or diminishes over the course of a professional life, in different contexts and the reasons for this, was limited in five important ways:

1   Studies on teachers' professional careers in England were relatively small scale (Ball and Goodson 1985; Sikes *et al.* 1985; Nias 1989; Bolam 1990). Research samples in previous studies were often from the same school phase. One important advantage of our VITAE research was that the research sample included both primary and secondary teachers. This enabled us to investigate the interaction between a greater range of school phases and teachers' professional lives.

2   In the past there has been an unhelpful conflation between 'career stage' and 'professional development phase', which has limited understandings and appreciations of the different needs of teachers, which are necessary to sustain effectiveness over a career. For example, the DfEE (1998) career structure for teachers sets out prescribed stages of recruitment, training and promotion, and targets aimed at rewarding teachers for role-related high performance. Though the Government's Teacher Development Agency (TDA) has now begun to promote CPD for a broader range of teachers, it remains the case that most resources are provided for role-related training and development. This reduces opportunities for more broad based and reflective CPD.

3   Studies on teachers and teaching have also defined teachers' careers in ways that closely relate them to role-related promotion: 'it (teaching career) implies a commitment on the part of a person to obtaining promotion through the status hierarchy that exists according to some time schedule' (Maclean 1992: 188; Hughes 1952, Pavalko 1971, Ritzer 1972, Butt and Raymond 1989, Huberman 1989, Prick 1989). The evidence from VITAE shows that for the majority of teachers, their original call to teach was the opportunity to work with children, and that pupils, not necessarily career promotions, remained the main source of their motivation and commitment (see Chapter 11). Their functional positions/ role-related career advancement only comprise part of these.

4   Studies viewing teachers' career patterns from the perspective of age ranges (Sikes *et al.* 1985) have not taken into account factors independent of age and, therefore, are limited in their ability to explain the complexity of teachers' professional life development. Our findings suggest that it is the complex interplay between teachers' professional and personal needs at different times in their work and lives, as well as between situated, professional and personal factors and external structures, that influences the trajectories of teachers' professional life journeys.

5   The impact of the interaction between professional and personal contexts on teachers' development tends to be overlooked in research on teachers' lives. Huberman (1993) emphasized that the importance of the concept of career is that it 'contains in itself both psychological and sociological variables. This means, for example, that we can explore the trajectory of individuals in organizations and thereby understand how the characteristics of these individuals influence that organization and, at the same time, how they are influenced by it' (1993: 4).

However, the analysis of teachers' professional life phases in our study, suggests that the portrayal of teachers requires an investigation into factors not only within the organizational settings, but also how these factors interact with, and are managed in conjunction with, factors arising from teachers' personal lives.

The notion of teachers' professional lives, rather than career lives, therefore, enabled us to form a holistic understanding of the complex factors which influence teachers in different phases of their work, and how these affect their effectiveness. We were able to analyse and interpret teachers' experiences, identities and professional trajectories, in the light of a wide range of influences relating to both teachers' professional worlds and their personal lives. The key influences identified as shaping teachers' professional lives were: i) situated factors, such as pupil characteristics, site-based leadership and staff collegiality; ii) professional factors, such as teachers' roles and responsibilities, educational policies and government initiatives; iii) personal factors (personal level), such as health issues and family support and demands (see Chapter 7). Over a professional life span, it is the interaction between these factors and the ways in which tensions between these and personal/professional identities are played out and managed, that produces relatively positive or negative outcomes in terms of teachers' motivation, commitment, resilience and perceived effectiveness; and such perceived effectiveness may itself influence effectiveness, as measured by value added attainments of pupils (see Chapters 8 and 9).

Six professional life phases: characteristics and trajectories

On the basis of their perceived identity, motivation, commitment and effectiveness, teachers within each of six professional life phases were further categorized into sub-groups. Key characteristics and sub-groups of the six professional life phases were:

Professional life phase 0–3 – commitment: support and challenge

Sub-groups: a) developing sense of efficacy; b) reduced sense of efficacy.

Professional life phase 4–7 – identity and efficacy in classroom

Sub-groups: a) sustaining a strong sense of identity, self-efficacy and effectiveness; b) sustaining identity, efficacy and effectiveness; c) identity, efficacy and effectiveness at risk.

Professional life phase 8–15 – managing changes in role and identity: growing tensions and transitions

Sub-groups: a) sustained engagement; b) detachment/ loss of motivation.

Professional life phase 16–23 – work–life tensions: challenges to motivation and commitment

Sub-groups: a) further career advancement and good pupil results have led to increased motivation/commitment; b) sustained motivation, commitment and effectiveness; c) workload/managing competing tensions/ career stagnation have led to decreased motivation, commitment and effectiveness.

Professional life phase 24–30 – challenges to sustaining motivation

Sub-groups: a) sustained a strong sense of motivation and commitment; b) holding on but losing motivation

Professional life phase 31+ – sustaining/declining motivation, ability to cope with change, looking to retire

Sub-groups: a) maintaining commitment; b) tired and trapped

Professional life phase 0–3 years – commitment: support and challenge

(N = 26: 9 × primary, 17 × secondary)

Commitment: support and challenge

The outstanding characteristic of the large majority of teachers (85 per cent) was their high level of commitment to teaching. This stemmed largely from their original motivation for entering the teaching profession. Over half of the teachers in this cohort (61 per cent) indicated that they had been primarily attracted to teaching because of their teaching family background and/or their expectation of a rewarding opportunity to work with children and contribute to their progress.

> My father was a teacher. I didn't really think I'd be anything else.
>
> (Ruth, secondary)

> I wanted to be part of children's education to inspire them.
>
> (Eleanor, primary)

Nineteen per cent, almost all secondary teachers, had entered the teaching profession because of a love of their subject.

> I like working with people and to pass on my love and understanding of English literature.
>
> (Cheryl, secondary)

Two sub-groups were observed within this professional life phase: one with a developing sense of efficacy (+15[5]) (6 primary = 67 per cent, 9 secondary = 53 per cent) and the other with a reducing sense of efficacy (−10) (3 primary = 33 per cent; 7 secondary = 41 per cent). As Figure 5.1 shows, a range of factors had positively or negatively impacted upon the work of these early years teachers. Figures 5.2 and 5.3 illustrate the weighting of the impact of these key influences on teachers within each sub-group.

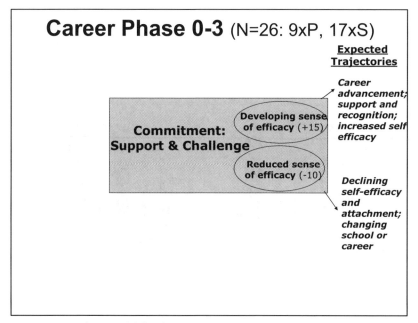

Figure 5.1 Professional life phase 0–3.

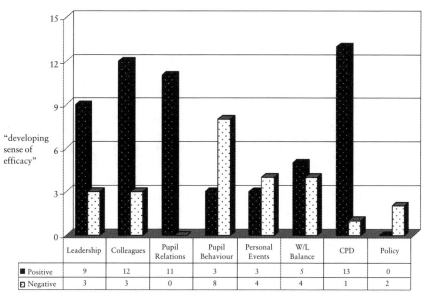

Figure 5.2 Developing efficacy (professional life phase 0–3) (N = 15).

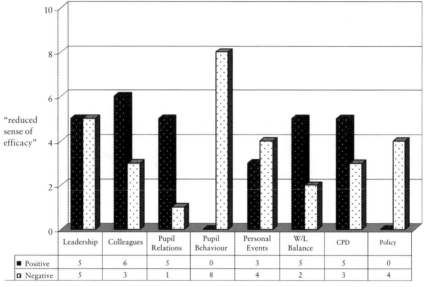

	Leadership	Colleagues	Pupil Relations	Pupil Behaviour	Personal Events	W/L Balance	CPD	Policy
■ Positive	5	6	5	0	3	5	5	0
□ Negative	5	3	1	8	4	2	3	4

Figure 5.3 Reduced efficacy (professional life phase 0–3) (N = 10).

Four late entrants to teaching were found in the former sub-group and three in the latter, which suggests that age is unlikely to be an important factor in the formation and change of teacher identity in this professional life phase.

Our findings confirm the view that teachers who had an 'easy beginning' benefited from a combination of influences that were more positive than those for teachers with a 'painful beginning' (Huberman 1993). Teachers in both groups reported the negative impact of poor pupil behaviour on their work. However, in contrast with the 'easy beginnings' group whose work had mostly benefited from leadership support, more teachers in the 'painful beginnings' group had experienced a lack of support from the school and/or departmental leadership. Thus, even at this time school/departmental leaders were a key mediating influence on the work and morale of beginning teachers. As in Huberman's (1993) work, the concept of 'survival' found resonance in teachers with two or three years' experience.

This is interesting, given the emphasis in recent years on work-based experience in initial teacher training courses. For new teachers who are struggling to survive the challenges of a new professional life in the reality of the classroom, the impact of combined support from the school/ departmental leadership and colleagues can be highly significant in helping to build their confidence and self-efficacy and deciding the direction of their next professional life path. In addition to the issue of support, the realization that teaching is indeed a 'demanding' job appeared to have a negative impact upon some new teachers' determination to stay in the teaching profession.

Possible trajectories

The key influences on these teachers' potential professional life trajectories, were found to be the level of support and recognition of their work from the school culture. As a consequence, teachers in this phase would be likely to follow one of two distinct professional life paths. These would be (Figure 5.1):

a) those who would enjoy career advancement with increased self-efficacy (N = 15, 60 per cent of 25); and
b) those who would suffer a declining sense of efficacy which led to change of school or career (N = 10, 40 per cent of 25).

Portraits of teachers

Nikita – developing sense of efficacy

Nikita was in her early twenties, and had been teaching for two years. She always wanted to be a teacher and had no additional responsibilities as yet. She taught English in a larger than average secondary school, with 1400 pupils on roll, aged 11–18 years. The percentage of pupils entitled to free school meals was in line with the national average (FSM2). The majority of pupils were white, with about 8 per cent from other ethnic groups, for whom English was an additional language.

Nikita felt that there was 'a big gap' between classroom teachers and the senior leadership team, especially heads of department, and that they had lost touch with what went on in the classroom. Staff relationships had a positive impact on her work as a teacher. Pupil behaviour had deteriorated, owing to having a number of supply (substitute) teachers in the past, but Nikita found that this was gradually improving. She reported that her relationship with pupils underpinned her high level of commitment to teaching. Nikita felt that her motivation and sense of efficacy remained high. She was undertaking further advanced study, because she wanted to carry on studying and developing her career further.

Darius – reduced sense of efficacy

Darius was in his early thirties, and had been teaching English for 2 years, in a mixed (FSM4) comprehensive school, with 710 pupils, aged 11–16. Having completed a degree, Darius had worked in business for a number of years. Since starting his teaching career, Darius had become literacy co-ordinator and had been temporarily given the responsibility of deputy head of year. He had also been nominated for best newcomer in the Teacher of the Year Awards.

Darius thought that, in general, the senior management were supportive and attempted to consult staff on potential changes, new initiatives, etc. However, he felt as if 'they (were) picking on me' during his newly qualifed teacher (NQT) year, because he was continually being asked if he could be observed. Towards the end of his first year he stopped spending much time in the staffroom, because the atmosphere had changed and the feelings of camaraderie had been lost. Pupil behaviour was given as the biggest negative impact on his work in his initial year, and this continued to impact on his work.

Not long after Darius had started his NQT year at this school (November 2002), a long-standing relationship ended. This meant that he had to move out of the house. Now that he was single, he spent a lot of his time marking, 'without someone else complaining about it!' Being single, he claimed, was an advantage in this phase of his career.

Although having remained highly committed to the school and to the students, Darius's level of motivation had decreased. This had been caused primarily by his resentment towards his department and the rest of the staff.

Professional life phase 4–7 years – identity and efficacy in classroom

(N = 75: 36 × primary, 39 × secondary)

Identity and efficacy in classroom

As Figure 5.4 shows, support from the school/departmental leadership, colleagues and pupils continued to be of importance to their work. Teachers in this professional life phase demonstrated a primary concern about their confidence and feelings in being effective, which is only partly in accord with Huberman's findings that teachers with 4–6 years of career experience move through a phase of 'stabilization, consolidation of a pedagogical repertoire' (1993: 13). In contrast with professional life phase 0–3, there were more frequent references made to heavy workload which was seen as reducing teaching effectiveness.

Unlike the context in which Huberman conducted his work, an important characteristic of teachers in this phase was that promotion and additional responsibilities had already begun to play a significant role in teachers' perceived identities, motivation and sense of effectiveness. There have been recent changes in the way that the teaching profession has been struc-tured, resulting in a greater differentiated pay scale to reward successful

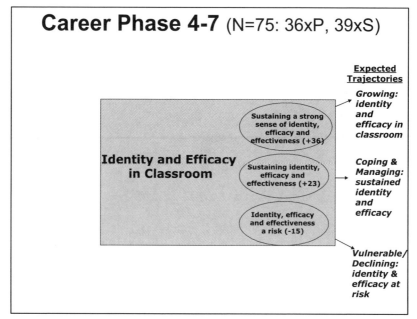

Figure 5.4 Professional life phase 4–7.

headteachers and teachers for high performance, and more posts of responsibility (DfES 1998; DfES 2003). Also, staff recruitment and retention is more difficult in some contexts (inner city and disadvantaged schools) and thus responsibilities and promotion may be more rapid for staff in such schools.

Fifty-eight teachers (78 per cent) of 75 teachers in this cohort (30 primary = 86 per cent; 28 secondary = 72 per cent) had additional responsibilities, and 23 (31 per cent) particularly stressed the importance of promotion to their growing professional identity (6 primary = 17 per cent; 17 secondary = 44 per cent). Among these 23 teachers, 16 (70 per cent) had 4–6 years' experience. This suggests that for many teachers this professional life phase is not a stabilization period. Rather, it is a period in which teachers, while consolidating their professional identities in their classrooms, also have challenges beyond these.

Figure 5.5 summarizes the association between levels of motivation and commitment of teachers in the three sub-groups. The difference in teachers' identities and perceived effectiveness, between the three groups, is reflected in their levels of motivation in the profession and commitment to the school.

Sub-group a) growing: teachers with a strong sense of identity, self-efficacy and perceived effectiveness. (14 primary (39 per cent); 22 secondary

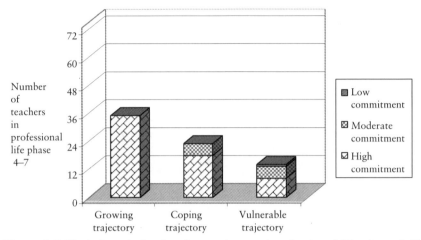

Figure 5.5 Variations in levels of commitment (professional life phase 4–7) (N = 75).

(56 per cent)) These teachers were most likely to experience positive career trajectories with a sense of increased efficacy in classroom. Huberman (1993: 7) discusses a phase of experimentation and diversification after the 'stabilization'/ 'pedagogical consolidation' phase. He suggests that teachers, with between 7 and 25 years' experience, 'having made an initial tour of duty in the classroom' set off in search of new challenges and new stimulations (1993: 8). In our study we observed a group of teachers with a strong desire for new commitments, but, in comparison with Huberman's work, these teachers were in an earlier professional life phase: the 4–7 phase.

Figure 5.6 illustrates the weighting of key influences on teachers' work. Substantial support from leadership and colleagues is a contributing factor in these teachers' growing sense of identity.

In this sub-group, 29 out of 36 had additional responsibilities (81 per cent) and 19 (53 per cent) (5 primary = 36 per cent; 14 secondary = 64 per cent) indicated the significance of promotion to their increased motivation, confidence and perceived efficacy. It is apparent that teachers in this sub-group had greatly benefited from their consolidated experience in the classroom, and that this was a contributing factor in their growing sense of professional identity, their feelings of becoming an effective classroom teacher and their ambition to progress their careers.

> Enjoying [my] job, absolutely love teaching the kids, and I love running the department.
>
> (Winona, secondary)

Sub-group b) coping/managing: teachers who had sustained a relatively moderate level of identity, efficacy and effectiveness and who were most

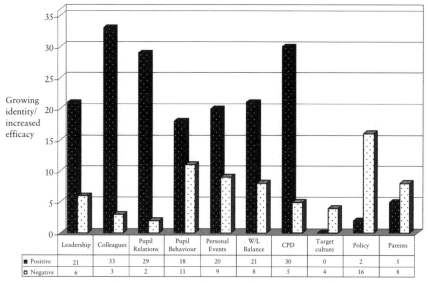

	Leadership	Colleagues	Pupil Relations	Pupil Behaviour	Personal Events	W/L Balance	CPD	Target culture	Policy	Parents
■ Positive	21	33	29	18	20	21	30	0	2	5
◻ Negative	6	3	2	11	9	8	5	4	16	8

Figure 5.6 Key influences on teachers with growing identity, increased efficacy (professional life phase 4–7) (N = 36).

likely to continue to cope with/manage their work in their next career phase (16 primary (44 per cent); 7 secondary (18 per cent)). In contrast with teachers in sub-group a), 18 out of 23 had additional responsibilities (78 per cent) but only four (17 per cent) (1 primary = 6 per cent; 3 secondary = 43 per cent) emphasized the positive impact of promotion on their motivation and self-efficacy. However, in common with sub-group a), most teachers in this group also expressed an enjoyment in seeing their experience and confidence increase.

> Feel more experienced, happier and more confident.
>
> (Jayne, primary)

> Increased confidence and effectiveness with experience.
>
> (Nadia, primary)

An important difference between sub-groups a) and b) appears to be that the latter group had a stronger concern over the management of their heavy workloads, and that some had shown an inclination to focus on classroom teaching in order to keep a balanced work and life.

> I enjoy it [teaching] I think. The enthusiasm I had a couple of years ago has waned a little and everybody used to say I made them sick how enthusiastic I was. Sometimes you just get tired or have a bit of a rough day with the kids. A lot of things affect it ... I don't think a lot

of people enjoy the fact that it [teaching] can push too far into your social life.

(Ricky, primary)

Figure 5.7 shows the key influences on the work of the 23 teachers in this sub-group. The overall weighting of the influences appears to be slightly more negative than those in Figure 5.7.

Sub-group c) vulnerable/declining: teachers who had felt that their identity, efficacy and effectiveness were at risk because of workload and difficult life events (6 primary (17 per cent); 9 secondary (23 per cent)). As a result, they might find their career trajectories vulnerable and see their identity and efficacy in the classroom decline. Few teachers in this sub-group mentioned the encouraging impact of promotion. Figure 5.8 indicates the impact of key influences on teachers' work. In comparison with the previous two sub-groups, a larger proportion of teachers reported a lack of leadership support, adverse personal events and work–life tensions.

The negative influence of workload and adverse personal events on teachers' declining identity and perceived efficacy is illustrated in the following quotation:

A major one [change] is going down with depression. I'm on anti-depressants at the moment. I've been going downhill since I started full

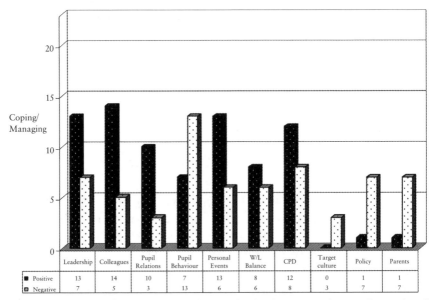

Figure 5.7 Key influences on teachers who had sustained a moderate level of efficacy (professional life phase 4–7) (N = 23).

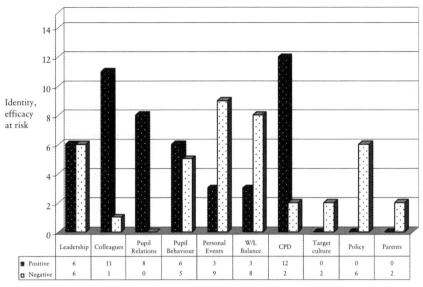

	Leadership	Colleagues	Pupil Relations	Pupil Behaviour	Personal Events	W/L Balance	CPD	Target culture	Policy	Parents
■ Positive	6	11	8	6	3	3	12	0	0	0
□ Negative	6	1	0	5	9	8	2	2	6	2

Figure 5.8 Key influences on teachers whose identity and efficacy are at risk (professional life phase 4–7) (N = 15).

time. It's just a combination of factors, teenage children, a husband with a busy job that needs supporting and the school as well . . . It's just more than I can manage.

(Faith, primary)

While analysis of the initial VITAE teacher questionnaire indicated that there is no statistically significant difference in the distribution of 'older' teachers (mostly late entrants and teachers with career breaks[6]) in terms of their motivation, commitment and professional outlooks; nevertheless, an analysis of teachers' worklines suggested that although these 'older' teachers exhibited a similar outlook to that of their younger peers, they appeared to have different concerns and face different tensions. The implication is that the influence of age and life experience on teachers' identity and professional life growth is not a linear one, but rather depends on issues such as their sense of vocation and how the tensions are managed.

While it has been argued that 'ageing, occupational development and identity are inextricably linked' (Sikes *et al.* 1985: 23) and in our research, age-related personal issues were found to impact upon teachers' work, we also found that chronological age alone does not adequately explain the complexity of teacher career development. First and foremost, viewing teachers' career patterns from the perspective of age ranges fails to take into account experiences of late entrants and teachers with career breaks.

For teachers with 4–7 years' experience, profession-related factors – promotion and recognition – were shown to have a more influential impact than biographical factors on teachers' sense of effectiveness and professional life advancement.

Discussions on professional life phase 8–15, below, indicates that this phase of a teacher's career, rather than the 'age 30 transition' as suggested by Sikes *et al.* (1985: 228), is a key watershed in teachers' professional lives. Sikes *et al.*'s model of the life cycle of the teacher describes teachers' growth through age patterns, presumably on the assumption that teachers all enter teaching at roughly the same age and remain in the profession with no career breaks. In our research, the investigation into teachers' professional development, through different professional life phases, enabled us to consider factors independent of age, such as an early promotion, and to understand teachers' professional development through a perspective which takes into account 'the arena where the expertise is played out' (Rich 1993: 138), and the complex and sometimes fragmented patterns of teachers' work and lives, which did not fit neatly into simple notions of growth stages.

Portraits of teachers

Eleanor – growing sense of positive identity
Eleanor was in her mid-twenties and had been teaching for four years at this small voluntary aided FSM1 school. Her school had a diverse socio-economic background and all pupils had English as a first language. Eleanor had been primarily attracted to teaching because she wanted to be part of children's education and to inspire them. In addition to being a Year 2 teacher, she was also co-ordinator for three other subjects.

Eleanor felt that, being a small school, the teachers and the headteacher got along well. Initially, she had seen pupils as the factor that had had the biggest negative impact on her work as a teacher. However, later in the project she enjoyed the respect of her pupils. Eleanor and her partner moved into their own home together during the project. Her family was very supportive and her mother had been into school to help her with displays. She also enjoyed going out with friends. She described herself as a confident, motivated and committed teacher. She joined in some of the extracurricular activities at school which gave her a feeling of being involved.

Ralph – coping
Ralph was 26 years old and had been teaching for six years at his first school, an urban low socio-economic status (FSM4) primary school of 391 pupils. He had been originally attracted to teaching because of the security it offered, which still applied. He was a Year 2 teacher, co-ordinator of three other areas. Ralph described the pupils in the school as 'challenging, lively

and interesting', and stated that the staff probably put up with a 'percentage of behaviour not tolerated elsewhere'. Ralph had experienced pupil behaviour problems in the past, particularly in Year 1 of the project, but had gradually found that his classroom management strategies had worked. He gained great satisfaction from the progress of his 'most stressful class' and his motivation and commitment had increased as a result.

Initially, Ralph thought that the recently established SLT (senior leadership team) structure was supportive, but later in the project he felt that the school management had negatively impacted on his work and motivation. He felt that the team leaders expected everyone to do everything in the same way, and that at times this undermined his professional judgement. He did not feel valued and found that his enthusiasm had begun to wane.

Scarlett – vulnerable/declining

Scarlett's experience illustrates a decline in motivation and commitment to teaching because of a perceived lack of support in the school culture and her heavy workload. She was in her late twenties and had taught English for five years, four of which had been at this urban, FSM3 school. She had wanted a different career on completion of her first degree, but because she could not afford the course, she undertook a teaching qualification and enjoyed it. At the beginning of the project, she said that she had grown to love teaching.

Her growing professional experience had increased her perceived effectiveness as a teacher. Her self-efficacy and confidence in managing the classroom had improved since she began teaching. At the beginning of the project she was highly committed to teaching and was very pleased to see that she could make a difference to pupils, both academically and personally. She saw teaching as 'a life as well as a job' and she enjoyed an extremely high level of job satisfaction.

Scarlett viewed the senior leadership team favourably, but felt less positive about the new leadership in her department. Nevertheless, staff at her current school were 'incredibly supportive and friendly' and she enjoyed the pleasant environment in the school. She had established a good relationship with her pupils, but found that, overall, pupil behaviour had become more challenging.

In her fifth year Scarlett reported that her motivation had decreased because of her increased workload and ill health. She had several months off school and believed that her illness was work-related. Although Scarlett had wanted to apply for promotion as second in department, she now felt that she was 'not utterly convinced' that she wanted to stay in teaching.

Professional life phase 8–15 years – managing changes in role and identity: tensions and transitions

(N = 86: 51 × primary, 35 × secondary)[7]

Managing changes in role and identity: tensions and transitions

This professional life phase is a key watershed in teacher professional development. Teachers in this cohort were beginning to face additional tensions in managing change in both their professional and personal lives. Figure 5.9 shows that the majority of teachers struggled with work–life tensions. Most of these teachers had additional responsibilities (68 out of 86 = 79 per cent; 47 primary = 92 per cent; 21 secondary = 60 per cent), and had to balance the effectiveness in their management role and teaching role. Heavy workloads worked against the effectiveness of their teaching.

Two sub-groups were identified on the basis of their current levels of motivation and commitment. Figure 5.10 summarizes the levels of commitment related to teachers' values and dedication to the profession, and their desire to actively participate in the processes of teaching and learning, of teachers in the two sub-groups. Once again, the difference in teachers' identity and perceived effectiveness, between the two groups, is

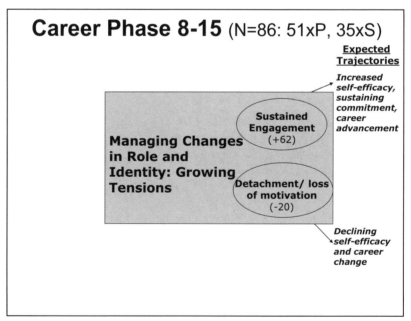

Figure 5.9 Professional life phase 8–15.

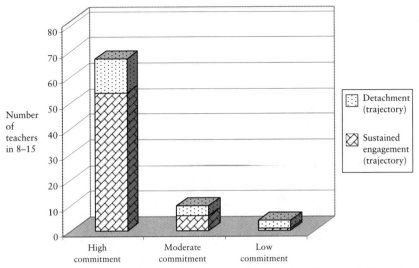

Figure 5.10 Variations in levels of commitment (professional life phase 8–15) (N = 86).

clearly reflected in their levels of motivation and commitment in the profession.

Sub-group a) teachers with sustained engagement whose expected trajectories were career advancement with increased self-efficacy and commitment (+62) (40 primary = 78 per cent; 22 secondary = 63 per cent). Forty-two within this sub-group (67 per cent) had additional responsibilities. The combined support from leadership, staff collegiality, rapport with the pupils and CPD was a contributing factor in this sub-group's positive sense of effectiveness. This is illustrated in Figure 5.11.

Leadership roles comprised an important part of professional identity for the majority of these teachers who:

- Were looking into further promotion, aiming at head of department, deputy headship and/or headship.
- Had become established in current managerial roles and were considering further career advancement.
- Were settling into leadership roles and experiencing a change in identity; and deciding whether to place more of their efforts into being an effective teacher or being an effective manager.

In his study on teachers, Prick (1986) observed a period of 'crisis' in men, between 36 and 55, and in women, between 39 and 45, in terms of questioning whether to remain in teaching. In our study, teachers with 8–15 years' experience and at an earlier life stage, were clearly experiencing a transitional

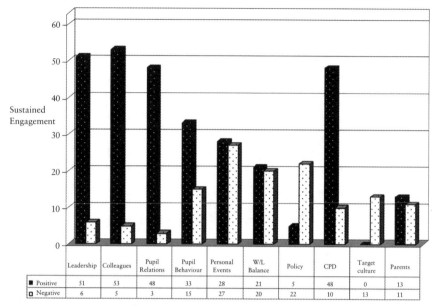

	Leadership	Colleagues	Pupil Relations	Pupil Behaviour	Personal Events	W/L Balance	Policy	CPD	Target culture	Parents
■ Positive	51	53	48	33	28	21	5	48	0	13
□ Negative	6	5	3	15	27	20	22	10	13	11

Figure 5.11 Key influences on teachers with sustained engagement (professional life phase 8–15) (N = 62).

period in their professional lives. However, they were not necessarily considering whether to continue or to leave teaching. Rather, they were at the crossroads of deciding the direction of their professional identity within the profession – whether to climb up the management ladder or to remain in the classroom fulfilling the original 'call to teach'.

A small group of teachers within this sub-group appeared to have already experienced this transitional 'crossroads' period. They were 'content' and 'happy' with their current work–life balance and had no intention of taking up any further additional duties. Some teachers wanted to focus on improving their effectiveness in teaching, whereas some late entrants were enjoying a high level of motivation, commitment and sense of effectiveness, but had no interest in promotion because they were nearing retirement age.

Sub-group b) teachers who felt a sense of detachment, a lack of motivation and were most likely to experience declining self-efficacy in their next professional life phase, or even a career change (−20), (7 primary = 14 per cent; 13 secondary = 37 per cent).

Figure 5.12 illustrates key influences on this sub-group's work. Around half of these teachers reported a lack of support from leadership (50 per cent) and colleagues (60 per cent). Adverse personal events and tensions between

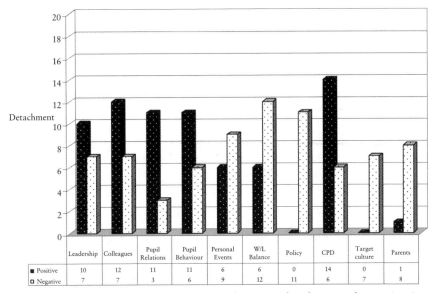

The following data appears in the chart:

	Leadership	Colleagues	Pupil Relations	Pupil Behaviour	Personal Events	W/L Balance	Policy	CPD	Target culture	Parents
Positive	10	12	11	11	6	6	0	14	0	1
Negative	7	7	3	6	9	12	11	6	7	8

Figure 5.12 Key influences on teachers with decreased motivation (professional life phase 8–15) (N = 20).

work and life were also important issues. CPD continued to be a positive influence on these teachers' professional lives. Three late entrants and one 'career break' teacher were identified here.

Eight teachers (40 per cent) reported their intention of leaving teaching. For Shaun, teaching had become 'a job' – he felt tired and did not take work issues home any more.

> I've made a conscious decision not to pursue promotion or extra work-load when I felt that I would rather spend that time at home . . . I think it's nice to be a father and it renews your faith in life, children, whatever, and it puts a smile on your face. As far as a hindrance, I'm more tired than I was. It also puts things into perspective that at the end of the day, work is work. Yes I'll work hard and try my best but it's not the most important thing in life, not now anyway.
>
> (Shaun, secondary)

Other key characteristics of this sub-group include: giving up management roles because of adverse personal events (e.g. ill health, increased family commitments); decreased motivation and commitment, which had led to early retirement (e.g. one late entrant and one 'career-break' teacher); and disillusionment/low self-efficacy/decreased motivation and commitment.

Portraits of teachers

Charlie – sustained engagement

Charlie was in his early thirties, with almost a decade of teaching experience and some of that outside primary – in secondary and adult education. Yet he had recently been appointed to headship. In his first interview, he said: 'It's my first term being Head. It's a whole new ball game. I found it really difficult.'

Charlie enjoyed working at his current school (FSM1) and pupils were the main source of his job satisfaction. Because of the decrease in the school roll, he felt stressed and was unhappy with the fact that his management role had distracted him from teaching. At that point, he described himself as being at the lowest point of his career. Charlie felt that there was 'no happy time whatsoever' in his personal life because of his worries about school. Nevertheless, he remained optimistic and confident that his morale and self-esteem would 'go up' in the future. Charlie believed that his promotion to headship was a positive turning point in his career: 'I just need to get through all the difficulties and carry on with my mission. Everything else has to be put on the backburner. It will get better.'

This teacher will be discussed from the perspective of identity in Chapter 6.

Katie – detachment/loss of motivation

Katie was a Year 6 teacher, in a rural high socio-economic status (FSM1) primary school. She was in her late forties, having taught for over a decade. Support and trust from the headteacher, and her colleagues, had a positive impact on her sense of efficacy. Katie felt that her sense of effectiveness varied, depending upon the make-up of her class. 'Sometimes I feel I can be more effective simply because I have less children in the class, but then I've got this one extra child who does make life difficult.' Pupil behaviour had been a detrimental influence upon her motivation and commitment – 'There is nothing more demotivating than a class that doesn't want to be taught.' She also felt demotivated and less committed when the parents questioned and complained about her methods of teaching.

The target driven culture was another negative influence on her decreased motivation in the profession. She was extremely negative about the excessive workload generated by the National Curriculum and the pressure from Ofsted inspections:

> This time last year . . . we were in the throws [*sic*] of Ofsted which was the most stressful experience I had ever been through, with the worst class in the school.

She also struggled with a lack of work–life balance:

I have to be very careful how I balance the support I give my own children, as I've got a pile of books to mark. Everything has to be planned like a military operation. If my husband wants us to go somewhere, like on Saturday, then I have to know. He can't tell me on Saturday morning that he wants to go out. He has to tell me the week before, so I can get my marking done, so that my Saturday can be free.

Katie felt that there was a slim chance of promotion for her in her current professional life phase.

Professional life phase 16–23 years – work–life tensions: challenges to motivation and commitment

(N = 46: 27 × primary; 19 × secondary)[8]

Work–life tensions: challenges to motivation and commitment

Almost all of the teachers in this cohort (41 out of 46 = 89 per cent; 25 primary = 93 per cent; 16 secondary = 84 per cent) had additional leadership responsibilities. In common with the previous two professional life phases (4–7 and 8–15), excessive paperwork and heavy workload were seen as key hindrances to their effectiveness. In contrast with teachers from the earlier professional life phases, events in personal lives, coupled with additional duties, had a stronger impact on the work of this cohort, and as a consequence, a larger proportion of teachers were struggling with a negative work–life balance. Figure 5.13 summarizes the key influences and characteristics of teachers in this professional life phase.

These teachers were categorized into three sub-groups on the basis of their management of the challenges of work–life and home events:

Sub-group a) teachers who had seen their motivation and commitment increase, as a result of their further career advancement and good pupil results/relationships, and who were most likely to see their motivation and commitment continue to grow (+23) (17 primary = 63 per cent; 6 secondary = 32 per cent).

Sub-group b) teachers who maintained their motivation, commitment and sense of effectiveness, as a consequence of their agency and determination to improve time management, and who were most likely to cope with work–life tensions in their next professional life phase (+15) (8 primary = 30 per cent; 7 secondary = 37 per cent).

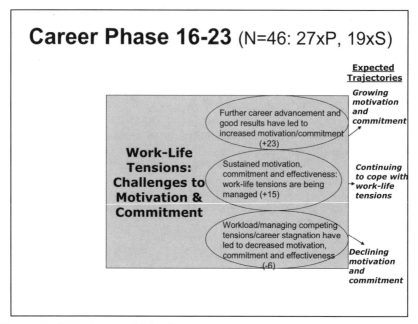

Figure 5.13 Professional life phase 16–23.

Sub-group c) teachers whose workload, management of competing tensions and career stagnation had led to decreased motivation, commitment and perceived effectiveness, and whose career trajectories were expected to be coupled with declining motivation and commitment (–6) (1 primary = 4 per cent; 5 secondary = 27 per cent).

Figures 5.14 and 5.15 summarize key influences on the work of two of these sub-groups. These show the negative influence of work–life tensions on teachers with 16–23 years' experience. Figure 5.15 shows that in addition to work–life tensions, the combined negative effects of pupil behaviour, personal events, policy, leadership and CPD had strongly contributed to sub-group c) teachers' decreased motivation and career stagnation. For example,

I'm tired. You're always dealing with three or four things at a time . . . You either draw a line and do not do what you know needs doing and spend time with the family and go out, or you do work and lock yourself away. I do a combination of both . . . I consider now I'm approaching my 40th year. Thinking of what I'm doing now for the next 20 years fills me with horror. I would like to ease back and keep the same salary.

(Jo, secondary)

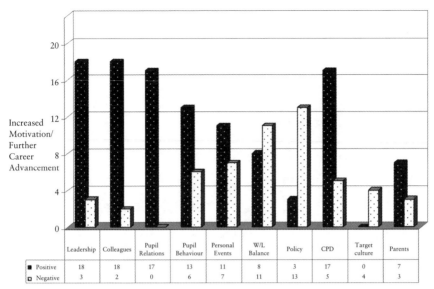

Figure 5.14 Key influences on teachers with sustained motivation (professional life phase 16–23).

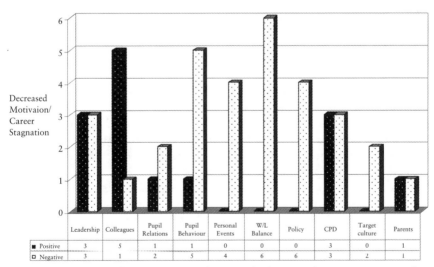

Figure 5.15 Key influences on teachers with decreased motivation (professional life phase 16–23).

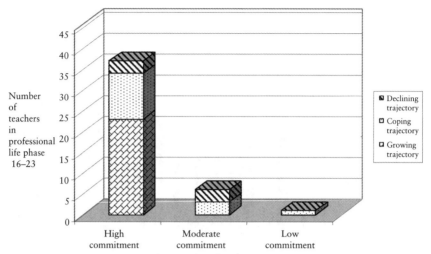

Figure 5.16 Variations in the levels of commitment (professional lilfe phase 16–23) (N = 46).

The impact of the above key influences on these sub-groups' commitment can be seen in Figure 5.16.

Portraits of teachers

Michael – growing motivation and commitment

Michael was in his late forties and had been teaching for over 20 years. He taught in two small, rural schools before taking his current post which he had held for 15 years. In addition to being a Year 6 teacher, Michael was also a subject co-ordinator. The school had 250 pupils on roll, drawn from a range of relatively advantaged backgrounds (FSM2).

Michael saw his school as a positive place to work, led by the head who was 'a strong character'. The headteacher had retired during the project and Michael was appointed acting deputy head, a post which he held for two terms. Although later he was not successful in his application for this permanent post, the experience had increased his confidence. He became more involved with other staff and in school activities. Michael saw the new head as 'a breath of fresh air' who was calm, approachable and supportive.

Pupils were the main source of his motivation and job satisfaction – 'The actual kids have motivated me more than anything else.' He resented the endless changes and excessive paperwork, and saw them as having a negative influence on his work as a teacher. Michael felt that he still looked forward to being at work. He was thinking of looking for promotion in other schools.

Cathy – continuing to cope

Cathy was in her mid-forties when the project began and had been teaching English for more than two decades, almost all in an 11–16 years, over-subscribed, suburban secondary school (arts college) with 1000 pupils and FSM at 21 per cent. She had responsibility for the library and had recently been appointed Key Stage 3 co-ordinator and deputy head of department. She regularly attended CPD events, all connected directly with her role. She had been attracted to teaching because she wanted 'to help pupils of all abilities achieve their full potential', and her motivation was still high. She worked 46–55 hours per week. Though she experienced high levels of stress, these only occasionally affected her work. In the late 1990s, pupil intake to the school changed. She now spent significant 'teaching' time in managing pupil behaviour. While her self-efficacy, commitment and motivation remained high, her job satisfaction was declining as she experienced deterioration in pupils' behaviour. The SLT did not provide leadership to combat this, being, in her view, 'over tolerant'.

Her recent promotion, however, had renewed her motivation and interest in her career which, prior to this had become 'a little stagnant!' Cathy had not really changed other than 'spending more hours working at home' because of her new responsibility. She was established in the school, having taught parents of present pupils, and was comfortable with her 'kind' approach with pupils. She spent more time now in 'training for the tests': 'They are having lessons before school, at break, after school as well as booster lessons. They're being overwhelmed.'

Gerard – declining motivation and commitment

Gerard was in his early fifties and had taught for almost twenty years. Currently he was a mathematics teacher, numeracy co-ordinator and form tutor in an urban (FSM3) school, of over 1000 pupils. Prior to teaching, Gerard worked in the family business for 12 years after leaving school, and went into teaching for its stability. In addition to coping with his own 'demanding' teenage children, he continued to devote himself to the family business. He did not have sufficient time for his hobbies and felt that his personal life and professional life were 'poles apart'.

Gerard found both the school and departmental leadership supportive. He felt that respect for teachers from parents was diminishing. His motivation and job satisfaction were decreasing mainly because of the deteriorating behaviour of his pupils. He disapproved of the results driven culture, and realised that his beliefs and values about education were different from those of others in his current school. Nevertheless, he still liked teaching his subject.

Gerard struggled with work–life balance – 'I worked too hard years ago and went off with stress, (which) made me more aware of life–work balance.' He found that his job satisfaction had declined – '[I] never get up wanting to go to school'. Family health issues were also a primary concern for him. On the whole, he felt that his professional life was in a 'survival' phase.

Professional life phase 24–30 years – challenges to sustaining motivation

(N = 52: 32 × primary; 20 × secondary)

Challenges to sustaining motivation

Teachers in this cohort faced more intensive challenges to sustaining their motivation in the profession (Figure 5.17). Forty-six out of 52 teachers (88 per cent) (31 primary = 97 per cent; 15 secondary = 75 per cent) had additional leadership responsibilities. In common with teachers in professional life phase 16–23, external policies and initiatives continued to exercise strong negative impacts on teachers' sense of effectiveness. Deteriorating pupil behaviour, the impact of adverse personal life events, resentment at 'being forced to jump through hoops by a constant stream of new initiatives', taking stock of their careers (and lives) and length of service

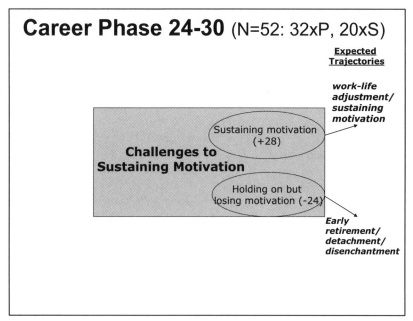

Figure 5.17 Professional life phase 24–30.

in the school, were key negative influences on the effectiveness of teachers in this cohort.

On the basis of their levels of motivation, two sub-groups were identified.

Sub-group a) teachers who had sustained a strong sense of motivation and commitment (+28) (19 primary = 59 per cent; 9 secondary = 45 per cent), and who were most likely to continue to enjoy an increase in their self-efficacy, motivation and commitment.

Sub-group b) teachers holding on but losing motivation, which was most likely to lead to a sense of detachment and early retirement (−24) (13 primary = 41 per cent; 11 secondary = 55 per cent).

The difference in teachers' motivation and commitment between these two sub-groups is illustrated in Figure 5.18.

Figures 5.19 and 5.20 illustrate key influences on these two sub-groups' work.

In common with teachers in professional life phase 16–23, policy diktats continued to demonstrate a strong negative impact on teachers' sense of effectiveness. It appears that the impact of work–life tensions and pupil behaviour, had made a major negative contribution to the professional outlook of teachers who were holding on but losing motivation, and who reported that they would consider early retirement or part-time teaching if their financial situation permitted.

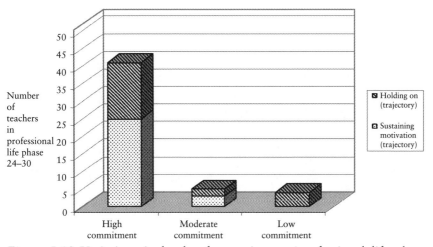

Figure 5.18 Variations in levels of commitment (professional life phase 24–30) (N = 52).

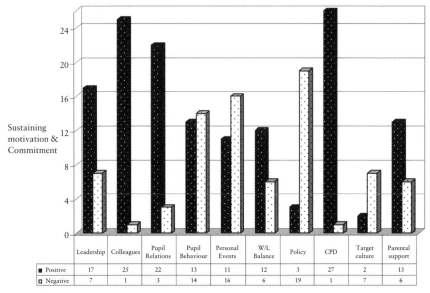

Figure 5.19 Key influences on teachers with sustained motivation (professional life phase 24–30).

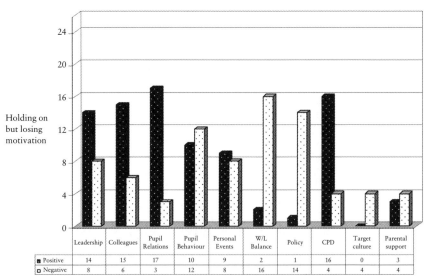

Figure 5.20 Key influences on teachers who were holding on but losing motivation (professional life phase 24–30).

Portraits of teachers

Lynda – increasing motivation and self-efficacy

Lynda was in her mid-fifties, a Year 2 teacher in a school with 173 pupils on roll. She had been teaching for more than 25 years, most in this school. The percentage of pupils eligible for free school meals was 54 per cent (FSM4). Sixty-four per cent of pupils were from ethnic minority backgrounds. Thirty-two pupils were on the register of special educational needs.

Lynda was also a subject co-ordinator. She liked working at her current school, and the staff played an important part in it. She felt that there was a lot of support from senior management for all staff, which had encouraged her to give more of herself. She was particularly positive about the headteacher and liked her open and approachable leadership style. Lynda described her colleagues as open and easy-going, friendly and welcoming. Everyone pulled together and tried to be helpful. Pupil behaviour was 'fine' in her school. There were learning support strategies in place to deal with challenging behaviour.

Lynda was married and her children had finished school. She believed that it was important to have time to herself, and strived to maintain a good work–life balance. Although considering early retirement, Lynda insisted that she remained motivated to try new things in her teaching.

Patty – detachment/early retirement

Patty was in her late fifties and had been teaching for 25 years. She had been primarily attracted to teaching by the chance of working with children, and developing their skills and personalities. Patty had taught in three schools, and had been in her current post for more than 10 years. In addition to being a Year 2 teacher, she was also the Key Stage 1 manager. She enjoyed teaching because she liked to see the progress that the pupils made during the year.

Changes in the school, and the struggle to balance demands at work and at home, had challenged Patty to sustain motivation. She felt that, owing to the school having a large staff, they did not always have the time or opportunity to talk to each other. However, she believed that colleagues were very supportive when there were personal problems. She was experiencing difficult pupil behaviour, especially from boys. Although her job satisfaction remained constant, her level of self-efficacy decreased. This was largely due to the amount of time she had to spend on the family business rather than on school work. Patty felt that in recent years this tension had become more difficult for her to manage, as she had to take more paperwork home from school. She had decided to retire soon. This teacher will be discussed from the perspective of teacher identity in Chapter 6.

Professional life phase 31+ – sustaining/declining motivation, ability to cope with change, looking to retire

(N = 22: 11 × primary; 11 × secondary)

Sustaining/declining motivation, ability to cope with change, looking to retire

Government policies, excessively bureaucratic results driven systems, pupil behaviour, poor health, increased paperwork, heavy workloads and the consequent long working hours, has had a negative impact on the motivation and perceived effectiveness of teachers in this phase. Pupils' progress and positive teacher–pupil relationships were the main source of job satisfaction for these teachers. This cohort was categorized into two sub-groups (Figure 5.21).

Sub-group a) teachers whose motivation and commitment remained high despite or because of changing personal, professional and organizational contexts and whose expected trajectories were strong agency, efficacy and achievement (+14) (7 primary = 64 per cent; 7 secondary = 64 per cent).

Sub-group b) teachers whose motivation was declining or had declined,

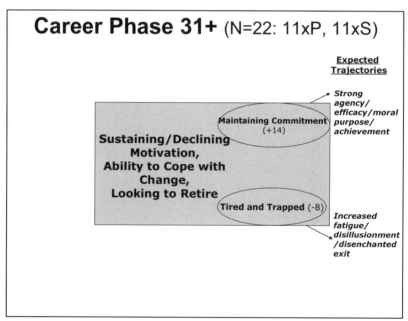

Figure 5.21 Professional life phase 31+.

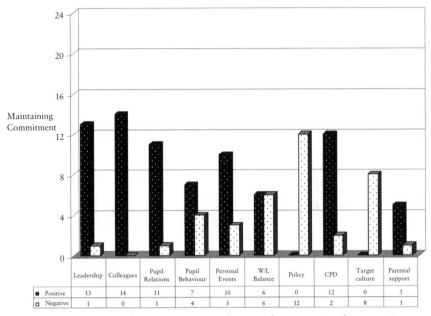

	Leadership	Colleagues	Pupil Relations	Pupil Behaviour	Personal Events	W/L Balance	Policy	CPD	Target culture	Parental support
■ Positive	13	14	11	7	10	6	0	12	0	5
□ Negative	1	0	1	4	3	6	12	2	8	1

Figure 5.22 Key influences on teachers who sustained commitment (professional life phase 31+).

and whose expected trajectories were increased fatigue, disillusionment and exit (−8) (4 primary = 37 per cent; 4 secondary = 37 per cent).

Figures 5.22 and 5.23 indicate key influences on these two sub-groups' work, the outcomes of which can be seen in Figure 5.24.

Huberman (1993) maintains that there is a 'distinct phase of "disengagement" (serene or bitter)' towards the end of teachers' careers:

> . . . the data of the present study do support the thesis of an increasing detachment near or at the conclusion of the career cycle, characterized mostly by a greater focusing on preferred classes, preferred tasks and preferred aspects of the academic programme.
>
> (Huberman 1993: 12)

Such a sense of bitter disengagement and disillusion was also found in our study, but not to the same extent. In contrast with Huberman's observation of disengagement, most of the teachers in the first sub-group had continued to demonstrate a high level of motivation and commitment, and a strong sense of 'active' engagement in the teaching profession. They remained highly committed to improving their knowledge within the classroom. Our analysis suggests, not only, that supportive school cultures

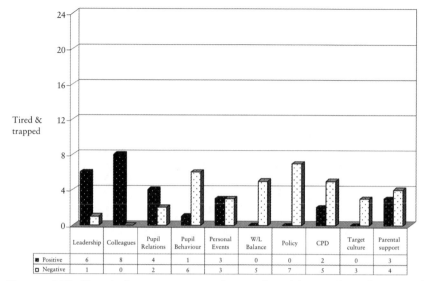

Figure 5.23 Key influences on teachers who felt tired and trapped (professional life phase 31+).

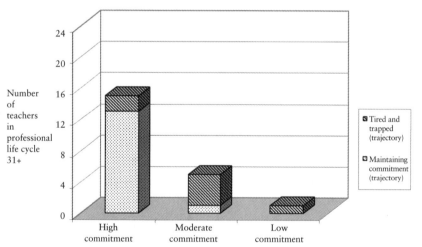

Figure 5.24 Variations in levels of motivation (professional life phase 31+) (N = 22).

were of crucial importance to teachers' sense of effectiveness across all six professional life phases, but that for teachers in this professional life phase, in-school support played a major part in teachers' continued engagement in the profession.

Portraits of teachers

Jeremy – sustained motivation and commitment

Jeremy was in his mid-fifties and had been teaching for over thirty years. Despite his ill health in the final phase of his career, he had remained highly motivated and committed to teaching and to his pupils. Since his promotion to head of department in his early career, Jeremy had seen a steady increase in his sense of effectiveness. He had been in his current school (FSM4) for around two decades, having served previously in several others. With several more years of teaching to retirement, he did not intend to move to another school.

Jeremy was well supported by the headteacher and the local authority, and felt that they had helped him in making improvements to the department, of which he was head, and the school more generally. He had recently been invited to be a member of the senior leadership team. Jeremy found that high staff morale has had the biggest positive impact on his work. He enjoyed teaching because of the success he had with the pupils and the department. Jeremy was committed to working with children from impoverished home environments and identified himself strongly with them, having high expectations. He acknowledged, however, that pupil behaviour was, on the whole, deteriorating.

Jeremy had been diagnosed with a health problem, and had tried to cut down on the amount of time he spent working 'after hours'. Nevertheless, he continued to work at weekends. He remained highly motivated and committed to teaching.

Jacqueline – tired and trapped

Jacqueline was in her early fifties and had taught for over thirty years. She was a Year 6 teacher and deputy head in an urban FSM2 primary school. She came from a teaching family and was originally attracted to teaching because of the opportunity 'to change things for the better through education'. This still applied but she found it 'harder to see the possibility'.

She appreciated support from the school leadership and her 'charismatic colleagues', but felt that the deteriorating behaviour of the pupils had a negative effect on her teaching. She also found that parental pressure had greatly increased over time.

She wanted either to take early retirement or become part-time, because she did not think that she 'could keep up this kind of pressure for the next five years'. She believed that she had maintained her commitment over the long term, but regretted that her enthusiasm had diminished. Because of government initiatives and changes, Jacqueline found teaching a difficult job – 'Nothing is ever finished.' She resented the paperwork – 'I didn't come into teaching to fill in bits of paper.' She was also strongly against the target-driven culture because she did not think SATS had much value in improving her teaching or her pupils' learning. After over 30 years' teaching, she felt tired and 'trapped'.

Conclusion

Our identification and analysis of teachers' professional life phases suggests that the understanding of teachers' professional life progression requires a consideration of factors, not only within the organizational settings, but also how these factors interact with, and are managed by, organizations and teachers in conjunction with factors arising from their personal lives. While there are a number of common influences which affect teachers positively or negatively across their professional life phases, there are variations in the impact of these which affect, positively and negatively, their diverse professional life trajectories. Teachers' professional life phases, then, are by no means static. They are dynamic in nature. The interaction between a range of influencing factors in their work and personal contexts is a sophisticated and continuous process, and impacts differentially on teachers' perceived effectiveness both within and across different phases of their professional lives.

An interesting finding regarding teachers' professional life phases is the unique experiences of late entry teachers. These 'older' teachers (in terms of age) exhibited a similar professional outlook to that of their younger peers in the same professional life phase. However, because of the age factor and its associated personal needs and concerns, they faced similar work–life tensions to those who were in the same age range but were in later professional life phases. This suggests that the influence of age and life experience on teachers' identity and professional life growth is not a linear one, but rather depends on issues, such as their sense of efficacy, resilience and how tensions are managed, together with the impact of sometimes hard to predict life events. This again points to the advantage of studying teachers' effectiveness from the perspective of their professional life phases rather than age.

An overview of teachers' six professional life phases reveals generational differences in teachers' professional experience and views of educational change. Poor pupil behaviour had a negative impact on both early and late years teachers. However, for the latter, it was more of a nostalgic attitude towards a 'golden past' (Welch 1987). Resistance to mandated reforms was found in most later years teachers and regarded as, to a larger or lesser extent, a denial of their values, status and experience which they might have treasured and enjoyed throughout their professional lives. Goodson *et al.* (2006) explain that:

> Resistance to change . . . is as much about generation as degeneration –
> the first being concerned with the construction, protection, and

reconstruction of professional and life missions; the second being about the deconstruction and erosion of physical capacities and professional commitment. Understanding resistance to change as a process of fulfilling, preserving, and protecting the missions and memories of one's generation draws attention to a positive sense of what teachers are fighting for (Fullan and Hargreaves 1996), rather than merely what they are opposed to or against.

(Goodson et al. 2006: 43–44)

However, contrary to their observation, an important finding of the VITAE research is that despite some later years teachers' 'embittered' experiences of the present (Lasch 1991) and nostalgia for the past, the large majority of these teachers continued to demonstrate a strong sense of commitment to their work.

These findings challenge traditional 'stage theory', which conceptualizes teachers' professional development as moving through a number of linear skills development stages – from being a 'novice' through to 'advanced beginner', 'competent', 'proficient' and 'expert' (Benner 1984; Dreyfus and Dreyfus 1986; Day 1999). Futhermore, as Chapter 9 shows, teachers in their later professional life phases – who are usually regarded as experienced or established – are not necessarily more effective in relation to their pupils' levels of attainment than their younger counterparts.

Key messages

Message 1   There is a difference between 'career' and 'professional life' phase. The former relates to out of classroom responsibilities and promotion. The latter relates to broader professional characteristics, concerns and needs.

Message 2   Chronological age alone does not adequately explain teachers' development and the influences upon this.

Message 3   Teachers may be grouped into one of six professional life/ experience phases, each with similar concerns, influences and positive and negative trajectories of effectiveness.

Message 4   There are key generic influences which affect teachers' sense of effectiveness across all phases: i) personal life experiences/events; ii) school (roles and responsibilities, classroom settings, leadership and colleagues); iii) pupils (relationships and behaviour) and iv) professional values and policies (national).

Message 5   Recognizing the impact of these and the interactions within and between them, is of crucial importance in understanding how and why teachers do, or do not, sustain their commitment and sense of effectiveness.

six

Emotional contexts of teaching: agency, vulnerability and professional identities

Introduction

This chapter focuses upon the ways in which the interactions between teachers' professional beliefs, work and life scenarios, and the extent to which they are able to manage these can affect their sense of professional identity. It suggests that identity is an important determinant, and plays a crucial part in influencing teachers' emotional well-being and effectiveness.

Teachers' sense of professional and personal identity is a key variable in their motivation, job fulfilment, commitment and self-efficacy; and is itself affected by the extent to which teachers' own needs for autonomy, competence and relatedness are met. Identity should, however, not be confused with role:

> Identity must be distinguished from what, traditionally, sociologists have called roles and role sets. Roles . . . are defined by norms structured by the institutions and organizations of society. Their relative weight in influencing people's behaviour depends upon negotiations and arrangements between individuals and those institutions and organizations. Identities are sources of meaning for the actors themselves, and by themselves, constructed through the process of individuation.
>
> (Castells 1997: 6–7)

Teacher identity, then, is how teachers define themselves to themselves and others, and is a construct that evolves over the duration of a career (Ball and Goodson 1985; Sikes *et al.* 1985; Huberman 1993).

In much educational literature it is recognized that the broader social conditions in which teachers live and work, the emotional contexts, and the personal and professional elements of teachers' lives, experiences, beliefs and practices are integral to one another, and that there are often tensions between these which impact, to a greater or lesser extent, upon teachers' sense of self or identity. If identity is a key influencing factor on teachers' sense of purpose, self-efficacy, motivation and commitment, and effectiveness, then investigation of those factors which influence identities positively and negatively, the contexts in which these occur and the consequences for practice, is essential. Surprisingly, although notions of 'self' and personal identity are much used in educational research and theory, critical engagement with individual teachers' cognitive and emotional 'selves' has been relatively rare (Nias 1998). Yet such engagement is important to all with an interest in raising and sustaining standards of teaching, particularly in contexts which threaten to destabilize long held beliefs and practices (Day *et al.* 2006a).

Development of teachers' identities

Personal and professional

The development of a teacher's identity is a dynamic process. It occurs over time through continued interaction with others (Cooper and Olson 1996). Several researchers (Nias 1989, 1996; Hargreaves 1994; Sumsion 2002) have noted that professional identities are not only constructed from technical and emotional aspects of teaching (i.e. classroom management, subject knowledge and pupil test results) and their personal lives, but also '. . . as the result of an interaction between the personal experiences of teachers and the social, cultural, and institutional environment in which they function on a daily basis' (Sleegers and Kelchtermans 1999: 579).

Reforms have an impact upon teachers' identities and, because these are both cognitive and emotional, create reactions which are both rational and non-rational. Thus, existing identities may become what MacLure has described as 'a continuing site of struggle' (1993: 312). Instabilities, whether of a personal, professional or situated nature, or a combination of these, create stresses in the fabric of identity and these need to be managed. Teachers need to be resilient and to be supported during these periods, in order that these may be managed in ways that build or sustain positive identities and existing effectiveness. Critical of earlier notions of an essential or substantial 'self', MacLure (1993) proposed the concept of an 'active' agential teacher self which is formed and informed through the 'discursive practices' and interactions in which individuals engage. Here identity is not a stable entity that people possess, but rather is constructed within given sets of social relations.

Contrasting the teachers in the Teachers' Jobs and Lives project with those within Nias' (1989) study, which took place in a more stable policy context, MacLure argued that the teachers in her study appeared to be more varied in their senses of themselves, much less secure in their identities as teachers, and less committed to teaching as a career. In doing so, she was acknowledging, perhaps, that in the period since Nias' work, teachers have more frequently come to occupy positions of increasing uncertainty and constraint. This need not imply that all teachers have a reduced sense of 'agency' *per se*. An increase in constraint can be seen to imply, however, that the 'opportunity costs' attached to teachers' agency (Archer 1996) have changed – that the 'costs' for teachers of asserting their agency in order to achieve their particular individual and/or professional satisfactions are now higher, for example, in respect of their personal relationships, health and well-being (discussed later in the chapter), and the quality of learning which they provide for their pupils. The importance of MacLure's work is that, like that of others (Day and Hadfield 1996) it indicates that teachers' identities are, in some cases, less stable, less convergent and less coherent than is often implied by notions of a 'substantive self' (Nias 1989).

The role of emotion

Over the past 20 years there has been increased interest in the role of emotions in teaching (Golby 1996; Hargreaves, 1996, 2000, 2001; Kelchtermans 1996; Acker 1999). One of the central arguments of early studies was that 'effective teaching and learning is necessarily affective, that it involves human interaction, and that the quality of teacher–pupil relationships is vitally important to the learning process' (Osborn 1996: 455). Other notions were those of stress and burnout which demonstrated that structural characteristics were central to the experiences of teachers and to their job satisfaction (Vandenberghe and Huberman 1999).

We know that the emotional climate of the school and classroom will affect attitudes to and practices of teaching and learning, and that teachers (and their students) experience an array of sometimes contrasting emotions in the classroom. Thus, a significant and ongoing part of being a teacher is the experiencing and management of strong emotions. Experiences of emotion are interconnected with personal beliefs, context and culture (Lasky 2000) and play, therefore, a key role in the construction of identity (Zembylas 2003). They are the necessary link between the social structures in which teachers work and the ways they act:

> . . . emotion is a necessary link between social structures and social actor. The connection is never mechanical because emotions are normally not compelling but inclining. But without the emotions category, accounts

of situated actions would be fragmentary and incomplete. Emotion is provoked by circumstance and is experienced as transformation of dispositions to act. It is through the subject's active exchange with others that emotional experiences is both stimulated in the actor and orienting of their conduct. Emotion is directly implicated in the actor's transformation of their circumstances, as well as the circumstances' transformation of the actor's disposition to act.

(Barbalet 2002: 4)

The literature suggests that identities are an amalgam of personal biography, culture, social influence and institutional values, which may change according to role and circumstance. They depend upon:

the sustaining of coherent, yet continuously revised, biographical narratives, [which] takes place in the context of multiple choice ... Reflexively organized life planning ... becomes a central feature of the structuring of self identity.

(Giddens 1991: 5)

Thus, the ways and extent to which reforms are received, adopted, adapted and sustained or not sustained, will not only be influenced by teachers' emotional selves but will exercise influence upon them.

There is an unavoidable interrelationship between professional and personal, cognitive and emotional identities, if only because the overwhelming evidence is that teaching demands significant personal investment of these:

The ways in which teachers form their professional identities are influenced both by how they feel about themselves and how they feel about their students. This professional identity helps them to position or situate themselves in relation to their students and to make appropriate and effective adjustments in their practice and their beliefs about and engagement with students.

(James-Wilson 2001: 29)

Thus it is not surprising that, because of their emotional investments, teachers can experience a range of negative emotions when control of long-held principles and practices is challenged, or when trust and respect from parents, the public and their students is eroded.

Conceptualizing teacher identity

Our conceptualization of teacher identity draws on the existing research on identity, as well as on the evidence from the 300 teachers involved in the

VITAE project. While this existing research is helpful in understanding teachers' professional identities, it does, nevertheless, have limitations:

1   Studies disagree over the issue of whether identities are substantive (essential) or contingent stable or unstable.
2   All are limited by their lack of longitudinal 'real time' data.
3   None seek to address possible relationships between identity and teachers' effectiveness, either perceived or in value added measures of pupil attainment.
4   More or less cognisance is taken of:

   • Macro structures: broad social/cultural features usually referred to in discussions of social diversity and/or government policy
   • Meso structures: the social/cultural/organizational formations of schools and teacher education
   • Micro structures: talked of in terms of colleagues, pupils and parents
   • Personal biographies: values, beliefs, ideologies
   • Emotional factors.

The longitudinal 'real time' data from teachers participating in VITAE provides an holistic picture of variations in teachers' lives, work and effectiveness across macro, meso and micro level contexts and different biographical and experience phases. This suggests that some teachers themselves do seek and find, in different ways, their own sense of stability within what appears from the outside to be fragmented identities. Furthermore, it suggests that neither stability nor instability will necessarily influence their effectiveness. On the contrary, the research indicates that many find and maintain meaning in their work through a strong sense of personal and professional agency and moral purpose; and that these contribute to their commitment and resilience which are key factors in their perceived and measured effectiveness (see Chapters 10 and 11 for a full discussion of these).

Dimensions of identity

A core message from the VITAE research is that identity itself is a composite consisting of competing interactions between personal, professional and situational factors:

1   Professional identity – open to the influence of long-term policy and social trends as to what constitutes a good teacher, classroom practitioner etc. It could have a number of competing and conflicting elements, such as local or national policy, CPD, workload, roles and responsibilities etc.
2   Situated or socially located identity within a specified school, department

or classroom – affected by pupils, support and feedback loops from teachers' immediate working context, connected to long-term identity.

3 Personal identity – based on life outside of school, it could have various competing elements, such as identity of being a father, son, partner etc. Feedback comes from family and friends and these often become sources of tension as the individual's sense of identity could become out of step.

Each dimension of identity is subject to a number of positive and negative influences. It is the degree of dominance which these influences have on each dimension of identity, and the way teachers manage them, which determine the relative stability or instability of teachers' composite identities and whether these are positive or negative (Figure 6.1).

Four scenarios were identified by the degree of dominance that each of these dimensions had on aspects of a teacher's life at a given time: dimensions in relative balance, one dominant dimension, two dominant dimensions and three conflicting dimensions. Our analysis of data collected from various sources (e.g. teacher interview, survey) over three years, showed that teachers, once in a particular scenario, were able to be grouped into one of four identity 'states': stable positive or negative, and unstable positive or negative. (Instability is not necessarily negative. It can stimulate a re-evaluation of current thinking and practices which may no longer be the most effective in the work situation.)

Figure 6.2 shows an identity that is stable, that is, the dimensions are being held in balance. Thus, although there might be mild fluctuation within and between these from time to time, no action would need to be taken *unless stability is negative*, i.e. resulting in continuing ineffectiveness.

However, when identity is unstable, i.e. when one or more dimension is

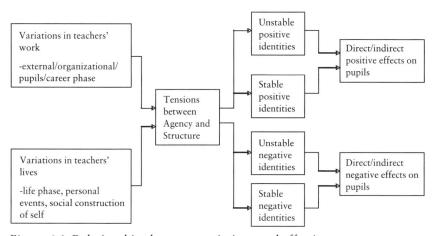

Figure 6.1 Relationships between variations and effectiveness.

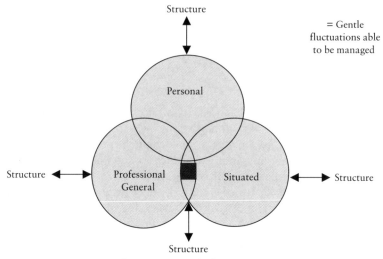

Figure 6.2 Scenario 1 – dimensions in balance.

disturbed by internal or external events (e.g. personal crises, policy changes, pupil changes, school changes), then additional effort would have to be made by the individual in order to manage the imbalance.

Any one (or more) of these three dimensions of identity may, at a particular time and/or in particular scenarios, become dominant, requiring additional time and attention from the teacher and affecting their sense of vulnerability, well-being, agency and effectiveness.

Vulnerability

For the purposes of this chapter, the term vulnerability is defined as an inability to find a suitable strategy for coping with challenging situations or scenarios, a lack of a strong sense of agency, a sense of helplessness, submissiveness or compliance which may be short- or longer-term depending upon the extremity of the scenario experienced and the strength of belief and purpose. In England, Jeffrey and Woods (1996) found professional uncertainty, confusion, inadequacy, anxiety, mortification and doubt among teachers when they investigated primary school teachers' responses to external (Ofsted) inspections, associating these with 'de-humanization' and 'de-professionalism'. Other negative emotions were: frustration; anger exacerbated by tiredness, stress and students' misbehaviour; anxiety because of the complexity of the job; guilt, sadness, blame and shame at not being able to achieve ideals or targets imposed by others.

More recently, vulnerability has been described as:

. . . a multidimensional, multi-faceted emotional experience that individuals can feel in an array of contexts. It is a fluid state of being that
can be influenced by the way people perceive their present situation as it
interacts with their identity, beliefs, values and sense of competence.

(Lasky 2005: 4)

As in our own conceptualization of teacher identity, Lasky suggests that
vulnerability is a fluctuating state, triggered by critical events in the lives and
work of teachers which results in individuals feeling as if they have 'no direct
control over factors that affect their immediate context, or feel they are
being "forced" to act in ways that are inconsistent with their core beliefs and
values' (2005: 4). The impact of this can result in defensive and protective
behaviour and create feelings of anger, frustration and inefficacy, as well as
the potential unwillingness of teachers to take on new ideas and change
(Lasky 2004). Vulnerability also poses challenges to commitment and resilience which are discussed in Chapters 10 and 11. Thus understanding this
vulnerability is crucial for its management.

Well-being

There are many definitions of well-being. Among these are those that follow developmental perspectives which emphasize the differing challenges
confronted in various phases of life and work (Erikson 1959; Buhler and
Marschak 1968; Neugarten 1973).

Suh *et al.* (1996) examined the interplay between positive and negative life
events and the impact of these upon well-being. They went on to suggest that
the events that have a direct impact on an individual's well-being (and vulnerability) depend on four factors: the stability of the event; adaptation;
structure of the event; and personality. We would add to these: professional
life phase influence, values, and a number of mediating factors which are
discussed in the next chapter.

These often competing demands that are experienced by individuals are
characterized by Grant-Vallone and Donaldson (2001) as 'work stressors'
and 'non-work stressors'. 'Work stressors' included the number of hours
worked and workload, whereas the 'non-work stressors' were described as
children, relationships, health etc. Also included in this latter category was
the interaction between work and family commitments (Higgins *et al.* 1994;
Frone *et al.* 1997). The potential impact of a lack of balance between work
and life has been found to lead to poorer health (Easterlin 2003), including
higher stress levels (Chapman and Harris 2004), increased depression
(Googins 1991), physical ailments (Frone *et al.* 1997; Grzywacz 2000),
decreased quality of family life (Higgins *et al.* 1992) and lower energy levels
(Googins 1991), of particular significance to teachers who are interacting

with thirty or more individuals for most of their working lives. Other recent research (Grzywacz and Marks 2000) has proposed a broader perspective on the work and home balance, which also encompasses the positive aspects of life and work satisfaction. For example, work may positively 'spill over' to home by developing a sense of purpose, respect and competence in a career, or by maintaining contact with friends and peers.

Seligman identifies two states relating to long-term well-being:

> (i) a feeling of gratification that arises when one is engaged in pursuing one's strengths, and the resultant feeling of 'flow'; and (ii) a sense of meaning that derives from pursuing goals in the service of something of wider significance than oneself . . .
>
> (Seligman (2002) in Huppert and Baylis 2004: 1448)

Teachers' sense of agency

The concept of agency has been applied in research studies (Gergen 1987; McAdams 1993) in order to explain the behaviour and perception of individuals, and to highlight aspects of their personality and identity etc. It has been defined as 'intentional acting aiming at self-protection, self-expansion, and mastery of social reality' (Pulkkinen and Aaltonen 2003: 146). Theorists (Brandt 1996; Russell 1996) have agreed that agency relates to actions that are intentionally initiated and, although reliant on various factors and opportunities, is ascribed to those who attempt to modify their environment according to their aims and necessity. Moreover, a sense of agency has to be driven by the individual.

Flammer refers to agency as an 'innate basic need for control' (1990: 115) which varies in strength throughout an individual's life as particular events arise.

> Thus, the various control needs are always goal-oriented and manifest themselves in specific control behaviours that are mediated and accompanied by corresponding cognitive and emotional processes, that is, control beliefs and control feelings or emotions.
>
> (Schneewind 1995)

Earl (1987) postulated a concept of self trust that he defined as 'the faith (belief plus action) in one's ability to fulfil a perceived task' (1987: 421), consolidating the position that agency is exercised through action and not purely on the basis of positive belief. That is, if an individual believes they can effect change, then they are more likely to find the most appropriate way of doing so.

The importance of agency in relation to teachers' work and lives is underpinned by Giddens' (1991) notion that human agency and social structure are not separate concepts or constructs, but two complementary ways of considering social action; the first comprising individuals who undertake social action and interaction in various situations, and the second involving the rules, resources and social relationships that are a result of social interaction (Giddens 1986). Agency is mediated by interactions between the individual and the structures of a given social setting (Lasky 2004). A sense of agency, therefore, is developed when an individual feels able to pursue their goals within the context of positive and negative interactions within and between internal situated (e.g. colleagues, school context, leadership) and personal (e.g. health, family) factors, and external professional factors (e.g. workload, career structure). Moreover, teacher agency impacts, and is impacted upon, by the structural and contextual features of the school and profession (Datnow *et al.* 2002).

We found a dynamic relationship between identity, agency and structure (external influences), and effectiveness (both perceived and measured). Agency in relation to identity is, therefore, concerned with: the fulfilment of each of the three dimensions; their reconstruction where necessary; the management of critical incidents and experiences which may threaten them or which need to be managed; and the extent to which people can live with contradictions and tensions within these various dimensions, and continue to be effective in their workplace.

Strategic management

In order to manage the balance (stability) or imbalance (instability) of identity, strategies were adopted, consciously or unconsciously, by VITAE teachers to deal with particular circumstances. Such management appeared to involve the conscious or unconscious use of one or a combination of a number of these:

- **Accommodating** by adjusting one or more component to the needs of the others
- **Tolerating** the imbalance to the system caused by the new circumstances
- **Subjugating** one or more component to accommodate the needs of the other(s)
- **Resisting** any change
- **Re-evaluating** the nature of the existing composite identity
- **Accepting** the imbalance positively
- **Separating** one part of work or life from another
- **Engaging** with one or more components with full commitment
- **Re-focusing** from one component to another
- **Adapting** to the new situation in a positive way.

Adopting these strategies was likely to affect existing identity. The impact upon motivation, self-efficacy, well-being, commitment, resilience and effectiveness related to a greater or lesser extent to: whether the dominant dimension(s) had to be managed over a short-, medium- or long-term (e.g. unsatisfactory relationships in the classroom, staffroom or home); individual biographies (i.e. the strength of their values and aspirations, their resilience/vulnerability to stress of different kinds, and physical health); personal and professional support (e.g. leadership, colleagues and friends etc.); and sense of agency.

The extent to which the scenarios were managed depended in part upon the level of disturbance or fluctuation and in part upon the combination of internal influences (e.g. strength of personal values) and external influences (e.g. school leadership, teacher–pupil relationships, pupil behaviour, colleague support, home circumstances). Teachers' sense of vulnerability, well-being or agency, related to the degree to which these influences were perceived by them as being positive or negative.

Key characteristics and influences within scenarios

Teachers were grouped on the basis of the degree of dominance of a particular influence (or combination of influences). Four scenarios were identified which reflected different relationships between these dimensions of identity. Table 6.1 shows the number of teachers in each of the four scenarios.

Analyses of the key features of teachers' professional life phases, school context, perceived effectiveness, motivation and commitment, and self-

Table 6.1: Number of teachers in each Scenario

Scenario	Dimension	Sub-groups			Total
Scenario 1	dimensions in balance				102 (35%)
Scenario 2	one dominant dimension	professional (N=46)	situated (N=57)	personal (N=28)	131 (44%)
Scenario 3	two dominant dimensions	professional and situated (N=15)	professional and personal (N=16)	situated and personal (N=13)	44 (15%)
Scenario 4	three dominant dimensions				18 (6%)
					295

efficacy revealed dominant patterns which characterized each scenario. Each scenario contained teachers who were resilient (i.e. were sustaining their commitment) and those who were vulnerable (i.e. were sustaining their commitment despite the scenario or not sustaining it).

The first was holding the three dimensions in balance. Over a third (35 per cent, N = 102) of teachers were in this group, with over half coming from primary schools and the majority coming from more advantaged schools. The dominant characteristics of this group of teachers included being highly motivated, committed and self-efficacious. In the second scenario, one dimension was dominant, for example, immediate school demands dominating and impacting on the other two. This was the largest group (44 per cent, N = 131 teachers), predominantly from the 4–15 years professional life phases and more likely to be female (82 per cent). Most were highly committed and saw themselves as effective. A third of these teachers were rated as vulnerable in terms of resilience, while less than a quarter reported positive well-being. Coping strategies included accepting the imbalance, subjugating one dimension ('life on hold') or tolerating it for the present.

In the third scenario, two dimensions dominated and impacted on the third. Over half of this smaller group (44) were secondary teachers. While their motivation levels generally remained high, they were more negative about their well-being and work–life balance. Half were judged to be vulnerable in terms of effectiveness and were likely to use strategies of resisting change and separating one dimension from another. Finally, the fourth scenario represents a state of extreme fluctuation in which each dimension is unstable. Of the 18 teachers in this small but vulnerable group, nearly three-quarters (72 per cent) taught in socially disadvantaged schools (FSM3 and 4). Teachers in FSM4 were more likely to be resilient than those in other schools, but were, also, more likely to experience health problems.

By drawing on the stories of four of the participating teachers, the following section provides an overview of the complex analyses of the professional identity of 295 teachers (Day *et al.* 2006a)[9].

Scenario 1: Identity dimensions in balance (N = 102)

Teachers in this scenario experience minor fluctuations in their professional, situated or personal lives but these are able to be managed and no one dimension became dominant. In general terms, teachers in this group have high levels of motivation and commitment, and their comments regarding well-being are generally positive.

A portrait of Lesley

Work and life contexts

Lesley was in her mid-thirties and had been teaching for four years. Before this she had worked in the financial sector for over a decade. She taught mathematics in a large comprehensive school of 1527 pupils in a relatively prosperous urban area (FSM1). At the start of the project, she was very enthusiastic about her teaching, particularly the support she had received from her head of department. Her relative effectiveness, measured by Year 9 pupils' value added attainments, was below what was expected at that time, although she had still felt that her self-efficacy and commitment were high.

Sense of vocation and commitment

Both of Lesley's parents had been teachers, and she grew up 'seeing how much work and pressure they were put under'. In spite of this she had always wanted to be a teacher since she was a child. She enjoyed being in a support- ive school and said that this was a major contributory factor to her sustained commitment, coupled with positive feedback from the pupils which provided her main motivation to remain in teaching.

Agency and vulnerability

The fact that Lesley was 'in balance', in terms of her identity, did not mean that that she did not experience minor fluctuations relating to one or more of the dimensions. During the first two years of the project, Lesley experienced the ill health of a child and the ending of a long-term relationship. Struggles during this period may have accounted further for pupils' 'below expec- tation' performance. However, she managed to 'accommodate' these events and sustain a strong sense of identity. In the third year of the study, her personal life increased in stability with the meeting of a new partner.

Lesley was in the 4–7 professional life phase. During this phase, teachers were more likely to be influenced by the level of staff collegiality, teacher–pupil relationship, and experiences of CPD. It was also seen as a time when teachers looked for the opportunity to take on additional responsibility, within the school, which further strengthened their emerging identities. The key characteristic was the increased confidence about being an effective teacher and the potential negative impact of heavy workloads that some teachers experienced. Teachers in this professional life phase were grouped as either: sustaining a strong sense of identity, self-efficacy and effectiveness; sustaining identity, efficacy and effectiveness; or identity, efficacy and effec- tiveness at risk (Chapter 5). Lesley wanted additional responsibility in the near future and was sustaining her identity and self-efficacy as a result of her strong sense of agency.

Based on the analysis of interview data, teachers in this scenario were identified as either likely to remain in teaching, or at risk of leaving the teaching profession as a result of the (im)balance of the dimensions of identity. Like 86 per cent (N = 91) of teachers in this scenario, Lesley demonstrated a strong sense of agency and so was not at risk of leaving her post. Moreover, she envisaged herself teaching for many more years. However, there were 21 (21 per cent of 102) teachers experiencing Scenario 1 who were thought to be vulnerable and at risk. These teachers were less likely, than their resilient colleagues, to be positive regarding their well-being and the balance they managed to achieve between the pressures of work and home life, commenting on tensions between teacher and manager roles, reduced social life, and difficulties in managing teacher, mother and wife roles.

Scenario 2: One dominant dimension of identity (N = 131)

This scenario comprises of teachers where one of the three dimensions of identity dominates, putting pressure on one or both of the other dimensions. Regardless of which of the dimensions is dominant, there are a number of core characteristics that apply to this group. These include strong and supportive leadership and colleagues, supportive family, positive pupil relationships, poor or challenging pupil behaviour, and high motivation and commitment. Many have additional responsibilities in the school or have recently been promoted. The well-being of this group was more likely to be negative with teachers saying that their workload encroached on their home life, that they were tired, needed more time to themselves, had diminished social life, and that the workload could cause arguments at home.

A portrait of Patty (dominant situated dimension)

Work and life context
Patty was a primary teacher in her late fifties and with almost thirty years of teaching, over a decade of which had been in this large, mainly white, Catholic primary school in a relatively deprived urban area (FSM3). She was the Key Stage 1 manager, and recent staffing changes, including the head and deputy, had affected her job satisfaction and self-efficacy. She encountered behaviour problems with some pupils and her pupils' value added attainments in both English and mathematics were below those predicted. She felt she balanced family demands, which included working in the family business, with her heavy school workload, and was not enjoying the pressure this put upon her. Patty was due to retire in the next year.

Sense of vocation and commitment
Patty was primarily attracted to teaching because she wanted to work with children in order to 'develop their skills and personalities'. She enjoyed watching the progression children made and working within the school community. Patty strongly believed in the school mission and hoped that the work in school had a wider impact on the community, offering a place for parents and children to come and speak to someone – to get support, and somewhere where children could feel safe in their own neighbourhood.

Agency and vulnerability
Patty's strategies to cope with these school-based factors had been to 'subjugate' and 'tolerate'. She felt as if her voice was not being heard within the school and that her opinion was not valued, despite being one of the longest serving teachers in the school. She was also feeling undermined by the retirement of two of the senior leadership team, who were friends as well as colleagues, and who were still to be replaced. Her main concern was that the new members of staff would implement many changes, including the increased use of technology, which Patty was not used to. The challenges of her recent classes had also had an impact on her, as it had resulted in her having to take more work home.

Patty was in the 24–30 professional life phase and, like many teachers in this phase, she was finding it difficult to sustain motivation. In her case, this was due to length of service in this school, challenging pupil behaviour and changes in leadership. Patty was under-performing. Maintaining motivation in the face of external policies and initiatives, which were viewed negatively, and declining pupil behaviour was the core struggle for teachers in this phase. Patty experienced this in her dominant situated dimension and had to subjugate and tolerate the situation in order to cope. While 60 per cent of primary teachers in this professional life phase were judged to have retained a strong sense of motivation, over half the secondary teachers were rated as losing motivation. Teachers in this phase were categorized as either sustaining a strong sense of motivation and commitment; or holding on but losing motivation.

Although a fairly stable scenario, the analysis found that there were a number of teachers who were either resilient but had a weak sense of agency (as in this case), or vulnerable but demonstrated a strong sense of agency. These teachers were subjugating (one or more dimension to accommodate the needs of the other(s)), accepting (the imbalance) or tolerating (the imbalance to the system caused by new circumstances).

Scenario 3: Two dominant dimensions of identity (N = 44)

A total of 32 teachers in the sample felt that two of the three dimensions of identity were dominant. In this scenario, the dominant dimensions impact upon the remaining dimension and, although they can be managed in the short-term, there is a greater dependency on the supporting factors (motivation, leadership etc.) for the scenario to be managed successfully.

A portrait of Charlie (dominant professional and situated dimensions)

Work and life context
Charlie was the headteacher of a small, rural primary FSM1 school with a falling register, a source of concern to him. He was in his early thirties and had been teaching for eight years. Over three-quarters of his time was spent classroom teaching, and balancing this with his headship was proving stressful. He married shortly after taking up the post. Though his pupils' value added attainment was in line with expectations, he reported only moderate self-efficacy because he believed his teaching was suffering.

Sense of vocation
Charlie initially wanted to become a teacher in order to teach young adults (secondary phase). It was later in his career that he moved into primary teaching and made his fast rise to headship. He had been through stages in his career when he felt that he had 'lost enthusiasm and thought nothing was good enough' (teacher questionnaire). He valued the relationship he had with staff but felt strongly about the pressures put on schools by external policies and initiatives.

Dominant professional factors
Charlie felt strongly about the pressures he and other teachers were put under by external policies and initiatives. He was still trying to adjust to his new role as headteacher, but found that he was spending a lot of his time supporting the implementation of new initiatives which he and his staff did not want. He refused to let the teaching and learning within the school be dominated by the Key Stage tests, and would rather they had been left alone to deliver the curriculum without interference. Charlie also reported that external pressures had a direct impact on teachers' sense of effectiveness, on their energy levels, and on their level of stress experienced.

Dominant situated factors
Charlie reported that it was a 'friendly school with a good family ethos and good staff collaboration' (teacher interview). He reported that he was

fortunate in not having some of the problems that larger schools had, such as bullying, disruptive pupil behaviour and high staff turnover, but was having difficulties:

> You try to keep up with other people's protocols but everyone has different ways of working.
>
> (Teacher interview)

He had clear ideas about what he wanted to achieve in the school but also realized he had to be sensitive to the opinions of others who had been working in the school for a number of years. One of his main concerns was the continuing fall in the school roll and he reported that the school situation was impacting negatively on his teaching. In the larger sample of teachers, those who were most stressed were headteachers and teachers in small rural schools all of who experienced difficulties in coping with the management, leadership and teaching workload.

Agency and vulnerability

Charlie's professional and situated dimensions had a negative impact on his self-esteem and he felt that he was at the lowest point in his career, wishing that he had not taken on the additional responsibility of headteacher:

> . . . it changes me as a person, what I'm dealing with . . . I was far happier before.
>
> (Teacher interview)

Although he felt confident that he would come through it and deal with the situation more effectively in the future, he admitted that his personal life had to be put 'on the back-burner' so that he could focus on his career. He felt tired when he got home and said that he had 'no happy time what-soever' and spent a lot of his time at home worrying about the situation at school.

Charlie's dominant situated and professional roles were causing tensions, but between his responsibilities of headteacher and class teacher. This was contributing to extreme tiredness when he got home. Charlie was demonstrating sustained engagement and commitment and was focused on his career advancement, and although he was still spending little time at home, during the 3-year fieldwork period his sense of agency strengthened and some of the pressure he was under began to decline as he settled into his new role (see Chapter 5).

Charlie was in the 8–15 professional life phase. The key characteristic of this phase was the management of tensions between conflicting roles. Charlie (dominant situated and professional dimensions) taught Year 6 in a school with less than 8 per cent free school meals. He experienced tensions between his headteacher role and his teaching role (which took four days of his time), but was performing 'as expected'.

Scenario 4: Three dominant dimensions of identity (N = 18)

This scenario describes teachers who feel that all three dimensions (professional, situated and personal) are dominant. The key influences in personal, situated and professional lives were overwhelmingly negative, such as workload, leadership, pupil behaviour, family responsibilities and personal ill-health. Their work–life balance was generally negative with teachers saying that they spent a lot of time at weekends working, that their workload encroached on their home life, that tension hindered life with family and caused lack of energy and additional stress. In one case this resulted in the teacher giving up their management responsibility. Unlike the previous groups, Scenario 4 involves extreme fluctuations which may or may not be manageable depending on the strength of support from internal and external factors, and may result in the need for longer-term management.

A portrait of Rosalind

Work and life context
Rosalind was a late entrant to teaching who had been teaching for ten years and worked in a multi-ethnic primary school of 220 pupils. A very high percentage (48 per cent) spoke English as an additional language and the percentage of pupils eligible for free school meals was high (FSM4). She was committed to helping children to achieve, and her pupils' value added attainments were above what would be expected. She was co-ordinator for science and for literacy, and for the gifted and talented programme. She did not feel she had the support of the senior leadership team and there was rapid staff turnover. Rosalind had a large family and had lost both her husband and another close relative in recent years. This, combined with her lack of job satisfaction, had left her uncertain about her future direction.

Sense of vocation
Rosalind was primarily attracted to teaching because she wanted to 'work with people' (teacher interview). She valued the time she spent with pupils and enjoyed watching them progress. The amount of enjoyment Rosalind experienced in the classroom had diminished over her career, owing to the lack of support within the school and the lack of teamwork.

Dominant situated factors

Rosalind had mixed feelings about the school – she enjoyed the facilities and resources and some aspects of the leadership, but did not always feel as if she had support from the senior leadership team. This had been compounded by the fact that a new deputy head had been appointed recently who Rosalind did not find inspiring. She tended to see relationships with colleagues as 'professionally functional, but not intimate'. Rosalind's class had required the support of a learning support assistant (LSA). The impact of having an additional adult in the classroom had not been easy for Rosalind and had substantially increased her planning and preparation time. She reported having developed good relationships with pupils, mainly owing to having taught the same class for a few years, but said she had started to look at the children in terms of percentages that could be achieved in the Key Stage tests.

Dominant professional factors

Rosalind was still seeking professional challenges but had recently decided not to apply for Advanced Skills Teacher (AST) status. This was largely because of her lack of enthusiasm brought about by the dominant situated factors. She had a number of co-ordinator roles and would have liked to progress into middle management, but did not feel that she was being given the opportunities to further her training, and was conscious of the additional time it would have meant being away from her children.

Dominant personal factors

Rosalind had a large family and was solely responsible for their welfare. This contributed significantly to the stresses in Rosalind's life outside school. She had also suffered two major losses over the past few years. She had received little support from school for her personal issues, and reported having been reminded of her teaching commitments while taking compassionate leave after the death of her husband.

> . . . a week after he was buried, the headteacher reminded me that I had taken time off during Science Week.
>
> (Teacher interview)

Agency and vulnerability

Rosalind's strategy for coping with these factors was to 're-evaluate'. She reported a lack of support from within the school from colleagues, and did not feel that there was any collaboration or teamwork, especially in relation to the LSA working in her classroom. Leadership was also an important issue and there was a sense that there had been little support for Rosalind's recent personal events. This was not the case for the majority of teachers in

FSM4 schools, who commented upon the positive support received when faced with personal issues (e.g. health, marriage break-up, caring for parents, children). These teachers also reported issues relating to classroom disruption, pupil mobility and the 'inclusion' policy which affected class composition, which often meant that pupil behaviour management took priority over the teaching and learning tasks. This was not the case for Rosalind, who maintained positive relationships with her class, although her focus had turned to the pressure of performing well in the Key Stage tests.

Rosalind was also in the 8–15 professional life phase. The negative influence of Rosalind's dominant roles had resulted in ongoing tensions between home and work which had affected the relationship she had with her children. This was largely owing to her discontentment at school, her responsibilities as a mother and her feelings of hopelessness regarding her career opportunities. However, she was managing to over-perform in terms of value added pupil attainments in a challenging FSM4 school. The strategy she had adopted was one of re-evaluation of the existing dimensions of her identity. This had led her to entertain the idea of leaving the teaching profession or moving to another school. Rosalind had demonstrated a weak sense of agency, her level of motivation was decreasing and she was feeling detached from her work.

Conclusion

Our analysis of teachers' identities found they comprised three dimensions that interact to form a composite of teacher identity. These dimensions, individually or in combination, became dominant as events occurred in teachers' work and lives which had a professional, situated and/or personal emphasis. Based on the interaction between these dimensions, teachers experienced one of four scenarios (based on the dominance of the dimension(s)) and adopted one or a combination of a number of strategies in order to address the (im)balance. The research suggests that variations in teachers' identities occurred in response to their capacities to manage the fluctuations in various scenarios, which exercised positive and/or negative influences upon their sense of stability, agency, well-being and vulnerability.

The combination of positive well-being and a strong sense of agency implies a sense of balance, a capacity to manage pressures in life and work, together with a sense of control. However, although an inevitable part of work and life, there are likely to be times when everyday pressures turn into pressures that make teachers more vulnerable which, in turn, can have adverse emotional effects. These can impact on teachers' well-being which can be positively and negatively affected by a number of issues, such as the management of the school, the school ethos and culture, staff morale and opportunities for CPD. Thus, while individual teachers' experience can be dominated (to varying degrees) in terms of professional, situated and personal influences, there are also a number of experiences and events that either 'support' or put additional 'pressure' on the teacher.

The evidence from VITAE suggests that teacher identities may change over time, as a result of such different experiences and school contexts, but that the extent to which they do so will vary. Although scenarios themselves cannot be attributed to specific professional life phases, there are particular points when certain professional and personal events are more likely to occur, as discussed above, for example, starting a family (4–7 and 8–15), taking on additional responsibility (4–7, 8–15 and 16–23). These events can be paralleled by situated factors, such as disruptive pupil behaviour or change of leadership. Identities are not, then, as earlier research suggests, either intrinsically stable or intrinsically fragmented. Rather, teacher identities may be more or less stable and more or less fragmented, at different times and in different ways according to the impact of personal, professional and situational factors or a combination of these, and the capacities of teachers to manage the different scenarios which they experience. These capacities will be influenced positively or negatively by a number of key 'mediating' or 'intervening' factors, and it is to a consideration of these to which we turn in the next chapter.

Key messages

Message 1   Effective teaching requires emotional and cognitive investments from teachers which draw upon their personal and professional experience, knowledge and skills.

Message 2   Maintaining a positive sense of identity is closely related to teachers' sense of well-being and agency. Variations in teachers' identities occur in response to their capacities to manage the fluctuations in various scenarios which exercise positive and/or negative influences upon their sense of effectiveness.

Message 3   Teacher identities are neither intrinsically positively or negatively stable, nor intrinsically fragmented, but will display characteristics of stability and/or fragmentation at difference times during a career. There are associations between the extent to which teachers are able to manage their identities, the support they receive in doing so, and their perceived effectiveness.

Message 4 Teachers in FSM3 and 4 schools which serve disadvantaged communities are more likely to need more resilience than those in other schools, and those in FSM4 schools are also more likely to experience increased health problems.

Message 5 School leaders need, as a priority, to establish school-wide structures and cultures which support teachers if they are to sustain their sense of agency, well-being and effectiveness in different professional life phases and in different identity scenarios.

seven

What helps and hinders teachers' capacities to be effective

We have known explicitly for at least thirty years, and probably implicitly for a good deal longer, that it is not the policy, or the programme, that directly produces the effect ... it is now virtually a given that variability in effects among sites within a given intervention exceeds variability between the interventions themselves, or between the intervention and the control condition ... interaction effects dominate main effects'.

(Elmore 2006: 4)

This chapter provides examples of key 'mediating' or 'intervening' factors within teachers' professional life phases and working contexts which interact to affect their effectiveness. It is organized in three parts. The first analyses how professional, situated and personal factors, which intervened in VITAE teachers' work and life contexts, affected their capacities to sustain their commitment in their different professional life phases; the second highlights the importance of the social context of teachers' work, focusing upon differences in the perceived effects of these, between teachers in primary and secondary schools and, between teachers in schools serving students from relatively advantaged and disadvantaged communities; and the third part discusses the role which continuing professional development played in their work lives.

Two broad groups of teachers were identified in VITAE: i) teachers who had sustained commitment (N = 229, 74 per cent). Within the group were those who had sustained commitment despite working in schools in challenging circumstances (N = 40); ii) teachers whose commitment was declining (N = 81).

i) Sustaining commitment

The combination of factors mentioned most frequently by teachers as contributing to their sustained commitment were:

1 **Leadership** (76 per cent)
  It's good to know that we have strong leadership who has a clear vision for the school (Larissa, Year 6).
2 **Colleagues** (63 per cent)
  We have such a supportive team here. Everyone works together and we have a common goal to work towards (Hermione, Year 2).
  We all socialize together and have become friends over time. I don't know what we'd do if someone left (Leon, Year 9).
3 **Personal support** (95 per cent)
  It helps having a supportive family who don't get frustrated when I'm sat working on a Sunday afternoon and they want to go to the park (Shaun, Year 9).

Teachers in this group were enthusiastic about their work, and confident in their ability to make a positive difference in the learning and achievement of their pupils:

Comments relating to teachers' professional and personal scenarios suggested that some teachers in this group (N = 40; 17 per cent) were managing to sustain their level of commitment despite working under considerable persistent and negative pressures largely connected to deteriorating pupil behaviour and attitudes, lack of parental support and the effects of government policies. For some, these negative pressures were mediated by one or more types of support – internal (values related), situated (in the school and/or department) and external (family and friends).

ii) Declining commitment

The combination of pressures identified most frequently in the comments over three years by teachers as challenging their sustained commitment were:

1 **Workload** (68 per cent)
  It never stops, there's always something more to do and it eats away at your life until you have no social life and no time for anything but work (Jarvis, Year 6).
  Your life has to go on hold – there's not enough time in the school day to do everything (Hermione, Year 2).
2 **Pupil behaviour** (64 per cent)
  Over the years, pupils have got worse. They have no respect for themselves or the teachers (Jenny, Year 6).

Pupil behaviour is one of the biggest problems in schools today. They know their rights and there's nothing you can do (Kathryn, Year 9).

3   **Leadership** (58 per cent)
Unless the leadership supports the staff, you're on your own. They need to be visible and need to appreciate what teachers are doing (Carmelle, Year 2).
I feel as if I'm constantly being picked on and told I'm doing something wrong (Jude, Year 9).

A total of 81 (26 per cent) teachers were in this group. Those who were considering leaving the teaching profession for a new career were either looking for promotion out of the classroom (e.g. to advisory roles) or, having suffered health problems connected to the stress of teaching, were seeking different kinds of work.

These broad groupings illustrate how, for many teachers, sustaining commitment and effectiveness in different phases of their professional lives is likely to be mediated positively or negatively by the effects of national policies, the quality of leadership, pupil behaviour, relationships with pupils, peers and personal support.

Support and challenge in teachers' professional life phases

In this part of the chapter, we provide examples of the key mediating influences and their effects upon teachers in particular professional life phases. It appears that continuing professional development is particularly important to teachers in the middle phases of their career, a 'crossroads' phase where teachers are gradually confronted with growing family issues and the tension of deciding 'where their career is going and what it has brought to them up to now' (Huberman 1993). CPD could well be seen by teachers as a means of recharging themselves professionally, and to help pursue further career advancement in the teaching profession.

Key findings were that: i) pupil behaviour appeared to be a consistent concern for teachers in all the six professional life phases. Teachers with 4–7 years' experience reported most negatively regarding the impact of pupil behaviour; ii) apart from teachers in the initial phase of their career, almost 20 per cent of teachers in the remaining five professional life phases all reported the most negative impact of external policies (e.g. OFSTED, DfES policies and initiatives) on their work as a teacher; and iii) teachers in the final phase of their career reacted most strongly to the negative impact of external policies on their motivation and perceived effectiveness.

Compared with other professional life phases, more teachers in the initial phase of their career reported on the negative impact of media portrayal on their perceived effectiveness. This may be because their self-image is relatively undeveloped and they are, therefore, more sensitive to outside views.

While there are a number of common influences which affect teachers positively or negatively across their professional life phases, there are also variations in the impact of these on their professional life trajectories. Figure 7.1 provides an overview of variations among the felt effects of key

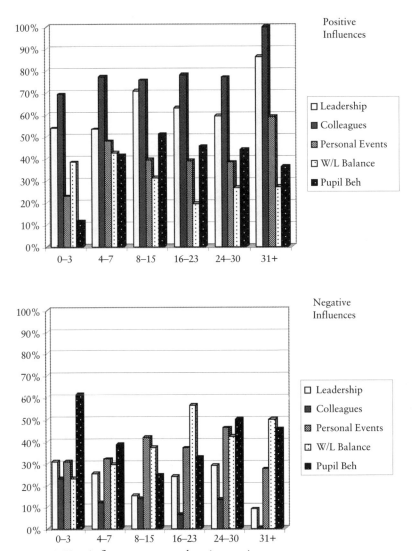

Figure 7.1 Key influences on teachers' experience.

mediating factors on teachers across six professional life phases. It illustrates how the shared and differing impact of these influences may contribute to teachers' perceived professional effectiveness as their professional lives develop.

Professional life phase 0–3 years

In-school support

The comments below by Celine (primary) and Janis (secondary), exemplify the growing sense of effectiveness and confidence of teachers who had greatly benefited from the in-school support available to them.

Celine:

> Everything seems to filter down really well, and everything seems to be discussed openly, and then decisions made as a whole staff . . . Everyone is allowed to develop. All ideas are listened to.

Janis:

> As an NQT Janis had seen her day-to-day experience improve from being 'so stressed all the time' to feeling 'more settled, confident and happier.' She began to feel that the workload was easier to cope with. Janis was highly motivated and committed to teaching. Her motivation remained high throughout the study because she saw herself continuing to develop. She was also encouraged by changes in the departmental leadership, as a result of which she had taken on extra responsibilities.
>
> Janis felt that her self-efficacy had greatly improved and was currently high – 'there aren't many students that I teach that I can't get through to and that I can't make produce work'. Her students' progress also contributed towards her high level of motivation – 'the more effort you put in then the more they get out of it'. She felt more effective as a teacher and was prepared to work harder (long term impact).

In contrast, Isaac's experiences represent those of another group of teachers who found that student behavioural problems, coupled with a lack of disciplinary support at school, had negatively impacted on their self-efficacy, job satisfaction and commitment to the school. As a newly qualified teacher (NQT), Isaac had been highly motivated and committed to teaching. He liked his subject and enjoyed 'being in the classroom' and 'the banter of the staff room'. But he indicated that because of poor pupil behaviour and the lack of discipline at his current school, his motivation and commitment had changed. Also, Isaac's job satisfaction was not as high as he thought it should have been at his current school – 'only at this particular school. At a different school I think it would be much higher.' He was thinking about looking for a new job.

> 'In terms of teaching within the classroom it's pretty good. In terms of overall with these other things it decreases somewhat. I'm quite happy being a teacher and being here, but there're too many pupils with no respect. Not just to me being a new teacher. I've seen them do it to teachers who have been here for many years. That's not satisfactory and decreases my job satisfaction.'
>
> (Isaac, secondary)

Professional life phase 4–7 years

Leadership support

Positive support from leadership and colleagues was a contributing factor in these teachers' growing sense of identity. For example,

> If you're unsupported then you're not going to feel as good about yourself, so then your motivation is lower. It is hard to be motivated if you don't have any support or encouragement or feedback. So yes, I think this [effectiveness] does increase as we have a very supportive team.
>
> (Hettie, primary)

The following comment exemplifies how a lack of staff collegiality may jeopardize teachers' motivation and commitment:

> There was a time I was really blunt and open with everybody and I got my fingers burnt a couple of times. The team spirit is very, very disappointing. There's also been a lot of turnover and a lot of people have left under a cloud. Some people have left because they simply could not bear to work here anymore. They weren't enjoying it.
>
> (Les, secondary)

The following story is an example of how a lack of in-school support may damage a teacher's motivation and commitment.

> I think mine has dropped with everyone else's. I don't feel quite as supported or valued in school and I feel less inclined to push myself or try out new things . . . I just don't enjoy it as much as I used to. I don't feel as supported or valued and if you feel like that your self-esteem goes down, you begin to question 'Are you doing the right thing?' and 'Is it actually worth it?'

It's getting harder and harder to get up in the mornings. It's more of a duty to come into school. I used to really, really love the job and a lot of that has kind of worn off now and that has been over the last year. It's been getting less fun and I've been less inclined to try new things and push myself that little extra as I used to do, as a teacher.

(John, secondary)

Adverse personal events/work–life tensions

The negative influence of workload and adverse personal events on teachers' identity and perceived efficacy is demonstrated by Lana. She was from Australia and has many Australian friends in London, but because of work pressures she had little social life. Work dominated, she was always having to turn down social invitations. She did not think she would stay in the classroom but was interested in moving to related work, such as writing children's books or teaching in adult education, rather than the 'daily grind of the classroom'. She didn't want to sound like a jaded teacher – the jadedness started at this school, not when she taught in Australia. She was finding teaching in the UK very prescriptive. She had 'had a life in Australia'.

Professional life phase 8–15 years

Policy

The significance of new roles and change to teachers' motivation and career advancement in this phase echoes Rippon's (2005) argument for an 'investment culture' in the modern teaching profession:

Each new role marked a transition point when the teacher had become confident in their current role and needed to face a new challenge, taking on challenges in their current posts which took them beyond the direct responsibilities of their remit or finding new posts entirely. All are forms of proactively investing in the development of their career for altruistic, intrinsic or extrinsic motivations.

(Rippon 2005: 284)

However, even for this group of teachers the negative influence of policy was increasingly significant as they considered the balance of life and work:

I feel I need to invest more time in my teaching. I find it difficult to find the time to do the paperwork, even though I have non-contact time.

(Jake, secondary)

I try very much to keep work as work and home as home. It doesn't always happen and sometimes I'll spend a whole weekend working, but on the whole the theory is that I'm happy to come in on a Saturday to do work if it's needed but I try not to take work home because that's my home and we don't talk about work at home. If there's been a problem at school I'll think about it at school.

(Maggie, primary)

Leadership Support

This also remained an important issue:

If support from the headteacher makes you feel better about yourself and your role, then it makes you a more effective teacher.

(Scarlet, primary)

We've had a change of leadership. It is a much better place to work in, much better atmosphere. Being treated like an adult. That's the difference ... I tell you what else has contributed to my motivation is the head thanking you when you do something. He does appreciate what you do. You do feel what you're doing is appreciated. He is a nice guy and he's got a bit more respect for you.

(Gavin, primary)

Motivation is probably better because [the head] leaves you to get on with it. He employs me to do a job and then trusts me to do it which I do ... Because I know he has the confidence in me, I feel more efficacious because I'm doing it.

(Geraldine, secondary)

I certainly have more job satisfaction in this school than, I have had in previous schools I've worked in. Again that's the management. That's the boss because he fields a lot of stuff that should be coming down. He realises we're doing a fine job.

(Katie, primary)

Professional life phase 24–30 years

Policy had a strong negative impact, not only on teachers' sense of work–life balance and their ability to manage this, but also on their sense of effectiveness:

I worked too hard years ago and went off with stress [which] made me more aware of work–life balance.

(Gerard, secondary)

Despite their continuing commitment to teaching, many in this group spoke of the erosion of job satisfaction:

> I still love teaching but the planning doesn't motivate me. I feel quite demotivated by the amount of planning and if I was to do this job well, it would involve 14 hours a day.
>
> (Alan, primary)

> It [OFSTED] was quite difficult and there were times when I felt this pressure was unnecessary and I wanted to jack it all in . . . It really attacked me. It can totally incapacitate me. The thought that these people could have had a team that come in and not like my style and irrespective of what happened, not liked the way I worked because it wasn't the way they worked. They could have totally destroyed me. I was very angry at that possibility.
>
> (Sadie, primary)

For others, commitment was declining:

> I think I have less [motivation] compared to maybe 10 years ago. I think I knew the direction I wanted my career to go in. Then so many areas came in, literacy strategy, numeracy strategy, and you had to have training for all these different areas and I lost focus really of what my main interest is, which is early years and early years curriculum, but I haven't been able to develop it in the way I wanted to develop it.
>
> (Agnes, primary)

> On a bad day I would say it [job satisfaction] has decreased. On a good day I would say it has remained the same. At this time of year (December) I would probably say it has decreased. It's generally things you deal with up to a point, but one day you wake up and say 'Yes, I can still deal with this but do I want to, have to?' When you have borne the brunt of so many changes over 30 years you start to think 'Can I actually cope with anymore change or yes, I can cope with it but do I want to cope with a new change?' I do not wish to teach until the end of my career and I have started to take steps at looking at this . . . the government pushes too many things . . . and I fear of being put in a situation of carrying on until my health does suffer.
>
> (Christine, primary)

Professional life phase 31+ years

Policy

Many in this phase also (86 per cent) experienced negative impacts of policy initiatives on their sense of job satisfaction.

I don't get job satisfaction from the paperwork, the endless planning and the marking . . . duplicating of paperwork that has to go on and the meetings and long-term plans, short-term plans and you know. I feel a lot of it is unnecessary but you feel under great pressure to have it in place.

(Katy, primary)

I just think we're a very close staff. We're a small staff, which does make things easier, but we do try whenever there's any stressful situation to get out for an evening all together, so we can sit and talk away from the environment, which is a big help.

(Aidan, primary)

Our analyses of the influence of mediating factors on teachers, in each phase of their professional lives, also revealed that there were similarities between groups of teachers within and across phases which related to the school phase and socio-economic contexts in which they worked. Figures 7.2–7.7, show that there are differences in teachers' attitudes towards pupil behaviour in different FSM schools. Figure 7.2 shows that teachers in FSM1 schools have the most positive views regarding pupil behaviour. The negative influence of pupil behaviour appears to be more dominant for teachers in FSM3–4 schools. Throughout the remaining five professional live phases, it was apparent that in contrast with teachers in FSM1 schools, those in FSM3 and 4 schools tended to have less positive views and more negative attitudes towards the impact of disruptive pupil behaviour on their classroom work. These findings caused us to undertake a more detailed examination of the influences of school contexts.

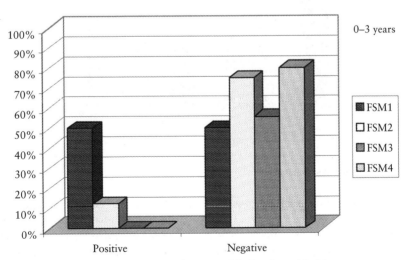

Figure 7.2 Teachers' views regarding pupil behaviour (0–3).

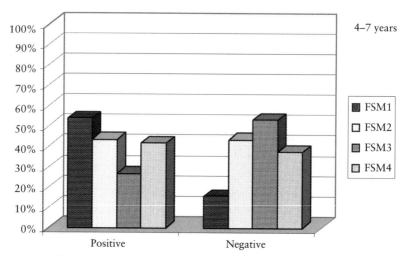

Figure 7.3 Teachers' views regarding pupil behaviour (4–7).

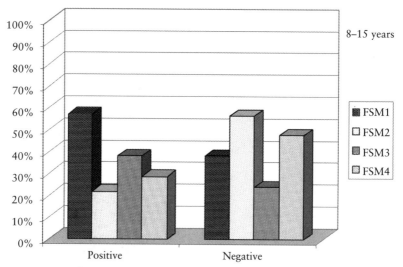

Figure 7.4 Teachers' views regarding pupil behaviour (8–15).

School contexts matter

Analyses of accounts by teachers within and across professional life phases of the factors which affected their sense of efficacy and effectiveness, revealed that there were clear differences between primary and secondary teachers (the former being generally more positive than the latter). More tellingly, they showed a significant difference between primary and secondary teachers

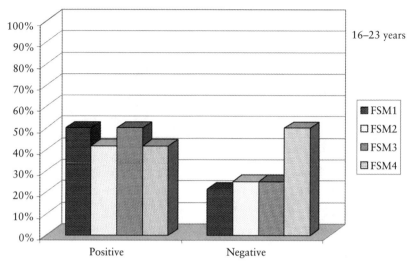

Figure 7.5 Teachers' views regarding pupil behaviour (16–23).

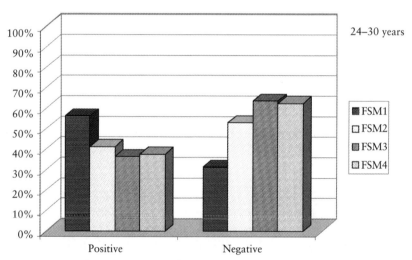

Figure 7.6 Teachers' views regarding pupil behaviour (24–30).

who worked in FSM1 and 2 schools and those who worked in FSM3 and 4 schools.

It seems that school context and phase both affect teachers' experiences of, and attitudes towards, professional factors (workload, national policies), situated factors (pupil behaviour, leadership) and personal factors (values, health).

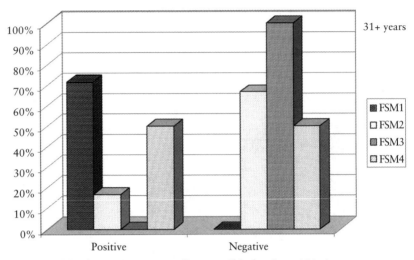

Figure 7.7 Teachers' views regarding pupil behaviour (31+).

Professional factors

Workload

> The massive workload takes away my personal life.
>
> (Sheila, Year 6)

Primary teachers

While all teachers identified workload as a key negative or positive medi-ating factor in their capacities to sustain commitment, there were also distinct differences between the responses of teachers in higher and lower SES schools.

The majority (72 per cent of 48) of primary teachers in FSM1 and 2 schools responded positively in terms of their commitment and motivation, despite the fact that they were working long hours and were experiencing increased paperwork. They reported that they were able to surmount the challenges of pupil attitudes, behaviour and results in spite of the workload.

> I feel demotivated by the amount of planning, but love teaching despite being absolutely knackered.
>
> (Agatha, Year 6)

> I still spend every waking hour through the week working to improve what I am doing. It's one of the best jobs and one of the most satisfying jobs you can have.
>
> (Violet, Year 2)

Rebecca (Year 2) was a self-confessed 'workaholic', and Hazel (Year 6) had 'to stop myself working 24 hours a day'. Michael (Year 6), Nancy (Year 6) and Sarah (Year 2) were among others who were confident that they were making a difference despite, 'endless change and paperwork' and changes 'being thrown at teachers'.

There were few overall negatives. Agnes (Year 2), the head of a small rural school, found that the cost of the job meant that she did not give enough time to her family; and Calvin (Year 6), also the head of a small rural primary school, found 'no happy time whatsoever in his personal life', because he worried about the school and his job while he was at home. Janice (Year 6) shared this pressure as a headteacher of a small school and was beginning to lose her sense of job satisfaction due to excessive workload. Violet (Year 2) had experienced a decrease in her effectiveness as her life 'revolved around the school' and her marriage broke down. Jeanne (Year 6), was a deputy head who wanted to retire and who resented paperwork – 'I didn't come into teaching to fill in bits of paper'. Gavin (Year 6), although deriving great pleasure from pupils' personal and academic achievements, did not think he would be in the job for too much longer because of the 'major demands that it makes on my time and energy'; and David (Year 6) also resented taking work home.

In contrast to the 72% of teachers in FSM1 and 2 schools who remained positive about their work, nearly half (43 per cent of 41, N = 18) of teachers in FSM3 and 4 schools reported that the workload was making them feel exhausted and that in some cases this meant that they did not get home from work until late evening, preventing them from having a social or personal life during the week. Many of them also commented upon the work that had to be completed at the weekend.

I go to bed at nine each night, exhausted.

(Ronald, Year 2)

The massive workload takes away my personal life.

(Sheila, Year 6)

However, nearly half (N = 19, 46 per cent) of the 41 primary teachers in FSM3 and 4 schools reported that, despite the heavy workload, they still enjoyed their job and found satisfaction in working with children:

It is really hard sometimes, but it's worth it in the end.

(Marion, Year 2)

Secondary teachers
Fifty-eight secondary teachers (42 FSM1/2, 16 FSM3/4) commented on their workload. Although 20 (48 per cent) of the teachers in FSM1 and 2 schools, who mentioned workload as a factor, felt they were unable to cope with

the pressures of work, 22 (52 per cent) were still enjoying their work and wholly committed, in spite of the workload. Leanne (Year 9, English) had 'improved' her work–life balance, and motivation and perceived effectiveness had increased. Ben (Year 9, mathematics) said that 'drive, enthusiasm, personal support' were the biggest influences in his effectiveness. On the other hand, Darrell (Year 9, mathematics) was 'trying as hard', but felt 'far less motivated' as a result of a combination of factors which increased his workload. Alexandra (Year 9, English) submitted her resignation because she had 'no life outside school', was caring for her elderly mother and dealing with a 'negative colleague'; and Nikita (Year 9, English) who had similar parental responsibilities reported that 'workload has taken over my life'.

Of the 22 teachers who remained positive, Ruth (Year 9, English) did not have much of a social life but still wanted 'to have a positive impact on young people's lives'. Ada (Year 9, mathematics) was only able to survive by taking work home in the evenings. Madelaine (Year 9, English) a part-time teacher commented:

> The more stressed I am, the less satisfaction I get out of my job . . . work on top of my teaching feels like drudgery.
>
> (Madelaine, Year 9)

However, Holly (Year 9, English) still 'loved the job' and her sense of effectiveness had increased despite 'external pressure from endless government changes'. Though Geraldine's (Year 9, English) personal life was 'squeezed out', she was 'more committed and more satisfied' with her increasing success in making a difference as a headteacher; and Adrienne (Year 9, mathematics) looked forward to coming to work each day and seeing results despite the 'long working hours and [little] amount of time for planning'.

Teachers in FSM3 and 4 schools echoed these sentiments. Of the 16 teachers who commented upon this issue, eight (50 per cent) still felt committed and found enjoyment in their work in spite of the pressures of workload. The remaining 8 (50 per cent) teachers were struggling to maintain motivation for teaching and were feeling 'run down'.

DfES/Ofsted/target driven policies

> It's like somebody's always looking over your shoulder.
>
> (Sasha, Year 9)

Primary teachers

Again, there were differences in emphasis between teachers in FSM1 and 2 schools and those in FSM3 and 4 schools. Of the 35 FSM1 and 2 teachers who commented, the majority (76 per cent of 35) did so negatively. Despite this, they still managed to find satisfaction from their work and would not let their teaching be dominated by the national (Key Stage) tests. Thirteen teachers (37 per cent) commented upon the restriction they felt when having to work to the National Curriculum and tried, whenever possible, to explore ideas creatively with the pupils. Twelve teachers (34 per cent) reported that they would like to be left alone to deliver the curriculum without interference.

A few teachers (20 per cent) held negative views about external initiatives and felt that they had a direct impact on their effectiveness and on their energy and stress levels. Of these teachers, four (57 per cent) commented upon there being too many initiatives, demands and targets, which caused low self-efficacy, and for some, a growing desire to leave the profession.

> There are so many initiatives; it's difficult to know when the teaching is supposed to happen.
>
> (Ricky, Year 6)

Finally, three teachers (9 per cent) commented on the accuracy of marking (of SATs), the intrusion of and impositions made by government, and the increased paperwork which left little time available for work with individual pupils' needs, marking and feedback.

Notwithstanding these negative comments, however, these teachers continued to find satisfaction from their work in spite of the policies. Nancy (Year 6) spoke of 'the spark of hope with children when you know you've made a difference – despite the inclusion policy'. Violet (Year 2) spoke of her pleasure in watching children develop 'despite SATs'. Gavin (Year 6) was highly committed, with teaching approaches not dominated by national tests:

> I'm determined to give them a range of experiences and opportunities in all areas of the curriculum.
>
> (Gavin, Year 6)

Rebecca (Year 2), similarly, felt she was not 'strait-jacketed', but was 'allowed to explore ideas with the children'. Carmelle (Year 2) wanted to be seen as 'human, not a machine saying do this and you'll get the mark', and Michael (Year 6) also believed that 'growing up socially and morally' was more important than 'bits of paper'. Leila (Year 2) felt strongly:

> I just wish the government would leave us to get on and deliver what we know we have got to deliver, raise their level of interest and self-esteem.
>
> (Leila, Year 2)

From a quite different perspective, of the 41 primary teachers in FSM3 and 4 schools who commented on professional influences, 37 (90 per cent) said they were struggling to deal with the various policies and initiatives introduced.

The inclusion policy (DfES 1998) was mentioned explicitly:

The inclusion policy brings rewards and hardships.

(Sheila, Year 6)

The lack of time with individual pupils and the fewer opportunities to interact socially with children, were also reported to be a result of the target-driven culture that existed in their schools.

Twenty-one teachers (57 per cent of 37) felt that they were increasingly under pressure to produce results and meet targets, which in turn, was having a direct negative impact on relationships in the classroom.

My biggest problem is time and energy. I put the children to bed at 8.00 pm and start working.

(Jenna, Year 6)

Secondary teachers
Nearly two-thirds (61 per cent of 72) of secondary teachers commented on this issue. The majority (77 per cent of 44) of these were FSM1 and 2 teachers (74 per cent). Although 12 teachers (35 per cent) were fairly positive about policies and initiatives, 15 (44 per cent) were extremely negative about external initiatives and their consequences. Nana (Year 9, English) felt that there were 'too many initiatives, demands and targets' which caused her to have 'a negative feeling of never being able to fulfil all that is required'. Ada (Year 9, mathematics) was 'thinking of leaving the school and possibly teaching' as a result of an Ofsted inspection; and Alexandra (Year 9, English) had 'no faith in the accuracy of SATs marking'.

For a further seven teachers in FSM1 and 2 schools (21 per cent of 34), 'impositions by government' (Sasha, Year 9, mathematics) left little time available for work with individual pupils, marking and feedback. Yet, although Catherine (Year 9, mathematics) was 'disillusioned, overworked, underpaid', she still gained 'a lot of satisfaction' from her teaching.

Of the 10 secondary teachers in FSM3 and 4 schools who reported policy as having an impact on their teaching, 8 (67 per cent) responded negatively.

Jo (Year 9, English) felt that she was 'teaching far more to the test than previously' and Sasha (Year 9, mathematics) was adamant that 'we are going down because of government policies – especially inclusion . . . It's like somebody's always looking over your shoulder'.

Although there were similar concerns expressed about DfES policies, there were differences in the incidence of ill health, degrees of stress experienced by secondary teachers in FSM1 and 2 schools (21 per cent of 47) compared with those in FSM3 and 4 schools (48 per cent of 25). The former also had a stronger sense of agency with regard to making a difference academically and socially to the lives of pupils. While similar negative and positive factors, which were perceived to affect their ability to do so were raised, the effects appeared to be more strongly felt by secondary teachers, and most strongly felt by secondary teachers who worked in schools in challenging socio-economic contexts.

Situated factors

Support from leadership and close colleagues

I know they care, even when nothing is said.

(Larissa, Year 2)

Two of the most frequently mentioned influences on teachers' work and lives were leadership and relationships with colleagues. The quality of the leadership, both at school and departmental level, plays a major role in teachers' sustained commitment and their motivation to remain in or leave a school. Eighty-one per cent of primary teachers said that the school leadership had an impact on their teaching, compared to nearly three-quarters (73 per cent) of secondary teachers. The aspects of leadership which teachers regarded as having a positive influence were: the ability to communicate with staff, being approachable, demonstrating a commitment to the school, praising and rewarding staff contributions to the school, feeling supported in decisions, being respected by parents, pupils and staff, and having a visible presence around school. Secondary school teachers also commented upon the mitigating influence of a supportive departmental leadership in the case of poor school level management and support.

The support of colleagues, on which teachers could draw and from whom they could seek advice and discuss issues relating to practice, emerged as a theme across both primary and secondary phases. Of the 261 teachers reporting on the impact of their colleagues, 87 per cent experienced positive support and 13 per cent a lack of support. A higher proportion of primary teachers (59 per cent) mentioned relationships with colleagues as important to their teaching, compared with secondary teachers (35 per cent). Teachers in FSM3 and 4 schools tended to mention the sense of teamwork and common purpose that they shared with other teachers more often (85 per cent, compared to 73 per cent in FSM1 and 2 schools), but regardless of school context, teachers stressed the importance of having someone to talk to when things went wrong and having the time and space to discuss problems and ways of dealing with them.

Primary teachers

Almost all (88 per cent, N = 70) of teachers in FSM1 and 2 schools spoke of their ability to take decisions affecting the teaching and learning in their own classrooms with regard to the academic, personal and social progress of pupils. This group, by implication, received support in this from their leaders and other colleagues. They did not feel that they were unduly dominated by national tests and were able to provide opportunities for a range of learning experiences. Naomi (Year 2) gained her greatest satisfaction from pastoral care, promoting 'honesty, fairness and relationships', while Laurette (Year 6) was 'trying to raise the profile of PSHE in school'. Edith (Year 2) wanted 'good SATs results and changes in children's attitude to school and learning', and Leila (Year 2) was 'not interested in league table results'. In essence:

> The school ethos allows teachers to define their own needs.
>
> (Sheila, Year 6)

Those who were suffering most from stress were headteachers in small rural schools, all of who experienced difficulties in coping with the management, leadership and teaching workload. For Margery (Year 6) there was 'freedom to use initiative and it makes people feel they are counted and they matter'; and for Joanna (Year 2) and Hazel (Year 6) there was good support from SLT on personal as well as professional matters.

These teachers experienced a supportive organization and appreciated the opportunities which they were given to exercise their own professional judgement in the classroom.

> . . . get on well as a team and we support each other whether we're going through a good time, a bad time or whatever.
>
> (Hazel, Year 6)

Of the 76 primary teachers who taught in FSM3 and 4 schools, 77 per cent (N = 59) reported that they valued the support they received from within the school from colleagues and particularly enjoyed the sense of 'family' or 'community' that was sometimes evident. Teachers who had experienced collaboration and teamwork felt that the sharing of ideas was important.

Leadership was also an important issue across primary schools in relation to support; and there were several positive comments regarding the openness of the school leadership and the recognition that life outside work was important. Teachers often highlighted the support they had when faced with personal issues (e.g. health, marriage break-up, caring for parents, children).

Secondary teachers

A total of 54 (64 per cent of 85) secondary teachers in FSM1 and 2 schools were unequivocal in their appreciation of support from colleagues and SMT;

20 (24 per cent) had mixed feelings; and 10 (12 per cent) felt negatively about the support they received. Liz (Year 9, English) appreciated management's 'willingness to listen' and their support on personal issues.

Ruth (Year 9, English) worked in a 'close knit' department and Hannah (Year 9, English) appreciated the support of her head of department. For Catherine (Year 9, mathematics) the staff were 'wonderful'.

Negative opinions included a perceived lack of support by the SLT for student behavioural issues and for career promotion. Mixed opinions concerned the differential levels and quality of support offered by the department and SLT. For example, although Claire (Year 9, English) did not 'feel valued' professionally by her SLT, she acknowledged their support on personal issues. Caroline (Year 9, English) and Abbie (Year 9, English) both experienced supportive departments but unsupportive SLT.

Thirty-one (58 per cent) of the 53 teachers in FSM3 and 4 schools reported negative feelings regarding the organizational support provided to the school, while 17 (32 per cent) were positive and 5 (10 per cent) were mixed. For Daniel (Year 9, mathematics), 'the school is singularly successful in the aims of giving each pupil the best possible support'; and for Jeremy:

> One way to manage this level of challenge is to work as a team . . . in this type of school there is no choice but to get on with everyone.
>
> (Jeremy, Year 9)

Jo (Year 9, English) experienced 'collaboration and teamwork at every level' and Sasha (Year 9, mathematics) experienced 'laughter and the sharing of ideas' in her department.

As with primary teachers, secondary teachers were particularly appreciative of support from school at times of personal crisis:

> Everyone was incredibly supportive . . . we do need that support because if you really felt isolated . . . I think you'd go off with stress . . . we have some very, very difficult pupils.
>
> (Siobhan, Year 9)

Sally (Year 9, mathematics) worked with 'incredible departmental support', and in an 'incredibly supportive school with a happy, dedicated staff'. For Jenni (Year 9, English) who began the job of head of department shortly following the birth of a second child:

> If it hadn't been for the intervention of the head, and his support, I would probably have had a nervous breakdown.
>
> (Jenni, Year 9)

Pupil behaviour

There are some kids who don't value education.

(Shaun, Year 9)

Primary teachers
Among all of the primary FSM1 and 2 teachers who commented (N = 80), only 11 (14 per cent) spoke negatively about pupil behaviour. Of these, Michale (Year 6) was concerned about the 'background of some pupils'; and Jackie (Year 6) was concerned about the 'constant drip of minor behaviour that wears you down'. Others commented that they continued to be highly motivated despite some poor behaviour. Gavin (Year 6) wanted children to 'make up their own minds – despite poor pupil behaviour'.

For Natasha (Year 2), pupils remained the main source of job satisfaction despite a number of children with behavioural difficulties in her class. Regina (Year 6) who associated poor behaviour with 'low motivation and lack of support from home', had experienced doubts about her effectiveness owing to the behaviour in her class. Jenny (Year 6) felt 'tired and trapped' by workload but retained her commitment despite this and 'more challenging pupil behaviour'.

For 69 of the 80 teachers, however, pupil behaviour was not an issue. Sadie (Year 6) was:

> . . . more satisfied working with a high calibre of children who could end up being very responsible, high achieving and articulate.
>
> (Sadie, Year 6)

Most of Kim's (Year 2) pupils had 'made progress in their academic work and all have made progress socially'; and Eleanor (Year 2) had 'total respect' from the pupils. Laurette (Year 6) gained satisfaction from achieving good results and improving pupils' behaviour.

Of the 76 teachers in FSM3 and 4 schools, comments tended to be more negative on the issue of pupil behaviour (N = 34, 45 per cent). They associated it with classroom disruption, pupil mobility and the national 'inclusion' policy which affected class composition. In the majority of cases (88 per cent), it meant that pupil behaviour management often took priority over the teaching and learning tasks.

Fourteen (41 per cent) teachers commented upon the lack of value pupils placed on education, those who did not want to work or achieve, and those who were disillusioned by the Key Stage tests and felt pressure to perform well.

Secondary teachers
In FSM1 and 2 schools, 65 (76 per cent) of the 85 teachers reported positive pupil behaviour, while 20 (24 per cent) commented on deteriorating

pupil behaviour. Of the positive remarks, 'the fulfilling part is when the students come up and say thank you' (Sasha, Year 9, mathematics) was a common theme. Great store was placed upon a combination of care and achievement:

Getting to know kids ... having them turn around and say they understand. Helping kids through their exams is a good feeling.

(Linda, Year 9)

Geraldine's (Year 9, English) satisfaction came through pushing the pupils, getting them 'to achieve their full potential, not just about exam results'; and Ben (Year 9, mathematics) also gained most satisfaction through 'seeing children achieve, parental comments, the good feeling at the end of the day, good results'. For him:

Meaning comes through change in people's lives. Targets will take care of themselves.

(Ben, Year 9)

Although the socio-economic background of pupils had 'a huge bearing' on what went on in Geraldine's (Year 9, English) classes, she was, nevertheless, more committed and satisfied with her successes. Catherine (Year 9, mathematics) was more cautious:

Teachers thrive on the idea that they do make a difference, although a lot of the time I feel I don't make a difference with the way they act socially.

(Catherine, Year 9)

Cheryl (Year 9, English) commented that 'a lot of pupils didn't value education' and Kathryn (Year 9, English) reported spending 'more time battling student behaviour' than teaching.

However, in contrast to teachers in FSM1 and 2 schools, more than three times the proportion, 39 (74 per cent) of the 53 secondary teachers in FSM3 and 4 schools, reported pupil behaviour as a negative factor. Lack of trust and the pressure that behaviour problems placed upon teachers, were two of the most commonly mentioned issues. For Winona (Year 9, English), 'It's hard work because the children don't trust you at first'. Jeremy (Year 9, mathematics) said that having to deal with disruptive pupils made him 'feel under pressure to perform'. The remaining 14 (26 per cent) secondary teachers in these schools commented positively with regard to pupil behaviour.

Personal factors

Personal health

Primary teachers
Of the 77 primary teachers in FSM1 and 2 schools who commented on personal factors, nearly one-quarter (25 per cent) of them had been away from work owing to ill health during the 3-year VITAE study. Agatha (Year 2) had been away from school for five months with a serious illness. Beverley (Year 6) and Sheila (Year 6) loved what they did, despite suffering from ill health. One teacher had suffered long-term ill health which had affected her ability to teach effectively.

The percentage of teachers suffering with health problems in FSM3 and 4 schools was higher, with over one-third (N = 25, 37 per cent) of the 69 teachers reporting illness. One teacher (Sheila, Year 6) had recurrent throat problems, another suffered from depression as work encroached more and more on her personal life (Leila, Year 2); and another (Alan, Year 6) had 'time off' for several operations and did not know if he could take many more years of teaching.

Secondary teachers
Thirty-two (42 per cent of 76) teachers in FSM1 and 2 schools reported that suffering from ill health was directly impacting upon their motivation and commitment. These included recurrent throat problems, miscarriage, depression, and the need for time away from school for recuperation/ operations. Other issues raised included being 'worn out' by young children at home, being the main carer for elderly parents, and emerging from a difficult marriage or relationship. Ruth (Year 9, English) had a major operation, returned to work too soon, had a relapse and had to take a term's leave; and Catherine (Year 9, mathematics) and Darrell (Year 9, mathematics) both complained of loss of energy and motivation.

A higher proportion (N = 31, 63 per cent of 49) of teachers in FSM3 and 4 schools (a higher proportion, also, than their counterparts in primary schools) reported health problems. Among this group of secondary teachers, Ben was worn out, in part because of looking after his young child, and Jo and Cameron, similarly, had two school age children to care for. Sasha (Year 9, mathematics) was emerging from a difficult marriage relationship and suffered from diabetes and high blood pressure. Shaun (Year 9, mathematics) had been diagnosed with high blood pressure, and Serina's health was causing her to lose job satisfaction. Jeanette (Year 9, English) had become worried at how tired she had become, and Danny (Year 9, English) was 'exhausted and disillusioned'.

Ten teachers (20 per cent) reported having a 'carer' role in addition to their work and parental activities. For example, Serena (Year 9, mathematics) was the main carer for elderly parents, as were Cheryl (Year 9, English) and Laurent (Year 9, mathematics).

Positive values

> It's a teacher's moral obligation to make a difference in pupils' learning.
>
> (Ben, Year 9)

Primary teachers

What kept the majority (75 per cent of 77) of the teachers in FSM1 and 2 schools motivated and committed to their teaching and learning agendas were their core values, their 'desire to make a difference to children's learning' (Larissa, Year 6); 'always looking for the good' (Adrian, Year 6); increasing their knowledge, independence, skills – getting their voice heard' (Abigail, Year 6); and giving them 'a range of experiences and opportunities in all areas of the curriculum' (Gavin, Year 6).

Being with children and 'developing relationships' was what interested Carmelle (Year 2) and these sentiments were repeated by almost all of the teachers. It was the satisfaction gained from working with pupils that kept them in teaching despite pressures from policy initiatives, the challenges of pupil behaviour, parental pressure and excessive workloads.

Teachers in FSM3 and 4 schools (N = 42, 63 per cent of 67) were also motivated by the challenge of their chosen context and what could be achieved with pupils:

> I get immense satisfaction from pupils' progress and achievements.
>
> (Larissa, Year 6)

> I can make a difference to what children think and learn.
>
> (Adrian, Year 6)

Secondary teachers

Fifty-one teachers (67 per cent of 76) in FSM1 and 2 secondary schools were motivated by their core educational values. They had entered teaching deliberately in order to 'help raise standards' in their subject discipline, to 'contribute to the community' and 'have a positive impact on the lives of young people'.

Teachers in FSM3 and 4 schools (N = 29, 59 per cent of 49) were also largely concerned with their ability to 'make a difference in pupils' learning' (Ivan, Year 9, mathematics). Darrell (Year 9, mathematics) loved working with pupils:

It's not a job you can do if your commitment's not there . . . I don't spend time moaning . . . I just do it.

(Darrell, Year 9)

Stella (Year 9, English) had always wanted 'to work with pupils, care for them and make a difference in their lives', while Gary (Year 9, mathematics) loved his subject and wanted to share it with others.

Jude (Year 9, mathematics) had entered and remained in teaching in the belief that 'pupils need a good education', as had Seth (Year 9, English) who had 'wanted to do something which was measurably worthwhile'. Shaun (Year 9, mathematics) had entered teaching because he 'thought I could do better' than his teachers. For him, it was 'a teachers' moral obligation to make a difference to pupils' learning'.

Isaac (Year 9, mathematics) remained 'absolutely and utterly committed to making a difference in social and academic terms' and for Stella too (Year 9, English):

What keeps me motivated is that I'm making a difference in kids' lives. If I wasn't doing that, then my motivation would go.

(Stella, Year 9)

Continuing professional development

This final part of the chapter summarizes the key findings of the analysis of VITAE teachers' views on CPD in response to questions in each of the three years about their interests in and experiences of CPD.

Most VITAE teachers (80 per cent) were satisfied with their experiences. CPD was described by teachers as an important professional life investment, a means of recharging their batteries. Previous analysis of the questionnaire responses of the original larger sample (see Chapter 4) showed that while there was satisfaction with CPD from teachers in both primary and secondary school phases, primary school teachers demonstrated higher satisfaction rates than secondary teachers in their attitudes towards CPD opportunities and the quality of what was offered. This was echoed in the responses of the case study teachers. In addition, VITAE teachers in primary schools were more satisfied with the overall focus and balance of CPD opportunities. However, teachers across all professional life phases felt that heavy workload, a lack of time and financial constraints were important inhibitors to their pursuit of professional development[10].

The most frequent reason for undertaking CPD was to enhance classroom knowledge (38.2 per cent) (such as 'subject matter update', 'the use of ICT in teaching' and 'classroom management'). This was closely followed by professional/personal development, such as 'renewal/refreshment' and promotion/career advancement (37 per cent). Grundy and Robinson (2004) stress the importance of taking account of factors which relate to teachers' internal needs and concerns. They argue that these 'personal drivers recognize life histories, personal circumstances and professional life trajectories as prime determinants of receptiveness to and enthusiasm for professional development' (2004: 163). The extent to which such 'personal drivers' of teacher professional development (Grundy and Robinson 2004: 146) dominated in teachers' reasons for undertaking CPD in all phases of their professional life phases was striking.

The third most important reason for undertaking CPD was role effectiveness (26 per cent). This was important for teachers with additional out of classroom leadership responsibilities (70 per cent of all teachers and 90 per cent of primary school teachers). These teachers found activities enabling them to improve their managerial abilities useful.

CPD and professional life phases

There was overall satisfaction with the current CPD opportunities and the focus, quality and balance of CPD by teachers in the six professional life phases identified in the study. Teachers with no more than three years of experience demonstrated the most positive attitude towards the above aspects of CPD, although the difference was minimal. Within the generally favourable attitude towards CPD among teachers in both primary and secondary phases, there were however, high levels of dissatisfaction (especially among primary teachers) with the time teachers had to reflect on their teaching (primary: 83 per cent; secondary: 71 per cent) and to learn with and from colleagues (primary: 75 per cent; secondary: 70 per cent).

A significant difference was found between professional life phases and teachers' views regarding the time they had to reflect on their teaching and the time they had to learn with and from colleagues. Teachers who were at the beginning of their professional lives, were the most positive about the time and opportunity they had had for self-reflection and a sharing of practice with their colleagues, in contrast with teachers in the final phase of their professional lives who had the most negative views. Further analysis of the interview data also revealed some patterned differences between teachers in different phases of their professional lives, and Figure 7.8 illustrates these.

Professional life phase 0–3 years

For teachers in their early years, CPD activities in relation to classroom knowledge were most frequently reported as having a positive impact on their morale, and as being significant to the stabilization of their teaching

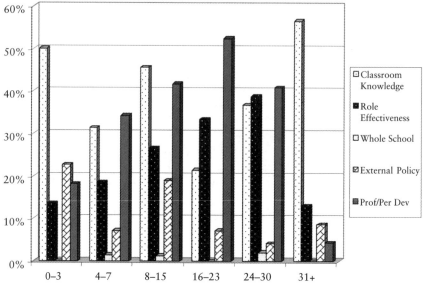

Figure 7.8 CPD focuses across six professional life phases.

practice. These activities included school/department-based training and INSET days, external (NQT) conferences, and visiting and working with teachers in other schools.

> There have been quite a few INSETs. I've been on a course on Tuesday on GCSE . . . I find it boosts your morale a little bit in that you are with other teachers who are in the same boat. Also I did spend a day in [. . .] School to observe the English department and that had an impact in watching other teachers teach.
>
> (Adrienne)

In this professional life phase, teachers with leadership roles also reported the importance of CPD opportunities that had helped to enhance their role effectiveness.

> I suppose it [a course relating to her ICT co-ordinator's role] makes you more aware of your job and feeling that you can do it.
>
> (Veronica)

Professional life phase 4–7 years

An important characteristic of teachers with 4–7 years' experience was that promotion and additional responsibilities had begun to play a significant role in their identities, motivation and sense of effectiveness.

Last year I did the leadership and management of small schools which was a four-day course and I shadowed two headteachers and how they managed their schools. I've looked at SDPs and just started on a new leadership programme where you have a mentor come to the school and the head and I go to meetings . . . The head is taking a secondment in January and I'm going to take over for the six weeks. I will be going on the performance management training so that I can carry that on while she's away. I tend to get to go on a lot of courses because of my role in school, e.g. special needs courses.

(Rhonda)

I think this current one is professional development of teaching, learning, planning and developing Key Stage 3 mathematics. I think that it plays such a big part in my role as second in department and Key Stage 3 co-ordinator that I think it's going to be invaluable to me. All the other courses have supplemented that.

(Cameron)

The need for classroom knowledge and knowledge of external policies was markedly less, role effectiveness similar, and CPD which focused upon professional and personal development needs was more important.

Professional life phases 8–15, 16–23 and 24–30 years

The significance of role effectiveness activities continued to be important for teachers in professional life phases 8–15 and 16–23, where respectively 77 per cent and 91 per cent of teachers had additional responsibilities.

These activities were also important for teachers in professional life phase 24–30, but declined for those in the final phase of their professional lives. Classroom knowledge updates were important to teachers in each of these phases; and more general professional/personal development needs were of great importance to teachers in all but the final professional life phase.

Professional life phase 8–15 is, it seems, a watershed in teachers' professional development, not only for personal and professional development needs in general, but also of teachers' desires to build knowledge of teaching and learning in the classroom. Not surprisingly CPD appears, also, to play an important role in preparing teachers for further professional life prospects, particularly for those who needed formal qualifications (e.g. National Professional Qualification for Headship (NPQH)[11]) to progress up the management ladder.

Everybody had a chance to do the course on behaviour management and that was a help . . . The one outside I would recommend because the speaker was brilliant and was giving us material with a bit of humour and he was doing exactly like situations you get in classes and you could talk to other colleagues who had similar problems with difficult students and you could exchange notes. The one in school wasn't bad. It was good but you were in a circle of friends from the school and with some colleagues you could discuss things but with some you wouldn't.

(Geri)

Professional life phase 31+ years

In contrast with Huberman's (1989) observation of disengagement conducted in a different era, country and context, the VITAE study found that a distinctive sub-group of the teachers in the final phase of their professional lives demonstrated a high level of motivation and commitment and a strong sense of 'active' engagement in the profession (see Chapter 5). As for their involvement in CPD, they showed a continuing interest in improving their knowledge within the classroom.

I'm always interested in finding new and better ways to facilitate learning – it fascinates me and motivates me . . . I'm very interested in developing a skill-based curriculum rather than a content-based one and I don't' have time to do this. I have a huge passion for working on this but I just don't have time apart from Saturdays when I take my mother out.

(Janet)

Sharing practice

An important message from teachers in all six professional life phases was their desire to share practice and expertise with their colleagues and teachers in other schools. This need for collaboration and network support appeared to be particularly important for teachers and leaders in small primary schools.

The professional learning activities for me which have worked best – but not necessarily increased my sense of professionalism – we work as a group of small schools heads, eight in this area as well as an academic council which I am chair and we sort out all our staff development ourselves.

(Alan)

In the VITAE study, collaborative learning with colleagues within teachers' own schools, as well as across schools, was also rated as a highly important and useful form of CPD activity.

Gender

Overall, male teachers were slightly more likely to be satisfied with their CPD opportunities, and the quality and balance of what was offered, than their female counterparts. Although both female and male teachers were highly dissatisfied with the time they had to reflect on their teaching and to learn with and from colleagues, females appeared to have a slightly more negative attitude than males, though this was not statistically significant.

Age

We found little association between variations in teachers' overall view of CPD and their ages. In comparison with their younger colleagues, teachers in their 40s and 50s were slightly more negative about the time they had to reflect on their teaching and to learn with their colleagues. However, teachers in their 50s reported a more positive attitude, although only marginally, towards the opportunities and balance of CPD. Younger teachers on this project (in age range 21–30) appeared to be the most satisfied with the overall focus and quality of CPD.

Despite the heavy investment in CPD over the past five years at policy level then, the teachers in the VITAE study did not appear to have experienced the wide range of CPD that the investment represents. What the VITAE teachers spoke about, in the interviews, were overwhelmingly in-service activities which focused principally upon updating and upskilling them to deliver the curriculum and assessment agendas which were promoted at national level. This may be because they were teaching Key Stage 1, 2 and 3 pupils, and so were focused upon the teaching, learning and assessment needs of these groups; or it may be because of the busyness of their working lives or out-of-classroom additional leadership responsibilities that short courses, which met short-term management and teaching needs, were the dominant experiences of which they talked.

Conclusion

As the data in this chapter demonstrate, CPD alone is unlikely to exert a major impact on teacher effectiveness. It needs to take place within professional, situated and personal contexts, which support rather than erode teachers' sense of positive identity and which contribute, in each professional life phase, to their capacities to maintain upward trajectories of commitment. The analysis of the influences on teachers in different work contexts revealed that there were clear differences in the experiences of primary and secondary teachers, and between those in schools in different socio-economic contexts. While almost all teachers referred to deteriorating pupil behaviour and the impact of central government initiatives on workload and class composition, it was those in schools in areas of social and economic deprivation who referred to these more frequently and to associated problems of demoralization, failing energy and ill health. It is this group of teachers, working in especially challenging circumstances, that may be said to be at greater risk of, sooner or later, losing their motivation and commitment to their work.

For primary and secondary teachers in schools in social and economically disadvantaged contexts, work is exacting. For many, excessive workload – largely perceived as being caused by a range of DfES policies over a number of years, not only during working hours but after them – is seen as intrusive on personal lives. These contexts must be of concern in terms of the focus upon raising quality in teaching, learning and achievement and the broader school improvement agenda. More important are the consequences upon teachers' ability to sustain motivation, commitment, job satisfaction and health.

There is no single factor which influences teacher effectiveness. Rather, it is a combination. However, it is clear that teachers in relatively more disadvantaged school settings are likely to have to be more resilient than others in the face of more persistent and a greater range of challenges to their commitment.

Increased workload, for teachers, means not only longer times spent in working outside the school for the purposes of planning and assessing, it means also calling upon reserves of emotional energy needed in order to teach in classrooms which contain a broader range of pupils in terms of ability and behaviour; it means that increased intellectual energy is likely to be needed in order to implement new curricula in new ways; and it means meeting the intellectual and emotional challenges of mediating between the increasingly instrumental focus of the 'performativity' and 'accountability' agendas and their own moral purposes in order to satisfy both.

Acknowledging the impact of interactions between socio-emotional, policy, personal, organizational/situated factors and CPD on teachers' professional lives is a necessary first step in planning for ways to support and build on their capacities for sustaining effectiveness. We now turn to an examination of the relationships between perceptions of effectiveness, and effectiveness as defined by value added measures of pupil progress and attainment.

Key messages

Message 1 The quality of leadership, both at school and departmental level, relationships with colleagues and personal support, are major factors in teachers' sustained commitment and their motivation to remain in or leave a school.

Message 2 CPD has a consistently positive influence on teachers across all professional life phases. Teachers in all professional life phases associated CPD with building their emotional, health and intellectual capacities in response to different scenarios of their professional lives.

Message 3 Teachers across all professional life phases felt that heavy workload, a lack of time and financial constraints, were important inhibitors in their pursuit of professional development. CPD experiences are likely to be limited in their effects if they focus predominantly upon updating professional and managerial knowledge and skills.

Message 4 There are likely to be differences in the incidence of negative stress and ill health experienced by teachers in secondary schools in different socio-economic contexts. Teachers in FSM3 and 4 schools are more likely to experience more complex scenarios with a greater intensity of challenges than those in FSM1 and 2 schools. These are principally concerned with negative pupil behaviour, policy effects and personal and professional health.

Message 5 Teachers need to have regular opportunities to experience a broad range of informal and formal CPD appropriate to their individual concerns and needs in addition to those of the school and national policies. Collaborative learning with colleagues within and across schools is a highly effective form of CPD.

Message 6 Policy-makers, organizations concerned with initial teacher and in-service training and schools themselves need to review their provision so that it is relevant to the specific needs of teachers who work in these contexts, in different professional life phases and in different scenarios.

eight

Teacher effectiveness, pupil attainment

Introduction

This chapter focuses on investigating teachers' effectiveness, in terms of their impact on pupils' academic attainment and progress. The (standards agenda) has received increasing attention in many countries during the past two decades, reflecting concerns about economic competitiveness, and controversy about the possible influence of more progressive approaches to teaching. This stimulated the introduction of a number of international surveys, such as TIMSS, PISA and PIRLS, to explore variations within and between different countries in the level of attainments achieved by pupils in basic skills or core areas of the curriculum (Sammons *et al.* 2004).

In England, as Chapter 1 has shown, major educational changes from 1988 onwards involved an emphasis on 'raising standards' through the introduction of a National Curriculum, and an associated programme of national assessments at different Key Stages of pupils' school careers (ages 7, 11 and 14). Regular inspection of schools, by Ofsted, was instituted to ensure the delivery of the National Curriculum, and hold schools accountable for the standards achieved by their pupils, with the intention of promoting 'improvement through inspection' (Matthews and Sammons 2004). The national literacy and numeracy strategies had a major influence on teachers' practice in the primary sector after 1998, and the Key Stage 3 strategy influenced practice for teachers of the lower secondary age group from 2001. All these developments sought to increase pupil attainments in the core subjects of English, mathematics and, to a lesser extent, in science. We have discussed teachers' experiences of these major influences on their classroom practice, and in the final chapter we will return to a discussion of the implications of our research findings for educational policy contexts and educational standards in more depth. Here we describe and analyse the way the VITAE research investigated teachers' effectiveness, in terms of pupils' outcomes measured by national assessment results, given their high profile in the English education system. Our findings are likely to be relevant to those working in other contexts where high stakes assessments are used to monitor student achievement and school performance.

So far, teachers' own perceptions of their effectiveness as classroom practitioners and variations in their perceptions of effectiveness over the course of their professional teaching lives, and in different scenarios including changes over the three years of the research, have been identified, analysed and discussed. In addition, and related to these, an important feature of the research was the use of external indicators of effectiveness based on the study of pupils' attainments in national assessments of two important core subjects, English and mathematics. This feature of the research drew on the concept of 'value added' (a form of analysis that seeks to measure the individual school's or teacher's contribution to pupils' progress, social behavioural or affective outcomes). It allowed the study to investigate relative effectiveness of individual teachers in the sample in comparison with each other, by establishing whether pupils in classes taught by some teachers in the study had relatively better outcomes, taking other factors into account, than those taught in other classes by different teachers in the sample.

The VITAE research design involved the collection of pupils' attainments in three consecutive school years in which fieldwork took place. The focus was on classes (Years 2 and 6) or teaching groups (Year 9) taught by the teacher sample. This feature of the quantitative component of our study was used to establish the relative effectiveness of different project teachers in promoting pupils' attainment in English and mathematics using value added approaches and multilevel statistical modelling (Goldstein 1995). The results of these analyses were then fed into the qualitative strand of the project and form a component of the chapters on professional life phase and identities; and an integral component of the chapters on commitment and resilience. They provided the means of exploring whether there were relationships between teachers' perceived effectiveness and their relative effectiveness in promoting pupils' attainment and progress. This illustrates both the limitations of quantitative and qualitative only designs and the advantages (to understanding the nature of effectiveness) of being able to explore the influence of antecedent, mediating and outcome factors when making judgements about effectiveness. In other words, multilevel modelling and value added pupil attainment themselves are important to identify the extent of differences in teacher effects on pupil outcomes, but cannot fully explain the reasons underlying any differences between teachers in their relative effectiveness.

The multilevel analysis was primarily used to identify, measure and categorize teachers' relative effectiveness, in promoting the pupil attainment and progress across three consecutive school years (2002/03 to 2004/05), and to investigate stability and consistency in effects for teachers of different year groups, different curriculum areas and differential effects for different pupil groups. These are important questions and have received very little attention in earlier teacher effectiveness studies. We sought to establish whether individual teachers varied in their effectiveness from one year to another (stability), and in the primary sector whether effects varied for the two different subjects of mathematics and English (consistency). We also explored similarities and differences in the results across the primary and secondary phases of education. From our results we were able to conduct an analysis ('data cut') of our qualitative findings to explore any differences between teachers found to be relatively more or by contrast, relatively less effective in terms of value added results.

School and teacher effectiveness knowledge base

Cognitive outcomes remain important in any definitions of effectiveness. It is well documented, by both cohort and other studies, that children with low cognitive outcomes and poor educational achievement are likely to be at higher risk of poor attendance and poor behaviour in school, lower motivation and of becoming involved in criminal or other anti-social activities later in life (Rutter *et al.* 1979; Parsons and Bynner 1998).

Our initial literature review highlighted several aspects, namely the importance of school effectiveness for enhancing the life chances for disadvantaged groups of pupils, centrality of teaching and learning, pupil learning and teachers' classroom activity, effectiveness across curriculum subjects, and the impact of context on classroom practice. The VITAE research collected information on SES context (measured by the percentage of pupils who were eligible for free school meals) to explore its role in relation to teachers' lives and work, as well as in relation to relative and relational effectiveness.

Multilevel modelling, contextualized and value added attainment results

The influence of pupil intake

The first part of the statistical analysis was used to identify the amount of variation that exists across our sample primary schools, in pupil attainment levels in national assessment tests, taken in Year 2, in comparison with the pattern in schools with similar intake characteristics[12]. These contextualized analyses adopt statistical control for differences in pupil intakes (in terms of both pupil and school characteristics) and create an attainment indicator for each school after adjusting for the net impact of statistically significant pupil background and school context characteristics. This measure of relative effectiveness indicated how well children from each of the 75 schools achieved, compared with the attainment levels of similar children in other schools[13].

The second phase of the statistical analysis was used to assess the extent of differences between teachers in Year 6 and Year 9, in pupils' progress over a school year, and their relative value added effectiveness, taking into account a range of pupil characteristics and measures of pupil prior attainment. This analysis produced value added measures of teachers' relative effectiveness for the Year 6 and Year 9 teacher sample in each year of the study.

The most recent contextualized value added models, adopted by the DfES, incorporate data on pupil characteristics as well as measures of prior attainment. These are very similar to the modelling approach adopted by VITAE, with the exception that the DfES examines overall performance (using a composite outcome covering English, mathematics and science at Key Stages 2 and 3), rather than producing separate models for English and mathematics. Another important difference is that, in VITAE, progress was assessed across individual school years rather than across Key Stages. Thus, the DfES models examine school rather than potential individual teacher effects by examining progress for all children in a given age cohort across several years in different Key Stages. The VITAE models thus provide a more fine-grained analysis of effectiveness, in both primary and secondary schools. They enabled us to focus on the question of relative effectiveness at the teacher level by studying progress over an academic year in different classes or teaching groups, while following the same teachers for three successive years.

To assess the impact of an individual teacher on the progress in attainment their pupils make over one academic year, it is important that intake factors, beyond the influence of the teacher that are related to pupil attainment, are identified. We used national datasets on individual pupils' characteristics, such as age, gender, whether English was an additional language, ethnic group, special educational needs status, and an indicator of socio-economic status (the pupils' eligibility for free school meals). Such factors have been shown to have strong statistical associations with attainment (Mortimore *et al.* 1988; Sammons *et al.* 1997a; Strand 2000).

The aim of the Year 2 contextualized analysis was to identify the contribution of particular pupil and school characteristics to children's outcomes (in this case Key Stage 1 attainment) when prior attainment was not available.

Thus, for example, the net impact of family socio-economic status (using the pupils' eligibility for FSM as a quasi-indicator of SES), is established while taking into account the influence of pupil gender, age in months, EAL status, SEN and ethnicity. These significant characteristics can then be adjusted for when producing a 'contexualized' indicator of a school's effectiveness in promoting attainment for the Year 2 sample. This sort of analysis is not as precise as the value added analyses of pupil progress over an individual school year adopted for the sample of Year 6 and Year 9 teachers (which included prior attainment as well as pupil/school characteristics), and cannot identify individual teacher effects related to the progress made by particular Year 2 classes, but is a fairer way of comparing schools than unadjusted attainment indicators, such as the percentage of pupils achieving level 2a, b or c, or level 3 at Key Stage 1.

The contextualized and value added score indicates whether a year group of children in Year 2 or individual classes (Year 6) or teaching groups (Year 9), show better or worse attainment than expected based on their pupil/school intake characteristics. These estimates (residuals) measure the difference between predicted and actual pupil attainment levels. In VITAE, we categorized the results into five 'effectiveness' groupings (shown in Table 8.1), ranging from significantly below (most negative) to significantly above expected (most positive). These helped us to distinguish groups of teachers who were relatively less or relatively more effective in promoting their pupils' academic attainments. Typical levels of teacher effectiveness were identified from the 'as expected' category. Here pupils had made progress in line with that predicted across the whole sample. Teachers of such classes, therefore, could be considered to be typical or average in their effectiveness, neither relatively better nor relatively poorer than the majority of teachers in the study.

Table 8.1: Categorization of teachers' relative effectiveness based on contexualized and value added residuals

Significantly Below expectation	Below expectation	As expected	Above expectation	Significantly Above expectation
——	–	As expected	+	++
95 per cent chance of the school or class performing worse than expected	68 per cent chance of the school or class performing worse than expected	The school or class performance is statistically as expected	68 per cent chance of the school or class performing better than expected	95 per cent chance of the school or class performing better than expected

Schools (Year 2) or classes (Years 6 and 9) were classified as 'statistical outliers' where the residual estimates in the multilevel model are statistically significant at the 95 per cent confidence interval. This means there is a 95 per cent chance that attainment (Year 2) or progress (Years 6 and 9) is significantly better (+ +) or, by contrast, significantly lower (– –) than predicted on the basis of their pupil intake and prior attainment.

The sample

Table 8.2 shows the number of pupils, classes and schools for which we had collected sufficient data for inclusion in the multilevel analyses for each successive cohort of pupils over the three years of the study.

Table 8.2: The numbers of pupils, classes and schools in the multilevel analysis

	Year 2 (Key stage 1)					
	Cohort 1 2002/03		Cohort 2 2003/04		Cohort 3 2004/05	
	Maths	English	Maths	English	Maths	English
Number of schools	66	66	52	52	69	69
Number of pupils	1955	1954	1543	1536	2014	2014
	Year 6 (Key stage 2)					
	Cohort 1		Cohort 2		Cohort 3	
	Primary year 6		Primary year 6		Primary year 6	
	Maths	English	Maths	English	Maths	English
Number of schools	63	63	45	45	29	29
Number of pupils	1232	1235	935	934	612	612
	Year 9 (Key stage 3)					
	Cohort 1		Cohort 2		Cohort 3	
	Maths	English	Maths	English	Maths	English
Number of schools	16	17	18	13	17	13
Number of classes	43	49	43	29	28	19
Number of pupils	1046	1068	1066	723	670	436

Because the analysis of Key Stage 1 outcomes was a contextualized analysis, the data were obtained directly from national datasets. Thus, all schools completing the national assessments could be included. However, new assessment arrangements were piloted in around 25 per cent of LEAs in cohort 2 (2003–2004). Because of this, some schools did not have test data to include in the cohort 2 analysis.

Not all of our case study teachers were able or willing to participate in every aspect of the data collection, particularly over three years. We found that, for various reasons, fewer teachers participated in the baseline assessment of pupils at the start of the academic year in Years 6 and 9 for cohort 3 (the third year of the study). Similarly, some teachers were reluctant to administer the pupil questionnaire survey, so attitudinal data was missing in these cases. Our analyses reflected these differences in response rate, and more weight was given to the value added analyses for cohorts 1 and 2, owing to the higher response rate which provided more robust evidence for comparisons of relatively more and less effective teachers.

Data collection

Data from multiple sources were collected to conduct the multilevel analyses and produce indicators of school or teacher relative effectiveness.

- Baseline prior attainment data for individual pupils in classes were collected from teachers by the VITAE project for Year 6 and 9 pupils[14]
- Outcome data in the form of Key Stage 1, 2 and 3 attainment (levels and test scores)
- Pupil background information, such as age within the year group, ethnicity, SEN, EAL etc. was collected from the PLASC dataset, also provided by the DfES
- Some school level information was also collected from the PLASC dataset, such as proportion of pupils in the school entitled to free school meals.

Key predictors of progress and attainment

As would be anticipated, prior attainment (at the beginning of the autumn term) was the strongest predictor of later Key Stage attainment for Years 6 and 9 in both English and mathematics. Including prior attainment enables adjustment for differences at the start of the academic year, so allowing relative progress rates for pupils to be investigated. The results are summarized in Tables 8.3 and 8.4 and display the pupil and school factors found

Table 8.3: Child and school factors significantly related to attainment (Year 2)

Year 2 (Key stage 1)

Total Maths – cohort 1		*Total Maths – cohort 2*		*Total Maths – cohort 3*	
Age within year	(+)	Age within year	(+)	Age within year	(+)
Gender (Boys)	(+)	Gender (Boys)	(+)	Gender (Boys)	(+)
FSM entitlement	(−)	FSM entitlement	(−)	FSM entitlement	(−)
SEN: any stage	(−)	SEN: any stage	(−)	SEN: any stage	(−)
New pupil*	(−)	New pupil*	(−)		
Ethnicity; Other white	(−)			Ethnicity; Other white	(−)
Bangladeshi	(−)			Mixed	(−)
Black caribbean	(−)			Black caribbean	(−)
per cent of school entitled to FSM	(−)	per cent of school entitled to FSM	(−)	per cent of school entitled to FSM	(−)
				per cent of school with statement	(−)

Total English – cohort 1		*Total English – cohort 2*		*Total English – cohort 3*	
Age within year	(+)	Age within year	(+)	Age within year	(+)
Gender (Girls)	(+)	Gender (Girls)	(+)	Gender (Girls)	(+)
FSM entitlement	(−)	FSM entitlement	(−)	FSM entitlement	(−)
New pupil*	(−)	New pupil*	(−)	New pupil*	(−)
SEN: any stage	(−)	SEN: any stage	(−)	SEN: any stage	(−)
				Ethnicity; Other white	(−)
				Indian	(+)
per cent of school entitled to FSM	(−)	per cent of school entitled to FSM	(−)	per cent of school entitled to FSM	(−)
				per cent of school with statement	(−)

* Joined school in this or previous academic year

to have a significant relationship (positive indicating better progress and negative indicating less progress) with progress for the whole pupil sample.

The VITAE results are broadly in line with those of other researchers on the factors that relate to pupil progress in studies of school effectiveness (e.g. Strand 1997, 1999, 2002). For example, girls showed better results in English, but boys made more progress in mathematics in Year 6. Pupils from

Table 8.4: Child and school factors significantly related to progress after control for prior attainment (Years 6 and 9)

Year 6 (Key stage 2)

Total Maths – cohort 1		*Total Maths – cohort 2*		*Total Maths – cohort 3*	
Age within year	(+)	FSM entitlement	(−)	Age within year	(+)
Gender (Boys)	(+)	Age within year	(+)	Gender (Boys)	(+)
Ethnicity:		Gender (Boys)	(+)		
Other	(+)			per cent of school entitled to FSM	(−)
SEN status: In progress	(−)	SEN: any stage	(−)		
		EAL	(+)		

Total English – cohort 1		*Total English – cohort 2*		*Total English – cohort 3*	
FSM entitlement	(−)	FSM entitlement	(−)	Age within year	(+)
Age within year	(+)	Age within year	(+)	Gender (Girls)	(+)
Gender (Girls)	(+)	Gender (Girls)	(+)	New pupil*	(−)
Ethnicity:					
Mixed	(+)				
Black other	(+)				
SEN: any stage	(−)	SEN: any stage	(−)	SEN: any stage	(−)

Year 9 (Key stage 3)

Total Maths – cohort 1		*Total Maths – cohort 2*		*Total Maths – cohort 3*	
FSM entitlement	(−)	FSM entitlement	(−)	Class ability level	(+)
Age within year	(+)	Age within year	(+)		
SEN: statement	(−)	EAL	(+)		
Class ability level	(+)	Class ability level	(+)		

Total English – cohort 1		*Total English – cohort 2*		*Total English – cohort 3*	
FSM entitlement	(−)	FSM entitlement	(−)		
		Age	(+)		
		SEN statement	(−)	SEN: any stage	(−)
Class ability level	(+)	Class ability level	(+)		
per cent of school with statement	(−)				

* Joined school After Year 1

low income homes (eligible for FSM) showed poorer attainment and made less progress in all years. Older pupils in each year group (autumn born compared with summer born) also tended to show higher attainment and make more progress than their younger classmates. Children with a SEN statement, as might be anticipated, made less progress and showed lower attainment than other children.

The impact of average ability level of the class

We found that the average prior attainment levels of classes in Years 6 and Year 9 varied significantly. In secondary schools at Key Stage 3 this was particularly marked and can be associated with setting by ability level, especially for mathematics. Earlier studies in other contexts have suggested (Sukhanandan and Lee 1998) that higher ability pupils make greater gains in high ability sets than if they are taught in mixed groups. However, lower ability pupils tend to attain less well if taught in lower ability sets. Research in the Netherlands and in Flanders has similarly pointed to the impact of the average ability level of the class (De Fraine *et al.* 2002).

Our analyses of pupil progress in VITAE confirms the impact of the average ability level of the class (measured at the beginning of the academic year) on pupils' subsequent progress in Year 9 of secondary school, though no significant impact was identified in the analyses of pupil progress in primary classes. Being placed in a higher ability group confers an advantage in terms of the amount of progress made subsequently, whereas being in a lower ability group is a disadvantage. These findings are in line with those reported on setting by Hallam (2002) which concluded that pupils with a similar level of prior attainments, make more progress if taught in a higher set rather than a lower set.

The explanation for the influence of the average attainment level, of the class, is not likely to be straightforward. A high ability class may be relatively easier to teach than a lower ability class, owing to better behaviour, or greater levels of pupil motivation. An alternative hypothesis is that more experienced or highly skilled teachers may be allocated to higher ability classes in some schools. It may also be that both teachers' and pupils' expectations are shaped by being in a higher or a lower set, and also curriculum coverage may be more rapid or extensive in higher ability classes, particularly in mathematics where setting is most common and where decisions may be made to teach at a slower pace or a reduced content in low ability sets. The tiering of mathematics papers is likely to have an important impact, as those in lower sets are less likely to be entered for higher tiers. There was particular variation in Year 9 mathematics classes in aspects of teacher behaviour as perceived by pupils. The impact of variation in class average prior attainment level was strongest in the Year 9 mathematics analysis.

Variations in teachers' relative effectiveness

Overall, significant school and class level variation in progress was identified in each year group (2, 6 and 9) and in each of the three years studied. Table 8.5 reports the intraschool correlations for each cohort in the value added analyses across three cohorts. Our consistent results over three years confirm the existence of important differences in teachers' relative effectiveness. These indicate that variations between teachers, in terms of promoting pupil progress in their classes or teaching groups, are highly statistically significant. For example, in Year 6 between 17 and 29 per cent of the variance in pupil progress (after controlling for prior attainment and background) was found to relate to the class in which a pupil is taught. In Key Stage 3, the results show that differences between teachers and classes in progress results are also strong (15–30 per cent in English; 10–26 per cent for mathematics). These teacher effects are considerably larger than differences between schools confirming the importance of teachers' classroom practice in shaping pupils' academic outcomes.

A substantial number of teachers' classes were identified as statistical outliers in each year group studied. In other words, the characteristics of pupils taught did not account fully for the differences in pupil attainment and progress. This indicates that teachers were not all equally effective in promoting pupil progress. The results are illustrated in Table 8.6 for the

Table 8.5: Intraschool correlations – Maths and English value added results

Year of study	Year 1	Year 2	Year 3	N classes English	N classes maths
Yr 6				Yr 1 = 63	Yr 1 = 63
English	0.29	0.27	0.17		
				Yr 2 = 45	Yr 2 = 45
Maths	0.15	0.17	0.11		
				Y 3 = 29	Yr 3 = 29
Yr 9				Yr 1 = 43	Yr 1 = 49
English	0.15	0.16	0.30		
				Yr 2 = 43	Yr 2 = 29
Maths	0.23	0.26	0.10		
				Yr 3 = 28	Yr 3 = 19

Table 8.6: Differences in Relative Effectiveness for Years 6 and 9 Classes

	Below expectation (95 per cent sig.)	Below expectation (68 per cent sig.)	As expected	Above expectation (68 per cent sig.)	Above expectation (95 per cent sig.)
Year 6 (Key stage 2)					
Cohort 1					
English	14 (22.2 per cent)	7 (11.1 per cent)	21 (33.3 per cent)	7 (11.1 per cent)	14 (22.2 per cent)
Maths	10 (15.9 per cent)	11 (17.5 per cent)	25 (39.7 per cent)	7 (11.1 per cent)	10 (15.9 per cent)
Cohort 2					
English	9 (20.0 per cent)	1 (2.2 per cent)	25 (55.6 per cent)	1 (2.2 per cent)	9 (20.0 per cent)
Maths	8 (17.8 per cent)	5 (11.1 per cent)	20 (44.4 per cent)	5 (11.1 per cent)	7 (15.6 per cent)
Cohort 3					
English	4 (13.8 per cent)	3 (10.3 per cent)	14 (48.3 per cent)	3 (10.3 per cent)	5 (17.2 per cent)
Maths	2 (6.9 per cent)	6 (20.7 per cent)	14 (48.3 per cent)	4 (13.8 per cent)	3 (10.3 per cent)
Year 9 (Key Stage 3)					
(Including average attainment level of class in multilevel model)					
Cohort 1					
English	8 (16.3 per cent)	3 (6.1 per cent)	26 (53.1 per cent)	6 (12.2 per cent)	6 (12.2 per cent)
Maths	7 (15.3 per cent)	3 (6.8 per cent)	19 (43.2 per cent)	5 (11.4 per cent)	10 (22.7 per cent)

Continued Overleaf

Table 8.6: Continued

Year 9 (Key stage 3)	Below expectation (95 per cent sig.)	Below expectation (68 per cent sig.)	As expected	Above expectation (68 per cent sig.)	Above expectation (95 per cent sig.)
Cohort 2					
English	4 (13.8 per cent)	3 (10.3 per cent)	16 (55.2 per cent)	3 (10.3 per cent)	3 (10.3 per cent)
Maths	8 (18.6 per cent)	9 (20.9 per cent)	13 (30.2 per cent)	4 (9.3 per cent)	9 (20.9 per cent)
Cohort 3					
English	5 (26.3 per cent)	1 (5.3 per cent)	7 (36.8 per cent)	3 (15.8 per cent)	3 (15.8 per cent)
Maths	2 (7.1 per cent)	3 (10.7 per cent)	18 (64.3 per cent)	2 (7.1 per cent)	3 (10.7 per cent)

++ $p<0.05$ cl = confidence limit

Year 6 and Year 9 samples. Overall, around 40 per cent of Year 6 teachers' classes were classified as significant outliers (showed significantly better or significantly poorer than expected progress in cohort 1 and 2) for English and around 33 per cent for mathematics. In Year 9 the results showed slightly more fluctuation across years but nonetheless results were broadly in accord.

Stability in effectiveness from year to year

An important question for the VITAE project concerned stability in teachers' relative effectiveness across years. Our analysis of this topic focused on cohorts 1 and 2 for which more value added results were available, and Years 6 and 9 where pupil progress was measured over the school year for individual classes. Our results suggested greater stability for mathematics than English in teachers' relative effectiveness from one year to another. For mathematics in Year 6, the correlation was significant and moderate (0.48, $p<0.01$) but was weak and non-significant for English. In Year 9, the correlation was 0.51 ($p<0.05$) for mathematics but was not significant when class ability level was controlled. Nonetheless, some teachers showed positive results across more than one year, whereas others showed negative results across more than one year. A small number showed positive results in one year and negative results the following year in the same subject. Table 8.7 illustrates these patterns for the 37 Year 6 teachers for whom value added results were available in English and in mathematics.

Table 8.7: Relationships between teachers' relative effectiveness (value added) across cohorts 1 and 2 for the Year 6 sample

English Year 6	Cohort 2 n=37		
Cohort 1	Positive	As expected	Negative
Positive	2	5	3
As expected	4	8	2
Negative	3	6	4
Maths Year 6	Cohort 2 n=37		
Cohort 1	Positive	As expected	Negative
Positive	5	5	0
As expected	3	10	4
Negative	0	5	5

In all, 14 teachers out of 37 (38 per cent) showed a stable pattern of results for English in Year 6 across the two cohorts, while 6 (16 per cent) showed unstable results (moving from negative to positive or vice versa). For mathematics in Year 6, 20 teachers out of 37 (54 per cent) showed stable results, and none moved from negative to positive or vice versa across the two years. At the primary level these results indicate greater stability in teacher effectiveness in promoting pupils' mathematics progress across years. We cannot offer firm reasons for the greater stability in teachers' relative effectiveness for mathematics, but it suggests primary teachers may vary their approach to mathematics teaching from year to year less often than they vary their approach to English.

Table 8.8 gives the equivalent results for Year 9 teachers. Around a quarter, 6 (26 per cent) of the 23 English teachers showed stable results across the two years, while only one moved from positive to negative in the same time period. For mathematics, 8 (31 per cent) of the 26 teachers showed stable results across the two years, but 6 (23 per cent) moved from negative to positive or vice versa.

Taken together these results indicate that some teachers' relative effectiveness levels remained broadly stable over time while, for a smaller number, there was quite a change from one year to another. In later chapters we explore the relationships between personal and professional factors and teacher identity that are associated with more or less favourable teacher

Table 8.8: Relationships between teachers' relative effectiveness (value added) across cohorts 1 and 2 for the Year 9 sample (controlling for class ability level)

English Year 9	Cohort 2		
Cohort 1	Positive	As expected	Negative
Positive	0	7	1
As expected	3	5	4
Negative	0	2	1
Maths Year 9	Cohort 2		
Cohort 1	Positive	As expected	Negative
Positive	3	2	5
As expected	4	2	5
Negative	1	1	3

trajectories in different professional life phases. Such qualitative analyses can help to illuminate changes in perceived and relative teacher effectiveness from one year to another.

In addition to studying whether some teachers were more effective than others, and whether relative effectiveness was stable over time, the VITAE research explored whether teachers were equally effective in teaching different subjects by comparing the value added results for Year 6 teachers in mathematics and English (Table 8.9).

Table 8.9: Comparison of teachers' relative effectiveness in English and maths – number of Year 6 teachers (cohort 1)

	Maths		
English	*Positive*	*As expected*	*Negative*
Positive	8	9	4
As expected	5	10	6
Negative	4	6	11

Here, to simplify the patterns, results were compared in terms of only three broad groups (positive, as expected or negative). Some teachers were found to be relatively more effective in enhancing progress in both English and mathematics while others were less effective in both. In total 29 (46 per cent) out of 63 teachers in the cohort 1 Year 6 analysis showed similar levels of effectiveness in both curriculum areas. By contrast, only 8 (13 per cent) were found to be more effective in one area but less effective in the other. This result was supported by the comparisons for cohort 2. In this year the analysis was based on 46 teachers. In all, 25 (54 per cent) of the 46 teachers showed similar levels of effectiveness in both English and mathematics, while in this year none was found to be more effective in one area but less effective in the other (Table 8.10).

Table 8.10: Comparison of relative effectiveness in English and maths – number of Year 6 teachers (cohort 2)

	Maths		
English	*Positive*	*As expected*	*Negative*
Positive	5	5	0
As expected	7	14	5
Negative	0	4	6

These results indicate that there is a tendency for primary teachers, who are more effective at promoting pupil progress in English, to be more successful also in promoting their pupils' mathematics progress. However, there is still some marked variation and small number of teachers were found to be relatively better in one of these core areas.

Overall, the quantitative findings in VITAE demonstrate that the typical pattern suggests a fair degree of stability in teacher effectiveness over time but also reveals that some teachers do not fit this pattern, either improving in their relative effectiveness from one year to another or declining. For those in Year 6, we also studied whether those better at promoting progress for their pupils in English were also better in mathematics and vice versa. The findings suggest that this is the most likely pattern. Nonetheless, some teachers buck the trend by promoting more progress in one subject than another.

Differential effectiveness

Do teachers vary in their relative effectiveness in promoting the progress of different groups of pupils? This was a question of interest to VITAE and has implications for our conceptions of effective practice. School effectiveness research has, in the past, found evidence of significant differential effects at the school level in studies conducted over key stages for several years. These apply mainly to secondary schools, and though statistically significant, tend to be relatively modest (Sammons 1996). Some schools may be better at promoting the progress of initial lower attaining than of initial high attaining pupils. Others may be more likely to foster the progress of boys rather than girls, for example. Our research on teachers' relative effectiveness found no evidence of significant differential effectiveness for teachers across the study. In other words, teachers who were more effective tended to be more effective for all pupils (boys and girls, those of low or high initial attainment, those from disadvantaged backgrounds and those from more advantaged homes).

The absence of significant differential effects at the classroom level is important because it suggests that teachers who are more effective promote the progress of all children in their classes not just some groups. This is in accord with the conclusions of earlier research, such as the School Matters study of primary schools, in inner London (Mortimore *et al.* 1988).

The characteristics of more and less effective teachers

In order to link the quantitative value added data on teachers' relative effectiveness with the qualitative datasets on teachers' relational (perceived) effectiveness, further analyses were conducted. Owing to the smaller number of teachers for whom value added data were available for cohort 3 (2004/05), this chapter concentrates on findings for cohorts 1 and 2, where the numbers give greater confidence in the robustness of the results.

There were 243 VITAE teachers who had a value added score for at least one cohort and 136 (56 per cent of the sample) teachers who had a value added score for two years (2002/03 and 2003/04). Tables 8.11 and 8.12 show the sample for which it was possible to link qualitative and quantitative datasets to explore the following hypothesis: There are both positive and negative relationships between variations in teachers' work and lives and their relative effectiveness, as measured by value added analyses of pupil progress.

Table 8.11: Number and gender of teachers with value added results for at least one of the first two cohorts

	Number of teachers	*Female*	*Male*
Year 2	74	70	4
Year 6	66	57	9
Year 9 English	49	39	10
Year 9 Maths	54	28	26
Total	*243*	*194 (80 per cent)*	*49 (20 per cent)*

Teacher profiles were compared for the 'more effective' and 'less effective' groups, as identified by the multilevel analysis of relative effectiveness. The criteria for greater or lesser effectiveness included teachers with above or below expectation (++ or + compared with –, or − −) in either of the two

Table 8.12: Percentage of teachers with value added results for both year cohorts

	Number of teachers with VA scores for at least one cohort	*Number of teachers with VA scores for both year cohorts*	*Percent of teachers with VA scores for both year cohorts*
Year 2	74	50	68 per cent
Year 6	66	37	56 per cent
Year 9 English	49	23	47 per cent
Year 9 Maths	54	26	48 per cent
Total	*243*	*136*	*56 per cent*

main year cohorts. Two broad outlier groups were thus formed, a group comprising relatively more effective teachers (those with largely positive results and no negative results, in either or both, of the two year cohorts), and a group of less effective teachers (those with mainly negative results and no positive results over the two years).

Of the 243 teachers, nearly 24 per cent (N = 58) were included in the more effective group and 23 per cent (N = 56) in the less effective group (Table 8.13). Other teachers had results broadly in line with expectation in both years or mixed results. These analyses point to important variations in relative effectiveness levels in all three Year groups (2, 6 and 9) studied.

Teacher profiles were then compared in order to illustrate some of the different experiences and characteristics of teachers included in the more and less effective groups. Our findings made clear that teachers' experiences were very varied and that some in adverse circumstances were highly effective, despite personal or professional difficulties. Some others were found to be less effective, even in circumstances where no difficulties were reported. We did not find any simple explanations for differences in effectiveness or changes over time in terms of teachers' identities, career phases, gender or responsibilities.

Relative effectiveness: key findings from the analysis of pupils' academic outcomes

We found considerable variation among the VITAE teacher sample in relative effectiveness in promoting pupils' academic outcomes. Pupils in different Year 6 classes and in different Year 9 teaching groups, made different amounts of progress during a school year in reading and mathematics.

Table 8.13: Numbers of broadly more effective and less effective teachers in cohorts 1 and 2 by Year group

	Total N	More Effective		Less Effective	
		per cent	N	per cent	N
Year 2	74	18	13	18	13
Year 6	66	26	17	24	16
Year 9 English	49	25	12	25	12
Year 9 Maths	54	30	16	28	15
Total	*243*	*24*	*58*	*23*	*56*

Both relatively more and relatively less effective teachers were identified in a range of school SES contexts. SES context was found to be important, and we conclude that value added measures of performance need to take this into account, as well as other pupil level predictors if comparisons are to be made fairly.

At Key Stage 3, average class attainment levels (that may in part reflect setting arrangements, especially in mathematics) accounted for some of the difference and indicates that this is an important within-school context feature of organization, just as SES is an important between-school contextual influence. Nonetheless, considerable variation remained even when this was included in the analyses. Our results also provide evidence that some teachers varied in their relative effectiveness from one year to another. Despite this, across years the tendency was for more effective teachers to remain more effective, or show typical levels of effectiveness (progress as expected) and less effective teachers to remain less effective, or move to typical levels of effectiveness. Relatively few teachers moved from effective to ineffective or vice versa over a two-year period.

Our findings, from comparisons of the profiles of more and less effective teachers, indicate that one feature for greater effectiveness may be how well the teachers were able to keep their work and lives in balance or in equilibrium (see Chapters 5 and 6 for more discussion of this issue). It seems that negative aspects affected teachers' stress levels, workload, efficacy, motivation and morale, particularly in more challenging contexts; and that these can influence both perceived and relative effectiveness. For those 'less effective' teachers who had mentioned at least one major negative aspect, the extent of perceived professional support within the school seemed to have a considerable impact on their professional lives. As we have seen in earlier chapters, the negative aspects reported were in the areas of practice, adverse personal events, concerns about poor pupil behaviour or the perception of 'negative' policy influences, such as changes related to new educational initiatives, and the impact of inspection.

Our Year 9 results indicate that in secondary schools, there are likely to be both school and departmental influences affecting teachers' relative effectiveness. Several of the more effective teachers were found to be clustered in the same school and department. Similarly, evidence of such clustering in different schools and departments was identified in several cases for less effective teachers. This may reflect school or departmental culture and climate but may also be related to accepted methods of organization and classroom practice not studied in this project. In summary:

- School context (level of socio-economic disadvantage) did not appear to differentiate between the more and the less effective groups. This may be accounted for by the inclusion of both the individual pupil's entitlement to FSM and an additional contextual indicator of the percentage of pupils' eligible for FSM at the school level in the value added models, due to their known links with both attainment and progress. This finding indicates that contextualized value added measures (which have since been adopted by the DfES to add to school performance tables), are likely to be fairer than raw comparisons in terms of key target indicators, such as the percentage of pupils at level 4 (Key Stage 2), percentage at level 5 (Key Stage 3) or percentage at 5A*–C (GCSE) because they are less biased by contextual features, such as the level of socio-economic disadvantage in a school.

- Individual personal background characteristics, such as teachers' age, years in teaching and gender, were not found to be associated in any systematic or linear way with differences in relative effectiveness. This confirms earlier research which suggests such factors are not necessarily the main features of importance in promoting better pupil outcomes. Teachers with different characteristics can be equally effective, and effectiveness does not necessarily increase or decrease as experience of teaching increases. Rather, it is a combination of factors which is likely to influence teachers' capacities to be, and remain, effective.
- The 'more effective' Year 2 teachers were more likely, than the less effective group, to make positive comments about professional practice and support and also about their perceived self-efficacy.
- For Year 6 teachers in particular, it appears that a better work-life balance tends to have positive associations with better pupil progress.
- The 'less effective' Year 9 English teachers were found to have reported more negative personal events in their lives (73 per cent compared with 20 per cent for 'more effective' teachers). However, the same trend was not observed for Year 9 mathematics teachers. Here the gender difference may be relevant since proportionately more male teachers taught mathematics while proportionately more females taught English in the VITAE sample.
- The 'more effective' Year 9 English teachers also made positive comments about their professional practice frequently – 73 per cent compared with 42 per cent for the 'less effective' teachers.

Conclusion

The conclusions we draw from our analyses of pupil attainment and progress and teachers' relative effectiveness in promoting pupils' academic outcomes are that:

- Differences in the characteristics of pupils do not account fully for the differences in levels of pupil attainment or progress between classes and teaching groups.

- Variations between teachers, in terms of promoting pupil progress in their classes or teaching groups in Years 6 and 9, are highly statistically significant and account for between 15 per cent and 30 per cent of the variance in pupil progress.
- Differences between individual classes in pupils' progress rates are generally larger than differences in effectiveness between schools.
- Overall, 40 per cent of Year 6 classes and 33 per cent for mathematics had value added results that were either significantly above or significantly below those expected given pupil intake characteristics and the results for Year 9 are broadly in accord.
- Of the 243 teachers with value added (Years 6 and 9) or contextualized (Year 2) effectiveness scores for 2 years, 24 per cent (N = 58) were classified as more effective and 23 per cent (N = 56) as broadly less effective. Only a small minority showed mixed results across years.
- Few teachers moved from more to less effective or vice versa over two years, the more common pattern was movement from more effective to typical levels of effectiveness (pupils making progress as expected) or to move from less effective to typical.
- There is no single or simple causal explanation for the extent of variation in relative effectiveness in terms of personal, pupil professional or policy factors.

The combination of our quantitative data on relative effectiveness and the qualitative teacher profiles provide indications of the strengths of the mixed method VITAE design. The quantitative component demonstrates that pupil background and prior attainment, as well as the socio-economic contexts of schools, are powerful predictors of performance. Because of this it is necessary to control for such influences, in order to make fair comparisons of relative effectiveness for schools and teachers serving different communities. Teachers were found to vary in their influence on pupils' cognitive outcomes, even when intake differences were controlled. In some classes, pupils made greater progress in a school year than in others. The use of profiles, to link the quantitative measures with information from teacher interviews and other sources, enabled us to explore the influence of a range of other factors. Our results show that social context, external policy initiatives, personal experiences and events and school phase and SES may be, but are not necessarily, factors which moderate teachers' relative effectiveness defined by value added measures of pupil attainment and progress. Further investigation of the influences of personal lives and values, school and departmental leadership, colleagues and pupils, as Chapter 7 has shown, revealed the significant positive and negative mediating impact of these on teachers' work, lives and effectiveness. In the next chapter, Breaking the Mould, we explore further our qualitative data in relation to teachers' relative effectiveness, by illustrating patterns of improvement, stability and decline through case studies over the three years of the fieldwork.

Key messages

Message 1   In making judgements about the quality of teachers' work and pupil outcomes, it is necessary to consider perceived effectiveness and relative effectiveness as defined by value added measures of pupil progress and attainment.

Message 2   'Effectiveness' does not necessarily grow in relation to time in teaching (experience). The growth of experience and expertise do not fully account for teachers' perceived or relative effectiveness.

Message 3   More effective primary teachers, in terms of value added measures, tend to be more effective in promoting attainment in both English and mathematics.

Message 4   Teachers vary significantly in their impact on pupils' progress, and these variations account for around 30 per cent of the differences between pupils in their progress after control for background influences. There was little evidence that teachers were differentially effective for different groups of pupils.

Message 5   For pupils in secondary schools, being placed in a higher ability group seem to confer an advantage in terms of progress. Being in a lower ability group is likely to be a disadvantage. Differences between teacher effects are larger than differences between school effects in shaping pupils' academic outcomes.

Message 6   Effectiveness can fluctuate from one year to another but teachers tend not to move from effective to ineffective over the shorter term or vice versa.

nine

Teachers who break the mould

We use the term 'breaking the mould' to describe those teachers whose effectiveness in promoting their pupils' academic progress is relatively better than predicted on the basis of the characteristics of the pupils they teach, or who are improving in their relative effectiveness. In addition we explore relationships between relative effectiveness and two important themes of the research: professional life phase and identity.

A number of portraits were selected of teachers with different degrees of relative effectiveness, based on our value added results and from a range of school contexts. They are included in this chapter to illustrate the variation in profiles and experiences, and some of the connections that we found to help illuminate patterns of change or stability, in relative effectiveness over the three years of the research. We believe that these illustrate the complexity of differences in the professional and personal experiences of teachers, their management of these, and their own perceptions and understandings of the influences on their work and lives. The case studies chosen support the main conclusion we drew from the systematic comparison of the more and less effective groups of teachers identified by VITAE, that there is no single causal explanation for the extent of variation in teachers' relative effectiveness to be found in terms of specific personal, pupil, professional or policy factors. Different teachers appear to respond differently to the combinations of influences, and show varying degrees of resilience and ways of managing work–life balance and tensions, and the increasing complexities and challenges that affect individuals at various points in their professional life phases. Some teachers seem to succeed against the odds in the face of very difficult pressures. By contrast a few, despite apparently more favourable circumstances, may be rather less effective. Nonetheless, patterns were found that suggest certain factors are associated with an increased risk of lower effectiveness in promoting pupils' academic progress and a greater likelihood of doing so; and these relate to the effects of professional life phases, scenarios and key mediating influences upon their commitment, resilience and effectiveness.

Our qualitative data suggested that teachers generally perceived themselves to become more effective over the course of their teaching career, although often with peaks and troughs that generally coincided with important personal or career experiences and events. Perceptions of such changes could include a trough associated with ill health (personal or of a family member) or divorce (including resulting financial pressures), a rise associated with promotion or a change of school, or a change of policy initiated from outside the school. As previous chapters have shown, some events could have different impacts for different teachers. For example, a change of head teacher may be viewed very positively by some but not other staff in a school, while others, such as the birth of a child, might be viewed very positively at a personal level but also be seen to add to complexities and pressures, especially in relation to work-life balance. Other events that might be perceived negatively at the time (e.g. Ofsted inspection) may nevertheless later be viewed as a turning point and catalyst for change by some.

We recognize that individual teachers' perceptions of effectiveness looking back over different timescales, depending on their professional life phase, are retrospective and made with the benefit of hindsight. Our value added data related to the progress made by particular classes, or teaching groups, over a specific school year. We collected value added measures for a relatively short period of time over the three years of the study and thus, we could only investigate short-term 'real time' changes in teachers' relative effectiveness. Our data sought to establish whether there were any relationships between the qualitative evidence over this period for teachers' perceived effectiveness and teachers' relative effectiveness. In particular, we investigated the relationship with professional life phases and identity scenarios and a number of mediating factors. These affected teachers' perceived effectiveness and we hypothesized that they might also affect teachers' relative effectiveness in different ways over different time scales. By doing this we were able to explore longer term changes across professional life phases with our value added data, given the size and range of teachers in our sample.

Professional life phase

One question of particular interest to the VITAE study, was whether teachers became more effective over time. Although teachers' perceptions suggest that they felt they generally became more effective over the course of their career, we found no evidence of a simple linear association between age or years of experience and teachers' relative effectiveness. Moreover, as we illustrated in Chapter 8, there was a fair degree of fluctuation in teachers' relative effectiveness in the short term, from one year to another. Nonetheless, we were able to classify teachers into several coherent groupings, based on our value added data, in terms of whether they were relatively more or relatively less effective than other teachers in the study, given the characteristics of the classes or groups they taught.

We identified three broad groups of teachers: i) those classified as relatively less effective, ii) those with mixed effectiveness, and iii) those with typical or above levels of effectiveness. We found patterns of association between these and their professional life phase. Here we made three broad distinctions: early (0–3, 4–7 years experience), middle (8–15, 16–23 years) and late (24+ years). We used the value added results for cohort 1 and cohort 2 of the study, as this was where we had the largest numbers. In each year we made comparisons by the three groups of professional life phase, to establish whether the pattern was consistent across two consecutive school years, as this provided greater confidence in our interpretations of any associations.

Our results revealed some interesting associations. As can be seen in the two graphs below (Figure 9.1), there was a clear trend for proportionately more teachers in early and mid-career phase to have results as expected or better than expected in both cohorts. In all groups the majority of teachers had as expected or better than expected results in our value added measures, but for those in late career (24+ professional life phase) proportionately more had a mixture (positive and negative or as expected and negative) or were negative. This association suggests that teachers are at higher risk of a decline in effectiveness in late career, even though the majority remain effective in promoting pupils' academic progress. The pattern is stronger for cohort 1, where the mid career phase teachers in particular show the best results in value added terms (73 per cent as or above expected, compared with 53 per cent of the late professional life phase group).

These findings suggest that teachers do not necessarily become more effective over time in promoting their pupils' academic progress, and confirm earlier findings in Chapter 5 where professional life phase was discussed in more depth, and the challenges faced by teachers in later career phases and their increased vulnerability were highlighted. Our results suggest that the 'common sense' belief that more experienced teachers are better at promoting pupil progress than those with less experience, is mistaken. This claim is not supported by the evidence of our data and adds to our earlier critique of 'stage theory' (see Chapter 5). They confirm the view that teachers in late professional life phases tend to be more 'at risk' of reduced effectiveness and suggest that additional support for such teachers may be beneficial.

i) Cohort 1

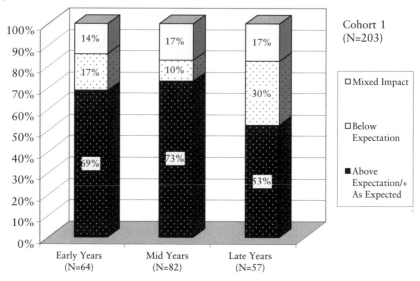

ii) Cohort 2

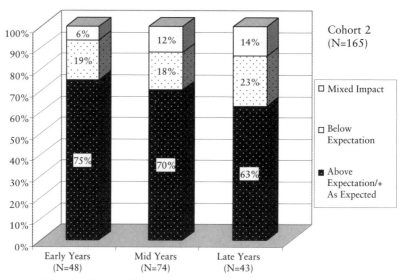

Figure 9.1 The relationship between teachers' relative effectiveness and professional life phase.

In Chapter 6, we drew attention, for example, to patterns of increased vulnerability across the professional life phases. Increased vulnerability, combined with a drop in commitment, is likely to underpin the relatively lower effectiveness for a substantial minority of those teachers in our research who were in the later professional life phases.

Scenarios

Following on from the investigation of the relationship between pupils' test results and teachers' professional life phase, we explored the links with identity through a data cut based on our analysis of different scenarios concerning the balance or imbalance in the way personal, professional and situated factors appear to affect individual teachers' sense of identity. We discussed these in detail in Chapter 6. Here our analysis explored the association between the four different scenarios ranging from: Scenario 1, in balance (personal, professional and situated) through increasing degrees of imbalance and tension between these sets of influences, represented at the extreme by the small number of teachers in Scenario 4. We found no obvious pattern of association with our value added measures of relative effectiveness. For cohort 1, the results suggest that proportionately fewer of the Scenario 4 group were in the average and above average group, but the picture is reversed for cohort 2 in the second year of analysis.

It may be that a more stressful, unstable scenario has a negative impact on teachers' relative effectiveness if sustained over a longer period of time, but we do not have quantitative data to test this hypothesis. Although there can be no doubt that teachers' effectiveness was more at risk of being eroded over the longer term, in the short-term we found no evidence of any consistent link between relative effectiveness and increased complexity of scenario. This was in contrast to the pattern of association with professional life phase.

Variations in relative effectiveness: portraits of teachers with different value added results

In this part of the chapter, we provide illustrative pen portraits of teachers selected as examples of those identified as relatively more effective and those identified as relatively less effective. We also provide examples of some teachers whose relative effectiveness had improved across years during the study.

Teachers who were relatively more effective

Three portraits of relatively more effective teachers are presented to reveal the range of profiles of teachers in this group. These cover teachers in different sectors (primary and secondary), and contexts ranging from relatively more to relatively less socially disadvantaged, as measured by the free school meal indicator of percentage of pupils from low income families. The findings show that more effective teachers have a range of backgrounds, but in these examples it is noticeable that most commented positively on their personal sense of effectiveness and also made reference to the value of team work and the support or contribution of other staff. This suggests that good relationships in a school or department and a supportive professional context, are advantageous in promoting a school or departmental culture conducive to greater academic effectiveness (see Chapter 7 for a detailed discussion of the influence of such mediating factors).

Michael (school context FSM2, attainment band 2)

Value added results: cohort 1 – above expectation; cohort 2 – above expectation

Michael was in his late forties and taught Year 6 in a primary school that was relatively advantaged in its context in FSM band 2 and attainment band 2 in national terms. He had been teaching for over 20 years. The headteacher of his school had retired recently and Michael felt his own confidence in his professional capacity was boosted when he secured the post of acting deputy head. He had much admiration for the new head and was positive about the school ethos noting a 'lovely atmosphere' where the staff supported each other. His self-reported sense of commitment, job satisfaction and self-efficacy were high, but he had described his motivation at the end of year three of the project fieldwork as only moderate. Michael felt that his personal life, professional role and current teaching situation were in general harmony and he enjoyed and looked forward to being at work, though he generally worked up to 55 hours per week. In the longer term he felt he would be looking for senior posts in other schools in the next few years.

Michael had considerable classroom support for several statemented pupils in his class. He made no mention of any personal or professional difficulties affecting his work as a teacher, although a close family member had died recently. In terms of our data about relative effectiveness, Michael was in the relatively more effective group for both English and mathematics value added measures over two successive years. He felt an ICT course had benefited his teaching and gained pleasure and satisfaction from his pupils' good 'SATS' results. He was categorized as being in the sustained commitment group. Commitment and resilience were to be identified as having close associations with effectiveness (See Chapters 10 and 11).

Simone (school context FSM1, attainment band 2)
Value added results: cohort 1: English – above expectation; mathematics – as expected; cohort 2: English – above expectation, mathematics – above expectation

Simone was in her early forties and taught Year 6 in a school with low levels of disadvantage. She was ICT co-ordinator. She had stayed at the same school and was in the 4–7 year professional life phase. Simone had some health concerns in year 2 of the project fieldwork which she felt had had a major impact on her and made her more realistic about managing her workload. She began to spend more time with her family and felt less stressed as a result. In addition, she thought that her level of self-efficacy had increased. Simone reported she had taught a low achieving class at the beginning of the project. She found this a struggle, but with the help of the deputy headteacher, she was pleased to see her pupils making good progress. In year 3 of the project she reported that she had a more placid class and that she felt more effective. She was also in the sustained commitment group.

Salman (school context FSM4, attainment band 4)
Value added results: cohort 1 – above expectation; cohort 2 – above expectation

Salman was in his early thirties and was in the 4–7 professional life phase. He was head of mathematics in a highly disadvantaged school and had been teaching Year 9 in his current school for the past two to three years, having previously served in one other challenging school with 'difficult children'. He reported that the recent change in senior management in his current school had 'a demotivating effect' on him.

He said he worked long hours and was very confident that he was an effective teacher, deriving immense satisfaction from his pupils' excellent achievements in exams. He was also very satisfied with his classroom behaviour management skills and liked to work independently without the assistance of support teachers. As head of department, he felt he had built an effective team and encouraged staff to used performance data to monitor and assess pupil progress. As a result of these positive pupil outcomes in challenging circumstances, his motivation and self-efficacy continued to develop. In our value added data, Salman was in the 'above expected' group in both years even when the ability level of the class was taken into account. Salman used value added approaches within his own department and on his own data noted he had the highest residual of the team and that his department was doing well. He still got a 'buzz' out of seeing the positive impact of his teaching. He felt his role as head of department had an adverse impact on his family life. He had not entered teaching for the money but, with children and a wife at home not in paid work, finances were a concern. In the last year of the project his wife's sudden ill health had changed his priorities and he decided not to move on up the career ladder so he could be more support at home. He was categorized as being in the sustaining commitment group despite the challenging circumstances.

Teachers who were relatively less effective

For a contrast, we selected several case study teachers who were classified as relatively less effective in terms of our value added measures. In several cases such teachers had experienced professional or personal difficulties although it is difficult to distinguish these teachers from the more effective group in terms of their personal or professional profiles.

Katie (school context FSM1, attainment band 2)
Value added results: cohort 1: English – below expectation, mathematics – below expectation; cohort 2: English – below expectation; mathematics: below expectation

Katie was in her late forties and a Year 6 teacher who had taught for over a decade. She felt she had good support and trust from the head teacher which she indicated gave her more motivation and job satisfaction. She also valued the professional support from colleagues. Although in a school with low levels of pupil socio-economic disadvantage as measured by the FSM context, she expressed many concerns about the deteriorating behaviour of pupils and commented that this had negative effects on her 'enjoyment of teaching'. She also complained about the influence of national educational policies and Ofsted inspection, and felt the financial constraints of her current school negatively impacted on her effectiveness.

Generally she felt dissatisfied with her ability to make a real difference to her pupils' learning. She said she worked up to 55 hours per week and experienced high stress levels. No specific personal difficulties were reported by Katie in the interviews. Katie's relative effectiveness in the value added results was below expected in both English and mathematics for cohorts 1 and 2 and she was classified as being at risk in sustaining her commitment.

Marvin (school context FSM4, attainment band 4)
Value added results: cohort 1 – below expectation

Marvin was a Year 9 teacher in his late forties and had taught English for over 25 years. He worked in a disadvantaged, low SES school. He believed the school had management and other difficulties and he did not get on with the headteacher or his line manager. He felt the school was badly run, but said he still loved the school and the staff. He wanted to resign but felt it was hard to move elsewhere at his relatively high current salary level. He reported good relationships with pupils, and felt that they liked his classes.

He had experienced several stressful personal issues in recent years and had recently divorced; he believed this placed him under emotional and financial pressure. Marvin felt undervalued at school and his job satisfaction had decreased in recent years. He felt his promotion prospects were poor in his present school.

His relative effectiveness in our value added data was below expected in cohort 1 and he did not participate in the value added assessment in cohort 2. His commitment trajectory was classified as declining.

Ivan (school context FSM2, attainment band 2)
Value added results: cohort 1 – below expectation; cohort 2 – below expectation

Ivan was in his early fifties and had taught for over 30 years. He was head of mathematics and had been teaching in this school for over 16 years, having previously served in three others. He taught a bottom set Year 9, working mainly with children who had special needs. He was remarried and had stepchildren together with children from his first marriage. These added to home pressures on work–life balance and finances. Ivan's motivation as a teacher had been decreasing because he felt there were no prospects for him in the current phase of his career. He felt 'stuck' in his current position. He knew that his low motivation was 'bound to have consequences' for his effectiveness, but said he tried not to let it affect his lessons. In our value added measures his pupils' results were below expectation in both cohort 1 and cohort 2 and he was placed in the declining commitment group.

Teachers who sustained their effectiveness

Next we include an example of a teacher whose results were consistently as expected (pupils making expected levels of progress taking into account their prior attainment and characteristics) in each year. The category 'as expected' in terms of levels of academic progress can be seen as typical or 'the norm' for the majority of teachers.

Julie (school context FSM3, attainment band 3)
Value added results: cohort 1 – as expected; cohort 2 – as expected

Julie, a Year 9 English teacher, was in her early 50s and had been teaching for over a decade, all in this current FSM3 school. Julie chose to be a teacher because she wanted to motivate children and pass on her enthusiasm and love of English. She believed she had become more effective over the years through growing experience and felt that she was respected more by the children now after earlier problems. Julie had strong religious beliefs and was considering a change of career in future in line with her spiritual interests for which she felt she was developing a vocation.

Julie felt that she had a good head of department who allowed teachers some independence and that her school was well managed. She had good colleagues in the school, though her particular friends had moved over the years. The overall behaviour of the pupils in the school was 'quite difficult', but had improved recently.

Personal stresses, some years in the past, included a divorce, other relationship and health issues, and caring for a family member with long-term illness. She tried to keep this part of her life separate from work. Currently, she felt her personal life, professional role and situation were in greater harmony and believed this had a positive impact on her teaching. Her value added results indicated that pupils' made progress in line with expectation in both cohorts 1 and 2. She was classified as positive and stable in terms of her commitment.

Teachers whose effectiveness was increasing

Two examples of teachers with upward trajectories whose value added results suggested they were improving in relative effectiveness moving from typical to above average effectiveness are also described. These were chosen to reflect different contexts and professional life phases. In one case the teacher worked in a school that had been in special measures recently but had improved.

Celine (school context FSM2, attainment band 3)
Value added results: cohort 1: English – as expected, mathematics – as expected; cohort 2: English – above expectation, mathematics – above expectation

Celine was a Year 2 teacher, science co-ordinator and recently became a member of the management team in an urban moderate socio-economic status (FSM2) primary school. She had been teaching for less than five years and this was her first school. It served an ethnically diverse population, and an above average number of SEN pupils. The school had been placed in special measures early in the project. The dilemma of being an effective teacher in a failing school had resulted in a dip in her motivation at that point. However, during the project the school came out of special measures under a new head's leadership.

Following this experience Celine reported that the school had improved. The school's new action plan had an important influence in relation to refocusing teaching. There was more freedom in some ways to develop the children's skills, without sticking to a too rigid timetable – looking more at individuals, not the whole class.

Celine had highly positive views on the school leadership – 'Everything seems to filter down really well, and everything seems to be discussed openly, and decisions then made as a whole staff.' Staff members at her school were extremely supportive of one another, both professionally and socially and her teaching colleagues kept her commitment strong. Celine had been on a number of courses for professional development and some had been very valuable.

Celine had always enjoyed teaching and working with the children. She felt discipline had improved, mainly owing to raised expectations in the school. Celine had a classroom teaching assistant for a child with a full statement in her class during the last year of the study.

She had a family and tried to keep her personal life and work life separate; in the last year of the fieldwork, she said that she felt more organized at school and less pressurized at weekends. A serious health scare and two bereavements in the project period had made her put school life into perspective. Because she was more experienced she felt she could teach without such detailed planning, and this was helped by the good framework provided by the school.

Celine consistently reported feeling enthusiastic and confident, and believed that she had made a difference to her pupils' learning. She stressed the importance of motivating the children and building their confidence and independence. She loved teaching and had a very high level of commitment. Celine described her effectiveness as having improved. Over the course of the project positive professional feedback from Ofsted, and praise from her mentor in the school and the LA advisory staff, had contributed to her self-confidence. Celine was optimistic and pleased with the way the school had pulled itself out of special measures and was continuing to improve.

In terms of relative effectiveness, year 2 results for Celine's school were as expected in cohort 1 and above expected in cohort 2. Her trajectory was upward in terms of increased commitment to teaching despite the challenging circumstances.

Abbie (school context FSM1, attainment band 2)
Value added results: cohort 1 – as expected; cohort 2 – above expectation

Abbie was in her late fifties and had taught for nearly 30 years with a career break of eight years to care for her young children. She was head of English and had recently become an advanced skills teacher in an 11–16, predominately white, rural comprehensive which was in band 2 of school attainment with low levels of socio-economic disadvantage (FSM1). Returning to teaching after the career break, as a supply teacher, Abbie had taught in a middle school rather than secondary, teaching subjects other than her own. She felt that both her confidence and her reputation as a competent teacher improved during this period.

Abbie emphasized that 'I like working in my department' and described the school leadership as 'good'. Hers was 'a happy department' where people had good relationships and communicated well. She felt that good staff relationships were 'the most important for the quality of your life'.

Abbie described the overall behaviour of the pupils in her school as 'good', and this had a positive impact on her relationships with pupils. She began to feel relaxed and more ambitious in teaching – to 'dare to do different things'.

Recently she had to spend time caring for an elderly parent. Her partner was retired. Though supportive at home, he was now keen for her to retire too. Abbie tried to separate work and personal life as much as possible but found time an issue.

Abbie worked with the head of mathematics in her current school on strategies to raise achievement across the school. This involved some school-wide research and then delivering school-based INSET to raise awareness and engage staff in developing strategies to improve teaching and learning. Through this whole school focus on achievement she became determined that in her department staff would work collaboratively, share good practice, and engage positively with new initiatives in ways that benefited their students. The experience greatly increased her job satisfaction, despite the extra workload. She had become an AST and this coupled with the whole school experience, led to increased motivation over the past three years.

She felt particularly motivated in this final phase of her career, although she speculated that she might be a more effective teacher if she were younger and more organized. She referred to the negative impact of restrictive curriculum, paperwork and assessment on her effectiveness as a teacher. Departmental support and her self-confidence had the greatest positive impact on her effectiveness during the last three years.

Although Abbie felt she coped, she emphasized that being an English teacher could be a 'particularly demanding' job. She still loved teaching but found the teaching situation 'much worse than 15 years ago' because of the greater pressures of accountability. Although she was preparing for retirement, she still felt a sense of sustained motivation and commitment.

In terms of relative effectiveness, Abbie's value added results were as expected in cohort 1 and above expected in cohort 2. She was judged to fit the sustained commitment group and was maintaining and improving her relative effectiveness despite testing personal circumstances.

Short-, mid- and long-term influences on relative effectiveness

Our evidence on academic effectiveness covers a timeframe of only three years, with two years of data being the most common period for which we had robust value added data for sizeable numbers of teachers in the sample. This allowed us to study variations over the short-term, from year to year in terms of teachers' relative effectiveness. However, because of our sample size and extensive qualitative data, we were also able to explore effects of differenct scenarios, mediating influences, and longer term influences on teachers in different professional life phases. This enabled us to address the question of mid- to longer-term variations in effectiveness, and this revealed that there were patterns of greater risk for teachers in the later phases of their career.

Thus, we were able to consider both short-term variations in relative effectiveness, from one year to another, as well as other mid- to longer-term trends related to professional life phase. We found that short-, mid- and long-term factors are likely to interact in different ways for different teachers at different points in their careers.

- **Short-term impact** – factors which are expressed within the three years of the project and whose impact accounts for year to year variations in perceived and measured changes in effectiveness.
- **Medium-term impact** – factors that account for year on year variations and trends, in their effectiveness over the three years of the project. Some of these factors will have come into play before the start of the project but their effect may only be expressed within the three years of data collection.
- **Long-term impact** – factors whose impact are not directly expressed within the span of the project but whose effects are to accelerate or depress the impact of other factors mentioned within the three years of data collection.

Different kinds of support may be important to enhance effectiveness in the longer-term than may be influential in promoting short-term improvement from one year to another. Changes in specific teaching practices or class organization, curriculum developments, guidance or mentoring, a change in school leadership and new national policy initiatives, such as the literacy or numeracy strategies, are likely to have more impact in promoting short- to mid-term improvements in pupils' outcomes. Short-term pressures may lead to fluctuation or decline, for example, a more difficult class in terms of pupil behaviour, shortage of staff in a department, or uncertainty over changes in leadership.

Over the mid- to longer-term, promotion and new responsibilities appeared to boost confidence and enhance satisfaction for many teachers, though this also generally led to increased workloads and added to pressures in terms of work–life balance (see Chapters 5 and 6). In general, greater demands and stresses were experienced, reflecting added complexity as teachers moved through early to mid and later professional life phase. They appeared to receive less support, perhaps owing to commonsense (but incorrect) assumptions that experienced teachers are 'better' and are assumed to be able to cope. They tended to be more critical of new initiatives and the pace and direction of policy changes in education. They were more likely to experience personal pressures related to their own health or that of elderly relatives, and reflecting more complex family roles and demands. These are important findings, given that a large proportion of the teaching force in England is in this mid to late professional life phase.

Our findings, on relative effectiveness, include recognition that there are no simple explanations for the significant differences in relative effectiveness we uncovered in the VITAE research. In summary:

• Teachers may differ in their abilities to influence their personal and professional contexts and in their abilities to manage the factors, both positive and negative, which impact upon them at different points in their professional life phase and in different school contexts.
• Current understandings of effectiveness are too simplistic. Our evidence reveals that it is not a linear path of ever increasing effectiveness associated with age and experience, but is likely to ebb and flow in the short-, medium- and long-term.
• School context is important in terms of risk and resilience, as shown in Chapters 7 and 10. While those working in more challenging contexts were often highly committed and the majority were effective in promoting their pupils' academic outcomes, they appeared to be more vulnerable to pressures both professional and personal in such contexts and were likely to have lower resilience in consequence. Teachers in late professional life phases and in challenging contexts can be seen to be at higher risk of ill health and appear less likely to maintain both their commitment and their relative effectiveness.

Given this, it seems that the most likely influences on teachers' relative effectiveness in promoting pupils' academic outcomes, especially in the short-term, are likely to relate to a combination of their sense of professional well-being, personal experiences and events, school contexts and specific aspects of their teaching and classroom experiences.

There is a need to consider the social and emotional well-being of teachers, the role of professional development and need for appropriate support and professional challenge during different professional life phases and in different school contexts and cultures. The accountability climate, pressures of assessment and inspection, and record keeping were seen by many teachers, particularly those in later professional life phases, to have increased the stresses of teaching and added to their workload. In addition, there was a general perception that pupil behaviour was more difficult, especially in more disadvantaged schools. Attention to developing strategies to support and enhance teacher resilience, commitment and effectiveness, and improve pupil behaviour (including the impact of the inclusion agenda), suggest that a stronger focus on human resource management is needed by policy-makers and senior management teams. They need to think more carefully about ways of supporting all teachers in different professional life phases and scenarios, especially those who are moving into the later phases of their careers – including more appropriately tailored professional development, in order to maintain their effectiveness in promoting their pupils' academic progress.

Our findings are supported and extended in Chapters 10 and 11 where we discuss the associations between commitment, resilience and teachers' relative effectiveness.

Key messages

Message 1 Teachers do not necessarily become more effective over time in promoting their pupils' academic progress.

Message 2 Pupils of teachers in late career (24 years +) are more likely to achieve below expectation or experience mixed impact in terms of value added results than those of teachers in early and middle professional life phases.

Message 3 Although there can be no doubt that teachers' effectiveness is more at risk of being eroded over the longer-term, in the short-term no evidence of any consistent link between relative effectiveness and increased complexity of scenario was found.

Message 4 There are associations between pupil outcomes, teachers' sense of well-being and efficacy, their professional life phase and their capacities to sustain their effectiveness. Policy-makers and school leaders need to provide appropriate support, especially for those in the later phase of their careers.

Message 5 Teachers respond to personal, professional and situated influences in different ways. Some are more resilient and remain more effective despite experiencing a range of difficulties.

ten

Real and resilient: how teachers sustain their effectiveness

Introduction

This chapter explores further the ways that teachers manage and sustain their motivation and commitment in times of change, by examining the role of resilience in enabling teachers to respond positively to challenging circumstances which they may meet over the course of a career. Portraits of three resilient teachers are provided in order to illustrate the range of professional assets and external factors and the interaction between these which, together, contribute to the positive role that resilience plays in enabling teachers to thrive, flourish and sustain their effectiveness. The chapter raises issues of leadership and colleagueship, pupil–teacher relationships, pupil behaviour and parental support; and it locates resilience in the discourse of teaching as emotional practice.

Resilience is of importance in teaching for three reasons. First, it is unrealistic to expect pupils to be resilient if their teachers, who constitute a primary source of their role models, do not demonstrate resilient qualities (Henderson and Milstein 2003). Second, teaching is a demanding job in an emerging 'age of diversity and sustainability' (Hargreaves and Fink 2006: 16). Third, resilience, defined as the capacity to continue to 'bounce back', to recover strengths or spirit quickly and efficiently in the face of adversity, is closely allied to a strong sense of vocation, self-efficacy and motivation to teach which are fundamental to a concern for promoting achievement in all aspects of students' lives. In the VITAE research, teachers were found to have common characteristics and concerns within six professional life phases (see Chapter 5). In these groupings there were those whose commitment was being sustained and others whose commitment was declining. As we will show in Chapter 11, in teachers' minds, and in the measured progress and attainment of their pupils, commitment is closely associated with effectiveness; and for commitment to be sustained, teachers need to be resilient.

The nature of resilience

The notion of resilience originated in the disciplines of psychiatry and developmental psychology as a result of a burgeoning attention to personal characteristics or traits that enabled some children, although having been classified as being at risk of having negative life outcomes, to adapt positively and thrive despite significant adversity (Block and Block 1980; Howard *et al.* 1999; Waller 2001).

Fredrickson's development of a 'broaden-and-build' theory of positive emotions (2001, 2004) provides a useful psychological conceptual framework. She found that a subset of positive emotions – joy, interest, contentment and love – promote discovery of novel actions and social bonds, which serve to build individuals' personal resources; and her work relates closely to that of those in educational research who acknowledge and affirm the importance of emotions in effective teaching and learning (see Chapter 6). These personal resources, ranging from physical and intellectual resources to social and psychological resources, 'function as reserves that can be drawn on later to improve the odds of successful coping and survival' (Fredrickson 2004: 1367). In other words, positive emotions fuel psychological resilience:

> Evidence suggests, then, that positive emotions may fuel individual differences in resilience. Noting that psychological resilience is an enduring personal resource, the broaden-and-build theory makes the bolder prediction that experiences of positive emotions might also, over time, build psychological resilience, not just reflect it. That is, to the extent that positive emotions broaden the scopes of attention and cognition, enabling flexible and creative thinking, they should also augment people's enduring coping resources (Isen 1990; Aspinwall 1998, 2001; Fredrickson and Joiner 2002).
>
> (Fredrickson 2004: 1372)

Most importantly, she suggests that 'the personal resources accrued during states of positive emotions are durable, (outlasting) the transient emotional states that led to their acquisition', and that 'through experiences of positive emotions . . . people transform themselves, becoming more creative, knowledgeable, resilient, socially integrated and healthy individuals' (2004: 1369).

Fredrickson's broaden-and-build theory of positive emotions, from a psychological perspective, contributes to the conceptual basis for understanding the resilient qualities of teachers who are doing a job that is itself emotional by nature; and it mirrors the work of a range of educational researchers on the nature of teaching (Nias 1989, 1999; Palmer 199; Fried 2001). Hargreaves (1998), for example, posits that emotions are at the heart of teaching:

> Good teaching is charged with positive emotions. It is not just a matter of knowing one's subject, being efficient, having the correct competences or learning all the right techniques. Good teachers are not just well-oiled machines. They are emotional, passionate beings who connect with their students and fill their work and their classes with pleasure, creativity, challenge and joy.
>
> (Hargreaves 1998: 835)

The VITAE research observed that in the emotional contexts of teaching, pupils' progress and growth constantly fuelled teachers' job satisfaction and motivation, but that these were mediated positively or negatively by a number of factors which affected their capacities to rebound from disappointments and adversity, maintain their commitment to the profession, and with this, sustain their effectiveness.

Resilience: a multidimensional, socially constructed concept

While the concept of resilience elaborated in the discipline of psychology helps clarify the internal factors and personal characteristics of trait resilient people, the social work literature advances a multidimensional and multi determined perspective, arguing that resilience is best understood as a dynamic within a social system of interrelationships (Walsh 1998; also Richardson *et al.* 1990; Benard 1991, 1995; Gordon 1995; Luthar *et al.* 2000; Henderson and Milstein 2003). As Garmezy emphasizes:

> Research on resilience provides critical opportunities to record changes in life-span developmental pathways – including the emergence of new vulnerabilities, strengths, or both at each period of the life course – which permits further validation of the dynamic nature of the construct of resilience.
>
> (Garmezy 1990, cited in Luthar *et al.* 2000)

We may all be born with a biological basis for resilient capacity, 'by which we are able to develop social competence, problem-solving skills, a critical consciousness, autonomy and a sense of purpose' (Benard 1995: 1). However, the capacity to be resilient in different negative circumstances, whether these be connected to personal or professional factors, can be enhanced or inhibited by the nature of the settings in which we work, the people with whom we work and the strength of our beliefs or aspirations (Benard 1991; Luthar 1996; Henderson and Milstein 2003; Oswald *et al.* 2003; Day *et al.* 2006c).

The social dimension of teacher resilience recognizes the interactive impact of personal, professional and situated factors on teachers' work and lives and contextualizes teachers' endeavours to sustain their professional commitment. Resilience, therefore, is not a quality that is innate. It is both a product of personal and professional dispositions and values, and socially constructed. It is a construct that is relative, developmental and dynamic, connoting the positive adaptation and development of individuals in the presence of challenging circumstances (Rutter 1990; Howard *et al.* 1999; Luthar *et al.* 2000).

The VITAE research provides comprehensive empirical data which supports the notion of resilience as a dynamic construct which is subject to influence by environmental, work specific and personal contexts. An individual may demonstrate resilience in a certain context and/or in a certain professional/life phase, but fail to display similar qualities at different times and under changed circumstances. Personal lives and working contexts may become unstable (e.g. failing health and classroom behaviour problems) in unpredictable ways, as we have seen among VITAE teachers, but whether the sudden changes are perceived as adverse conditions by the individual will vary depending on his/her scope of experience at the time of change, perceived competence and confidence in managing the emerging conditions, views on the meaning of engagement, and the availability of appropriate support within the context of change. The portraits of three teachers, later in this chapter, demonstrate that the socially constructed concept of resilience provides a fresh and more informative perspective to theories of teacher resilience and our understandings of how and why this varies among teachers over time.

Resilient teachers: their contexts and stories

In the VITAE research, we found that teachers' capacities to sustain their sense of positive professional identity and commitment (i.e. their resilience), were influenced by their professional life phases and the management of the interaction within the 'scenarios' in which they lived and worked. Chapter 7 has discussed the mediating influences upon teachers' effectiveness in detail. For example, as the scenarios in which teachers work became more complex – as in the case of FSM4 schools – so it might be expected that, in order to maintain commitment and effectiveness, teachers would need to exercise their resilience more frequently. In other words, the more extreme the scenario, the more energy it takes to manage and the more likely it is to test teachers' resilience. The data from the VITAE research show that this is indeed the case. Thus, teachers' capacities to be resilient will be influenced – positively or negatively – by key influencing factors, such as professional life phases, teacher identities and mediating factors, i.e. the personal, the situated and the professional. As Chapter 6 has shown, where teachers experience relatively mild fluctuations they are less likely to need to call upon their resilience.

Figure 10.1 shows that teachers in relatively unstable scenarios were relatively more likely to work in FSM3 and 4 schools. In other words, teachers who worked in FSM1 and 2 schools were more likely to experience relatively stable scenarios than those who worked in FSM3 and 4 schools. In addition, teachers who worked in FSM4 schools were more likely to experience extremely unstable scenarios than others.

However, the incidence of resilience among teachers is not always directly connected to school context as measured by the school FSM. For example, Figure 10.2 shows that the large majority of teachers in FSM4 schools were still resilient. This may be because in order to survive in these challenging circumstances, it is necessary. However, our data have shown that many of these teachers were committed by disposition to working with pupils from disadvantaged backgrounds. This may, therefore, account for the higher levels of resilience.

Figure 10.2 shows that teachers in FSM3 schools were less likely to be resilient than those in other schools. This may be because these schools are still disadvantaged but, because they are not severely disadvantaged, do not receive as much extra support or enhanced resources. It may be, also, that teachers in these schools were less likely to be committed to working in the particular disadvantaged socio-economic contexts to which those in FSM4

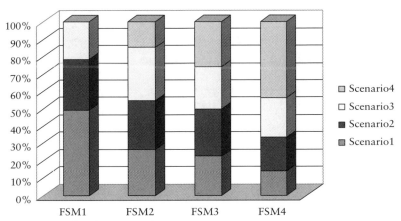

Figure 10.1 School contexts by scenarios.

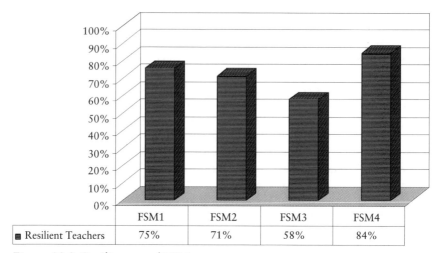

Figure 10.2 Resilience and FSM.

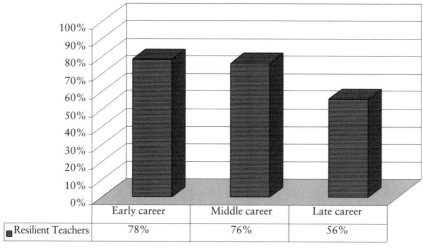

Figure 10.3 Resilience and professional life phase.

schools had committed themselves, and so find it more difficult to sustain resilience.

Figure 10.3 shows that teachers within early and middle careers were more likely to retain resilience than those in late career. As we have seen in Chapter 5, for late years teachers, government policies, disruptive pupil behaviour, increased paperwork, heavy workloads and the consequent long working hours, coupled with poor health, constantly challenged their capacities to exercise resilience and sustain effectiveness.

There were no significant differences between primary and secondary school teachers' resilience in different school contexts and professional life phases.

Stories of resilient teachers

The good news from VITAE is that of the 300 teachers in the study, 218 (73 per cent) were sustaining relatively positive identities across all professional life phases over the three-year period of the fieldwork. However, in each phase there were a number who did not. For the purposes of this chapter, we have selected the stories of three teachers in their early, middle and late careers who illustrate different degrees of resilience in response to the differing challenges. Their stories chart the mediating factors within different scenarios which helped or hindered them in this. While the experiences of these teachers are not representative of the whole VITAE teachers sample, their profiles are typical of teachers within their professional life phases, of the key personal, professional and situated factors that impact on their work and lives, and of the ways they manage these factors to sustain their motivation and commitment in the face of adversity.

Story 1 Sam – a teacher in his early years: from declining self-efficacy to growing attachment

Sam, in his late twenties, a Year 6 teacher in an urban very low socio-economic status primary school, saw his vulnerable professional life trajectory change as a result of his promotion and increased self-efficacy and confidence in the profession.

Declining self-efficacy and attachment in an unsupportive environment
Sam had worked in his current school for over four years, originally taking the job because of his ideological commitment to the school's poor socio-economic context. But having experienced some unpleasant incidents with parents, he admitted that he felt a little depressed because of the lack of parental support.

A lack of support from the school leadership was another negative influence on his work as a teacher. He felt that he would sometimes like management to give him more support – rather than the children. He was 'getting fed up' of doing things that others really ought to be doing and felt there was some unfairness in the school. People did not always pull their weight and this was largely because of unclear management who did not always recognize Sam, or others, for what they had done.

> When I started this school I was expecting to be told I'd done something good or bad and I wasn't praised or told off for doing things, so I didn't really know where I was. I've been here a little bit now so I don't expect praise or to be told off unless I do something really bad. It is just a lack of communication.

Ill health was, at the time, a critical issue for him. During the project, he had had time off for several hospital operations.

Sam enjoyed teaching and the rewards that he gained from working with children, but noticed that he did not have as much free time as his friends in other professions. He was happy for work to dominate at this early stage of his career but felt that 'I don't know if I can take many more years of doing what I am doing. While I am young I'm fine. But as I get older, I don't know, as other commitments take over. I just want a bit of life really'. Professionally, he had been becoming unhappier.

Career advancement and increased self-efficacy: conditions and outcomes of positive adaptations

In May of his fifth year in teaching, Sam was given more responsibility in the school. He was pleased to have the extra responsibilities and saw taking these on as a good move in terms of promotion and professional life development. This positive move, coupled with the appointment of a new deputy head, greatly improved his motivation and sense of effectiveness. The new deputy head had taken the school 'out of the comfort zone,' which Sam thought was basically good, although a little challenging. Nevertheless, he was keen to prove himself. Taking on extra responsibilities was hard at the outset and had had a detrimental impact on his teaching, but he felt that he was now managing better. Generally he felt more comfortable, more confident and knew what he was doing. He was considering changing schools and interested in taking on new roles. See Table 10.1.

Story 2 Abi – a mid-years teacher: from efficacy and effectiveness at risk to growing motivation and sense of positive identity

Abi's previous professional life phase (4–7) was characterized by her efforts to settle in her current secondary school, her struggle with a lack of work–life balance and her deep resentment towards the performativity agenda. As a result, her professional identity was at risk and she was considering leaving teaching. This downward trajectory had, however, changed radically for the better at the beginning of her current professional life phase (8–15). Contributing influences were her new job (with promotion), her increased

Table 10.1: Summary of variations in Sam's experiences

Declining self-efficacy and attachment	*Career advancement and increased self-efficacy*
Scenario 3: Situated & Personal dimensions dominant	*Scenario 2*: Professional dimension dominant
Positive influences:	*Positive influences:*
Staff collegiality, pupil behaviour	Staff collegiality, pupil behaviour, *promotion, school leadership*
Negative influences:	*Negative influences:*
School leadership, personal (illness), lack of parental support, lack of work-life balance	Lack of work-life balance

confidence in working with the performativity agenda, and the prospect of an improved work–life balance. Abi ultimately regained her high levels of motivation, commitment and sense of efficacy in teaching.

Abi was in her early thirties and had taught English for almost ten years. She taught in Canada for four years before coming to England, where she worked in other schools. Abi had always wanted to be a teacher and entered teaching with a sense of vocation. This still applied although she felt that she had lost 'some rose-coloured ideas' that she had had when she first became a teacher.

Abi taught Key Stage 3 mixed ability classes of 23–25 pupils in her school – a large 11–16, rural, moderate socio-economic status (SES) Beacon Community College which had GCSE results well above those in similar schools. The teaching of pupils from 'council estates' was a new experience for her and she had been shocked by the adverse home conditions for learning that some of the pupils faced.

Educational ethos at odds with professional values: identity, efficacy and effectiveness at risk

Abi's school provided strong professional and personal support. She liked the collegial working environment at her school and had good relationships with her colleagues. However, her department was less supportive. Having been in the school for a year, Abi felt 'a lot more at ease'. She knew her students better and had established excellent rapport with them.

She found it difficult to 'switch off' easily. Her personal drive to enable students to succeed was the cause of her high self-efficacy. When she arrived home she still had more work to do and spent half a day at weekends doing school work. She described herself as sometimes being in trouble at home for being 'in teacher mode'. She could not imagine 'not being in teaching'.

Abi's partner was living in a different city. They had been separated for over a year, and this had negatively affected both her work and personal life. Abi felt tired and less organized because of her weekend travelling to visit her partner.

The performativity agenda had had the greatest negative impact on her morale and motivation to teach because it ran counter to her personal philosophy of teaching. She felt that testing and marking seemed to be more important than fostering pupils' independent learning. There was a fall in her motivation during the project. Abi began to feel increasingly that she had 'less control over what I teach and how I teach it'. The accompanying pressure meant that she 'had less time to build relationships'. She spent a lot of time 'marking, reading, filling in results, feeling under pressure to teach something well and quickly'. This had led to a feeling of being 'overwhelmed' and 'more grumpy at work', with no time to teach fun, creative lessons that would help with social skills as well as learning.

Abi was not sure whether she would remain in teaching long-term as she found it 'emotionally draining' and 'mentally tiring', although she did like it and achieved good results.

Support and recognition – growing efficacy, motivation and identity – restoring mastery and control

The beginning of Abi's new professional life phase also meant a new beginning of her professional and personal life. She was more settled in her current school and began to get on well with her head of department. Abi found the overall pupil behaviour 'challenging', nevertheless, 'the rapport with the children' in the classroom continued to motivate her as a teacher. She still liked teaching and enjoyed seeing the children progress. Support and recognition from the school and departmental leadership, coupled with staff collegiality, contributed to her high sense of effectiveness. The opportunity to mentor PGCE students had made her think more about her own teaching and had also positively impacted upon her perceived professional identity and effectiveness. The target-driven culture remained a negative influence on her work, but Abi did not feel as strongly about this as before. She had found ways to 'get around' the rules, tests and targets and learned to inject her own interests in teaching.

Abi was moving to a school in a different city with a promotion in the new academic year. She looked forward to her new job because it also meant her reunion with her partner and improved work–life balance. She did not want to leave her current school, but felt that her personal relationship was equally important. She was also thinking of getting married and having a family – 'all the stuff you do in your 30s'. Her decision to move to Canada in the future had also helped in that it gave her hope of working in a place where she could enjoy pursuing her student-centred teaching. See Table 10.2.

Table 10.2: Summary of variations in Abi's experiences

Identity, efficacy and effectiveness as risk	*Growing motivation and identity*
Scenario 3: Professional & Personal dimensions dominant	*Scenario 2*: Professional dimension dominant
Positive influences:	*Positive influences:*
School leadership, staff collegiality, teacher-pupil relationships	School/departmental leadership, staff collegiality, teacher-pupil relationships, promotion (new job), personal (relationships)
Negative influences:	*Negative influences:*
Educational policies, target-driven culture, personal (relationships), lack of work–life balance, pupil behaviour, lack of support from departmental leadership	Educational policies, target-driven culture, pupil behaviour

Story 3 Sadie – a late years teacher: sustained commitment and a strong sense of self-efficacy

Sadie, 47 years old, was headteacher in a small, rural, high SES Church of England primary school. She came from a teaching family and had always wanted to be a teacher. She had taught for 26 years and still enjoyed working with children. She suffered from relentless pressure as a consequence of adverse personal events and heavy workload. Nevertheless, she had managed to sustain high levels of motivation, commitment and sense of effectiveness, both as a teacher and as a manager. Sadie's high levels of self-efficacy and agency, together with support from her small, friendly school, had made major contributions to her positive professional outlook.

Thriving against the odds
When she first joined the school, Sadie found that there was 'a competitiveness in the school, to the degree that it became destructive in the classroom and between parents and staff, so the whole situation was grim'. Pupil behaviour was 'appalling' too. She appointed a new, highly committed and enthusiastic teaching staff, created a positive teaching culture, and turned the school around. Good relationships between the staff and the pupils and parents had benefited from the small friendly school environment. For Sadie, the professional and personal support from the staff and the governors had had the greatest positive impact on her feelings of effectiveness.

Her husband was very insistent that she had a work–life balance. During the week, Sadie often worked late in the office so that she could spend most of the weekends with her family.

I think the teaching profession, if you're not careful, can totally destroy your home life – I think the hardest thing for people to do is to find the balance – I've only realistically found the balance in the last five to six years . . . I also live away from school now – I travel many miles a day – that has actually helped because without living so close to school I can't pop in during the holidays or weekends – and it's good reflection time sitting in the car with nobody hassling.

Personal events had recently had a detrimental effect on her work. Sadie's husband was suffering from severe depression, which, coupled with an Ofsted inspection, put her under tremendous pressure. Coming to work became a relief and remedy for her at the time. In the end she became ill with shingles. But she insisted that she had never felt out of control because she believed that she had the ability to manage tensions and bring back her work–life balance. Her husband's condition had gradually been improving and Sadie found herself more relaxed at home.

Despite these negative factors, Sadie continued to enjoy working with children and high levels of motivation and commitment in her job. 'Seeing children enjoy learning' had been the main source of her motivation and commitment.

I enjoy being a teacher. I love being a teacher. I'm very enthusiastic about my job. If I wasn't, I wouldn't stay in the job. I do feel there are expectations that are unfair from the government and from parents, and I do feel that there is a cultural element of parental responsibility being passed to our shoulders by the government as well as parents.

Sadie was also highly confident in her ability to be an effective teacher and an effective manager and, enjoyed a high level of job satisfaction. Although she derived great pleasure from her pupils' good National Test results, she did not think that the target-driven culture had affected her approach to teaching at all. She disapproved of this culture and believed that exam results were only a snapshot of her pupils' achievements. She was proud that her school was not driven by government initiatives and tests because she saw herself as being now well placed, with her enhanced experience and confidence, to implement the actions that she believed were in the best interests of her children's learning. She commented, 'I feel positive about what I'm doing.'

Confident in lots of ways. Confident from what the statistical data shows me, also confident because I have feedback verbally and written from children, parents and staff. We did a questionnaire on the effectiveness of the school for the parents and it was the most incredibly positive response you could imagine. Things have moved forward and the school has become a community.

As for her next career move, she thought that she might apply for a headship in a larger school, but there was 'no burning desire' yet. See Table 10.3.

Developing the professional assets of teachers

Sustaining a sense of vocation

The sense of vocation is an important professional asset of teachers. It fuels teachers' personal resources with 'determination, courage and flexibility, qualities that are in turn buoyed by the disposition to regard teaching as something more than a job, to which one has something significant to offer' (Hansen 1995: 12). Sam had deliberately joined his school to make a difference to students from socio-economically deprived backgrounds. Both Abi and Sadie had a strong calling to teach since childhood and continued to enjoy the pleasure of working with children in their current schools. Their response to the original call to teach had formed an important part of their professional identities, and had interacted with 'an inner incentive which prevents [the] person from treating his work as a routine job with limited objectives' (Emmet 1958: 254–5). This interaction had helped them to sustain commitment in the profession.

Hansen (1995) argues that in contrast to a profession which has an emphasis on public recognition and larger rewards, the language of vocation 'takes us "inward" into the core of the (teaching) practice itself', that is, 'what many teachers do, and why they do it' (1995: 8). More than a decade later, for the majority of VITAE teachers this was still the case. For all of the three teachers, pupils' progress had clearly stayed at the heart of their strong sense of vocation, or 'sense of mission' (Nieto 2005: 204). Abi struggled to

Table 10.3: Summary of variations in Sadie's experiences

Sustained a strong sense of efficacy and commitment	
Scenario 3: Professional & Situated dimensions dominant	Scenario 2: Personal dimension dominant
Positive influences:	*Positive influences:*
Personal (husband support)	Staff collegiality, teacher-pupil relationships, pupil behaviour
Negative influences:	*Negative influences:*
Pupil behaviour, teacher-pupil relationship, lack of staff collegiality, educational policies, target-driven culture	Personal (husband's illness)

separate her identity as a teacher from her identity as a person, i.e. not be in 'teacher mode' while at home. Both Sam and Sadie gained rewards and their motivation was sustained by seeing their children learn and develop. These three teachers' 'missionary zeal' and 'moral values' (Nias 1999: 225) had, to a larger or lesser extent, functioned as internal psychological and emotional supports for them, encouraged them to be 'vocationally and professionally committed' (Nias 1999: 225), and helped them to find strength and power to achieve 'personal autonomy and personal significance' (Hansen 1995: 6). Thus, teachers' vocation is associated with a strong sense of professional goals and purposes, persistence, professional aspirations, achievement and motivation – the essential qualities that Benard (1995) has observed in resilience. It is an essential component of teacher commitment, and contributes to their capacities to be resilient.

Developing a sense of efficacy

Gibson and Dembo (1984) suggest that teachers' efficacy beliefs influence their persistence and resilience when things do not progress smoothly. Similarly, Rutter (1990) describes self-efficacy as one of the very robust predictors of resilience; and, according to Hoy and Spero (2005: 343), teachers' sense of efficacy is their 'judgements about their abilities to promote students' learning'. These self-judgements and beliefs 'affect the effort teachers invest in teaching, their level of aspiration, the goals they set' (2005: 345). For Sam, Abi and Sadie, their perceived efficacy made differing contributions to their endeavours to develop. As a teacher in his early years Sam suffered from the inadequacy of management support, which he greatly regretted. The VITAE findings suggest that in-school support has a significant impact upon early years teachers' self-efficacy, as they are in a phase of gaining experience and establishing their professional identity in the classroom as well as in the profession. Promotion, which is often associated with recognition from the management, was shown to have greatly improved his motivation and efficacy. Sam was no longer considering leaving teaching. Instead, he had a clearer vision of his work and was keen to prove himself.

In common with Sam, Abi had also experienced a period of developing her sense of efficacy. However, in contrast with Sam, Abi had prior teaching experience in another country. The source of her stress and struggle was the mechanism and structure of the English education system. Nias (1999) traces the connection between teachers' moral purposes and vulnerability, and postulates that 'guilt and loss of self-esteem through the betrayal of deeply held values can be emotionally damaging as appropriating or resistance' (1999: 225). Her observation to a large extent explains the emotional strain that Abi had experienced. She, sadly, found that her personal interests and professional values were out of line with the government target-driven initiatives and regretted that she no longer had the time and energy to provide care for her pupils. The recovery of her self-efficacy had been the result of improved support from the departmental leadership, her successful self-adjustment to her department and school, and her improved work–life balance. More importantly, the 'rebounding' process itself reflects her high level of personal efficacy. It was a process in which she managed structural (macro), situated (meso), professional and personal (micro) factors. Bandura (2000) introduces self-efficacy belief as 'a vital personal resource' and explains why it may affect individual's self-motivation and life trajectories:

> When faced with obstacles, setbacks and failures, those who doubt their capabilities slacken their efforts, give up, or settle for mediocre solutions. Those who have a strong belief in their capabilities redouble their effort to master the challenges.
>
> (Bandura 2000: 120)

Bandura argues that, 'among the mechanisms of self-influence, none is more focal or pervading than belief of personal efficacy' (2000: 120).

In contrast with Sam and Abi, Sadie, with 26 years of teaching experience, believed strongly in her problem-solving capabilities. She possessed a very high level of self-efficacy and remained strong and positive, regardless of adverse influences either at work and/or in her personal life. She was particularly proud of her capabilities of leading her school to accommodate, rather than unquestioningly accept, the tide of government's target-driven initiatives and pursue the best education for the children. In Bandura's terms, her exercise of control over adversity and positive (emotional and psychological) well-being require 'an optimistic sense of personal efficacy' (Bandura 1986, 1989):

> This is because ordinary social realities are strewn with difficulties. They are full of impediments, failures, adversities, setbacks, frustrations and inequities. People must have a robust sense of personal efficacy to sustain the perseverant effort needed to succeed. Self-doubts can set in quickly after some failures or reverses. The important matter is not that difficulties arouse self-doubt, which is a natural immediate reaction, but the speed of recovery of perceived self-efficacy from difficulties ... Because the acquisition of knowledge and competencies usually requires sustained effort in the face of difficulties and setbacks, it is resiliency of self-belief that counts.
>
> (Bandura 1989: 1176)

Thus, a strong sense of self-efficacy is another essential component of teacher resilience. To rebound from setbacks and adversity, teachers need the strength of self-efficacy beliefs; and conversely, their sustained effort and perseverance in the face of difficulty will strengthen their sense of efficacy and result in a stronger sense of resilience. In other words, the development of teachers' self-efficacy consistently interacts with the growth of their resilient qualities. It is by nature a dynamic, developmental process – the key characteristic of resilience.

Meeting the challenge of the environment

Studies on resilience also emphasize that both positive and negative external environmental factors 'create the resilience phenomenon' (Gordon *et al.* 2000: 2) in the process of resilience building. According to Henderson and Milstein (2003), the environment impacts on an individual's resilience in two ways. They note that the changing expectations about schools and the composition of the student population are key environmental factors that challenge teachers' sense of effectiveness and well-being.

> First, the internal protective factors that assist an individual in being resilient in the face of a stressor or challenge, are often the result of environmental conditions that foster the development of these characteristics. Second, immediate environmental conditions present, in addition to the stressor or challenge, contribute to shifting the balance of an individual's response from one of maladaptation or dysfunction to homeostasis or resiliency
>
> (Henderson and Milstein 2003: 7)

In the VITAE research, we also observed the significant impact of various mediating factors on teachers' commitment and resilience. Managing the complex interactions between their professional assets and the professional, situated and personal scenarios, which teachers experience in each professional life phase, is a sophisticated process which contributes strongly to the relative strength of their resilience. In particular, situated factors – leadership of school and department, staff collegiality, teacher-pupil relationships and behaviour of pupils – were found to be contributing influences which contributed positively and/or negatively to teachers' efficacy, commitment and perceived effectiveness. It also extended previous work on teachers' careers by investigating the variations in the impact of critical influences on teachers and their effects in different phases of their professional lives.

External policy contexts

External policy contexts, heavy workload and work–life tensions appear to have had stronger influences on teachers' self-efficacy and sense of effectiveness in the middle and later professional later phases (from 8–15 years) (see Chapter 5).

Teachers' expertise is context dependent and 'highly idiosyncratic in nature' (Bullough and Baughman 1997: 131). Huberman (1989) observed that when contexts change, tensions emerge. Abi's initial struggle in her new school exemplifies such tensions. For Abi, moving to a new education system imposed an extra layer of emotional strain on her. In comparison to situated in-school factors, structural factors – standardization and the performativity agenda – had a greater impact on her declining motivation. In addition, she had to deal with growing tensions between her work life and personal life and began to feel the need to consider the next direction of her professional life – typical characteristics of teachers within professional life phase 8–15.

Sadie was the very essence of what Boyle and Woods (1995) describe as a 'composite leader' who meets statutory requirements and stays true to her own beliefs. With years of experience, she was able to enjoy a strong sense of 'responsible freedom' (Rogers 1969) in the profession in pursuit of what she believed was the best for the growth of the children. While Woods (1999: 123) claims that successful adaptation to initiatives and change is 'very hard', Sadie's determination and sustained commitment to her professional and moral beliefs suggest that teachers can develop in strength in such an emotionally stressful process, and derive joy and fulfilment from 'those components of his/her job which s/he values' (Evans 1998: 11). In other words, adversity may also promote the development of resilient qualities (also see Rutter *et al.* 1979; Benard 1991; Wang *et al.* 1993; Pence 1998; Henderson and Milstein 2003; Oswald *et al.* 2003).

School contexts

For both Abi and Sadie, staff collegiality was a contributing influence on their positive professional outlooks. Nieto (2003) suggests that to retain teachers' commitment in the profession, schools need to become places where teachers find community and engage in intellectual work. In addition to supportive leaders and colleagues, good teacher–pupil relationships had also had a positive effect on these three teachers' upward professional life trajectories.

In the early years of teaching the importance of in-school support predominates. Sam's enhanced confidence and desire to 'broaden horizons' in the teaching profession had greatly benefited from the positive effects of supportive school leadership and 'appropriate collegial relations' (Nias 1999: 223). His experience is typical of early years teachers (Sikes *et al.* 1985; Bullough and Baughman 1997; Hoy and Spero 2005).

In their study on teacher turnover, wastage and movements between schools, Smithers and Robinson (2005) observed that:

Teachers are more likely to stay in schools where there is a clear sense of purpose, where the teachers are valued and supported, and where appropriate appointments have been made. The impact of good leadership could be outweighed, however, by factors largely outside a school's control, such as location, cost of living, demographics and teachers' personal plans.

(Smithers and Robinson 2005: i)

Sam's and Abi's experiences illustrate that they would have been lost to the teaching profession if there had not been a positive change in the leadership. Elsewhere, Werner (1990) warns that 'when stressful life events outweigh the protective factors, even the most resilient ... can develop problems' (1990: 111).

The professional and personal experiences of each of the three teachers described, can be seen as being reflected in their journeys of self-adjustment and professional growth within particular contexts or scenarios which mediated these. In all their journeys the teachers were confronted by professional and personal pressures, tensions, and challenges to their values, beliefs and practices. But what shines through was their capacity to build upon favourable influences and positive opportunities in their work and life contexts, to overcome the emotional tensions of the scenarios in the environments which they experienced, and to maintain positive emotions and a sense of vocation.

For all three teachers, their 'inner motivation to serve' (Hansen 1995: 6) had called them into teaching and it had been this very motivation and a sense of meaning and moral purpose that underpinned the pursuit of effectiveness. These internal values and motivations, fuelled their capacities to exercise emotional strengths and professional competence and, subsequently provided them with the resilience which enabled them to meet the challenges of the changing and challenging environments in which they worked. As a consequence, then, the potentially negative effects of experiencing stressful work and life events were managed and translated into positive personal and professional resources upon which these teachers could draw and benefit, when developing and sustaining their positive professional life trajectories over the course of their careers.

Conclusion: the retention of quality

The evidence suggests strongly that resilience is a multi-faceted (Oswald *et al.* 2003) construct. The nature of resilience is determined by the interaction between the internal assets of the individual and the external environments in which the individual lives and grows (or does not grow). Thus, the manifestations of resilience vary from person to person and fluctuate over time, according to the scenarios which they meet and their capacities to manage these successfully.

Previous research on teachers' work in contexts of performativity, has tended to focus on factors affecting teachers' decisions to leave the teaching profession. Our research suggests the need to distinguish between two forms of retention in the teaching profession: their physical continuation in the role; and the maintenance of motivation and commitment as key indicators of the retention of quality. While the answer to this second form of retention is less easily observed, being located essentially in teachers' values and resilience to meet the challenges of different scenarios in their work and lives, it has major implications for their effectiveness and well-being and for school improvement. We call this second aspect of retention 'quality retention'. Underlying resilient teachers' endeavours to exert control over difficult situations, is their strength and determination to fulfil their original call to teach, and to manage and thrive professionally.

The interaction between teachers' sense of efficacy, professional/personal identities and their management of the interaction between these and the professional, situated and personal scenarios which they experience in each professional life phase, is a sophisticated process which contributes strongly to their resilience, and resilience (sustaining commitment) is a necessary condition for their effectiveness.

What is required by all concerned with enhancing quality and standards in schools, is a better understanding of the factors that enable the majority of teachers to sustain their motivation, commitment and effectiveness in the profession. It is, therefore, likely to be fruitful to examine why and how generally teachers maintain a continuing positive contribution, despite the range of experiences they encounter in their work environments which challenge their commitment, and how commitment relates to effectiveness. This is the focus of the next chapter.

Key messages

Message 1 The capacity to remain resilient is a key factor in sustaining teachers' effectiveness.

Message 2 Schools need to have strategies in place to help identify and support teachers at vulnerable points in their personal and professional life phases.

Message 3 Similarly, schools need to identify and support vulnerable groups of pupils whose achievement may be affected by disruption to their learning experiences due to staff difficulties.

Message 4   Teachers in FSM3 primary and secondary schools are likely to be less resilient that those in FSM1 and 2 schools.

Message 5   Creating positive work conditions, meeting teachers' professional and personal needs and minimizing teacher burnout, is the key to encouraging teachers' resilience, promoting teacher well-being and positive professional life trajectories, improving the conditions for teachers' effectiveness in relation to pupils' performance, and, ultimately, school improvement.

eleven

Commitment and effectiveness: contexts which make a difference to standards

Introduction

Commitment is a key factor in teachers' work, and the level of this varies between primary and secondary teachers within and across each professional life phase and varies also, for a significant number of teachers in secondary schools, according to the level of socio-economic advantage and disadvantage of the school. It represents a significant emotional as well as cognitive investment; it is not static or necessarily stable and, as earlier chapters in this book have shown, it is affected primarily by teachers' sense of identity, professional life phase, the influences upon these and ways that teachers manage them. Commitment is thus located in the personal values, professional interests and micro-political, emotional, social and political contexts of their work (Kelchtermans 2005). It also has consequences for pupils' learning and achievement; and the VITAE research provided the data from which both perceived and statistically significant associations between teacher commitment and pupil attainment were able to be identified. This chapter focuses, therefore, on the connections between commitment, effectiveness and standards in teaching.

Teacher commitment has been defined as the degree of psychological attachment teachers have to their profession (Chapman 1982). It is a term often used by teachers to describe themselves and each other (Nias 1981; 1989) and is a part of their professional identity (Elliott and Crosswell 2001; Crosswell 2006). Its outward expression is to be found in teachers who are motivated, willing to learn, and who believe that they can make a difference to the learning and achievement of students. Such teachers also make huge personal investments in their work, such that their sense of personal worth becomes closely bound to their sense of professional worth (Haigh 1995; Woods *et al.* 1997). Commitment is a predictor of teachers' performance, burnout, attrition as well as having an important influence on students' cognitive, social, behavioural and affective outcomes (Firestone 1996; Day *et al.* 2005). In a different context, others (Goodlad 1990; Jackson *et al.* 1993; Sockett 1993) have written of the 'moral purposes' of teachers, using words such as 'courage', 'integrity', 'honesty', 'care', 'fairness'; and it is easy to see how these may be associated with commitment. Nor should we forget the more obvious signs of commitment, such as enthusiasm and passion for the job and the people with whom one works (Day 2004). Some research suggests that teachers' commitment tends to decline progressively over a course of a career and that this is caused by a number of factors – pupil behaviour, changes in national policies, parental demands (Huberman 1993; Fraser *et al.* 1998; Louis 1998; Helsby 1999; Tsui and Cheng 1999). The problem in the past has been that much research on commitment, while informative and worthwhile, has been of limited value in relation to understanding effectiveness because, for the most part, it has not provided a holistic view of commitment in the context of the inevitable variations which will occur in the contexts of teachers' work and lives over a teaching career.

The nature of commitment

> Scholars distinguish three kinds of 'work orientation': a job, a career and a calling. You do a job for the paycheck at the end of the week . . . It is just a means to another end . . . A career entails a deeper personal investment in work. You mark your achievements through money, but also through advancement . . . When the promotions stop . . . alienation starts, and you begin to look elsewhere for gratification and meaning.
>
> A calling (or vocation) is a passionate commitment to work for its own sake. Individuals with a calling see their work as contributing to the greater good, to something larger than they are. The work is fulfilling in its own right, without regard for money or for advancement. When the money stops and the promotions end, the work goes on.
>
> (Seligman 2002: 168)

If you talk with any teacher, teacher educator, schools inspector, principal or parent about reform, raising standards or the quality of education, it will not be very long before the word 'commitment' enters into the conversation. They 'know' that while the headteacher's commitment to change is essential to its success, so too is that of their staff. Without commitment, change efforts – especially those which are initiated from outside the school or other organization – will be limited in their success. Research in the USA indicates that teachers with low commitment are less likely to develop plans to improve the quality of their teaching (LeCompte and Dworkin 1991; Firestone and Pennell 1993). Commitment is also associated with their identification with the goals and values of the school (Reyes 1990). A number of studies have examined the impact of workplace conditions on teachers and found that:

> commitment to teaching reflects commitment to the school as much as commitment to students and subjects.
>
> (Tyree 1996: 296)

Yet the meaning of 'commitment' rarely is made explicit. To some it may mean being prepared to work longer hours, or more intensively to ensure that change is not merely implemented but also embedded in the belief systems, attitudes and improvement practices of the individual and organization. To others it may be associated with professionalism itself, an indication of the difference between those who take their job seriously and those who put their own interests first (Nias 1989).

In a recent report of empirical research in Australia, Crosswell (2006) suggests that there are six dimensions of commitment:

- Commitment as passion
- Commitment as investment of extra time
- Commitment as a focus on the well-being and achievement of the student
- Commitment as a responsibility to maintain professional knowledge
- Commitment as transmitting knowledge and/or values
- Commitment as engagement with the school community.

> (Crosswell 2006: 109)

This echoes earlier research on teacher professionalism in England, where Helsby *et al.* (1997) identified that behaving as a professional among secondary school teachers involved:

> displaying ... degrees of dedication and commitment, working long hours as a matter of course and accepting the open-ended nature of the task involved ... [making] ... the maximum effort to do the best you possibly can and a constant quest for improved performance ...
>
> (Helsby *et al.* 1997: 9–10)

Tyree (1996), also, in a study of primary school teachers, reported four dimensions of commitment: commitment as caring, commitment as occupational competence, commitment as identity and commitment as career continuance. If the results of these researchers and VITAE are to be believed, then policy-makers and school headteachers who are serious about the need to raise standards of teaching, learning and achievement, and teachers themselves, will need to pay attention to teachers' emotional and intellectual commitment needs throughout all professional learning phases of their careers.

Commitment is the passionate determination in practice of one's values, moral purposes and beliefs, where you put your life energy and meaning; and it contributes to the realization of teachers' personal and professional identities:

> the ways in which teachers achieve, maintain, and develop their identity, their sense of self in and through a career, are of vital significance in understanding the actions and commitment of teachers in their work.
>
> (Ball and Goodson 1985: 18)

Ebmeier and Nicklaus (1999) connected the concepts of commitment and emotion, defining commitment as part of a teacher's affective or emotional reaction to their experience in a school setting, and part of the process regarding decisions about the level of personal investment to make to a particular school or group of pupils. This connection is central to understanding teachers' perceptions of their work, colleagues, school leadership, the interaction between these and personal life and their effectiveness.

There seems to be little doubt, therefore, that commitment (or lack of it) is a key influencing factor in the performance effectiveness levels of teachers (Kushman 1992; Bryk *et al.* 1993). Initial commitment, however, may rise, be sustained or decline depending on teachers' life and work experiences and their management of these scenarios.

Early commitment: teachers' motivation for teaching

Teachers' initial commitment is closely associated with their motivation to enter the teaching profession. However, their motivation to remain in the job can be affected by a number of professional, situated and personal factors which impact upon and thus, mediate their capacity to sustain commitment (i.e. be resilient).

Those who select teaching are frequently influenced in their career choice by family members and by significant teachers in their own schooling. While some variations occur over time, these basic themes emerge in the many studies of the reasons for teaching as a career choice (Lortie 1975; Woods 1978; Jantzen 1981; Andrews 1983; Zimpher 1989; Hutchinson and Johnson 1993; Weiner *et al.* 1993; Wong 1994).

Recent research has shown that alongside those who become teachers by choice, are those who become teachers by chance (Bush and Middleton 2005). There were relatively few of the latter in the VITAE research. Regardless of teachers' motivations for entering teaching, however, it is important to acknowledge that these can change during a career. For example, as in this research, those who are teachers by chance may develop a passion for the job, a sense that teaching is a worthwhile and a positive career choice where they can have an impact on the lives of children. Conversely, those who choose to become teachers may find that commitments to other priorities (personal events, for example) or to fulfilling the demands of the job itself, may exceed the expectations of their initial commitment.

Murname *et al.* (1991) found also that job opportunities, salary, and costs to enter or re-enter teaching all influenced the decision to teach. The extrinsic motivating factors reported by teachers participating in that study were:

- Pay
- Prestige
- Working conditions.

For those who decide to become teachers, however, these extrinsic rewards are secondary in importance to other, more altruistic, motivations.

Research by Dinham and Scott (2000) conducted with over 4000 teachers in five countries as part of the Teacher 2000 Project, found that teachers were motivated intrinsically by:

- A desire to work with children
- A desire to make a difference
- A desire to promote their subject
- A natural impulse to nurture.

Participants in VITAE were asked why they had entered teaching. Their responses were:

1 Making a difference – including having a positive impact on pupils' lives, helping them improve themselves, making a difference, contributing to the community and working with children.
2 Professional challenge – including the variety, creativity, interest and reward offered by teaching.
3 Personal – including holidays and job security.
4 Identity – including reasons associated with the identity of being a teacher, such as status within the community, the role played in the lives of pupils and increased self-worth.
5 Subject – comprising teachers who had primarily wanted to teach their subject area.
6 Accidental – a small group of teachers who had not intended to teach.

1 Making a difference

This was the most common reason given by 57 per cent of the 309 teachers (N = 176), for choosing teaching as a career. Primary teachers' responses were largely focused on working with children, the fact that they had always wanted to be a teacher, and the impact of their job on children's lives. For example, Phoebe (Year 6) said that she wanted to be 'part of the development of children' so that she could help in their future careers; and Carmelle (Year 2) reported wanting to be a teacher 'in order to make a difference in [children's] lives'. It was also felt that being a teacher meant playing a part in addressing some of the social inequalities to which pupils were exposed. For 61 per cent (N = 101) of the 166 primary teachers, their pupils remained the main source of their job satisfaction, together with the ability to contribute to their all round education:

> You have to have a special relationship – the children have to feel secure in their friendship with you and trust you.
>
> (Abigail, Year 6)

> The main thing is you want all children to do their best – not just academic work – to develop their full potential in as many areas as possible. That's always been my driving force.
>
> (Sharon, Year 6)

Over half (52 per cent, N = 75) of 143 participating secondary teachers also gave responses in this category. Like the primary teachers, their responses also focused on giving pupils 'the best start in life' (Shaun, Year 9) and allowing pupils to develop academically and socially:

> I really wanted to be a teacher so that I would be doing something that made a difference to someone.
>
> (Shaun, Year 9)

> You get the opportunity to see them grow, become more social and develop more skills.
>
> (Peter, Year 6)

2 Professional challenge

Eleven per cent (N = 34) of the 309 teachers gave the need for a professional challenge as their primary reason for becoming a teacher:

> Stimulating, varied work within my subject of interest and the opportunity to facilitate learning . . . This still applies.
>
> (Kathleen, Year 9)

I like the challenge of working with children and helping them improve themselves.

> (Noel, Year 9)

Teachers also reported wanting the variety and the stimulus that is provided by an ever-changing working environment.

3 *Personal*

Ten per cent (N = 31) of the 309 teachers gave reasons within this group for becoming a teacher.

Something that was meant to be for security became a vocation.

> (Sharron, Year 6)

The most commonly cited reason was the flexibility of teaching, which enabled the job to be accommodated around family life. Teachers reported being able to spend time with children during holidays and be at home when they finished school:

It's great to be able to be at home to oversee my children's homework and to meet their friends.

> (Magdelana, Year 9)

I chose teaching because I thought it would be a good job to fit around having a family, being able to have time to go to the dentists with them and see them in sports days.

> (Jake, Year 6)

4 *Identity*

A further ten per cent (N = 31) of the 309 teachers gave identity related responses, including the feeling that they had always wanted to teach, grew up in a family of teachers, were influenced by role models among their own teachers, or perceived themselves as having the appropriate skills for a career in teaching.

Always wanted to have an effect on pupils' lives and learning ... wouldn't do anything else, despite the long hours.

> (Sandra, Year 2)

It's what I always wanted to do.

> (Philip, Year 9)

Sara's (Year 9) comment summed up the views of many secondary teachers in this group when she stated, 'It's a life as well as a job'.

Eight teachers (26 per cent of 31) in total made a connection between being a teacher and their own socio-economic background. One of these teachers was Jeremy, a head of mathematics in his 50s who, despite suffering ill health, was still motivated by wanting to help pupils from a similar background to himself:

> I came from a similar background to these children and want to be able to get them out of the cycle . . . that's what motivates me.
>
> (Jeremy, Year 9)

5 Subject

Nine per cent (N = 28) of the 309 teachers gave responses suggesting that they initially chose teaching as a career because they wanted to teach a specific subject area and further their expertise in this subject.

> I always loved English at school and really wanted to do something as a career in that area. Teaching was the obvious choice.
>
> (Juliet, Year 9)

> It's really satisfying when a student who doesn't see the reason for a particular module in mathematics suddenly understands how useful it can be in life.
>
> (Alexander, Year 9)

The majority of the teachers in this group (N = 17) taught in the secondary phase (61 per cent of 28).

6 Accidental

A small number (N = 9) of the 309 teachers had entered because of the security offered by the job, had 'fallen into' teaching by accident, or, in one case, 'couldn't think of anything else to do' after having had 'a series of grotty jobs' previously.

> I came into it accidentally . . . but it was the best decision of my life.
>
> (Wilma, Year 2)

> I had no idea what I wanted to do . . . [now] . . . I am absolutely and totally committed to teaching.
>
> (Leon, Year 9)

The majority of teachers in this group (N = 7) were in the primary phase (78 per cent of 9).

In summary, research tells us that teachers who are committed, have an enduring belief that they can make a difference to the learning lives and achievements of students, through who they are (their identity), what they know (knowledge, strategies, skills) and how they teach (their beliefs, attitudes, personal and professional values embedded in and expressed through their behaviour in practice settings). Commitment is an expression of moral purposes (not morality). It is the expression, over a career, of a desire to be the best possible teacher, and provide the best possible teaching, for all students at all times through care and competence. Commitment exists, then, in both real time and as an enduring aspiration. At its best it is both a cognitive (intellectual) and affective (emotional) endeavour. Thus, commitment to teaching involves sustaining the initial investments over time of emotional understanding (Denzin 1984) and 'emotional labour' (Hochschild 1983), which demands that teachers 'manage and moderate their emotions in order to match what the job demands of them' (Hargreaves 2005).

Sustaining commitment: problems and possibilities

> It's something that the school's just managed to grasp and I don't know if it's the type of people that work here or it comes from above, I don't know, but the staff on the floor themselves seem to fit and support each other. If that side wasn't there I wouldn't still be here because if you didn't have your staff members to turn to or go for a drink on a Friday night, it is a very tough school to teach in, and the problems and the workload, and if you didn't have the backup from the staff you wouldn't put up with it.
>
> (Cheryl, age 21–30, secondary)

Regardless of initial commitments to teaching, motivation, self-efficacy, sense of identity, emotional investment and agency – key components of commitment – will be subject to challenge. Indeed, this research, like that of others, has found that teacher commitment, while grounded in teachers' biographies, may be enhanced or diminished by factors, such as student behaviour, collegial and administrative support, parental demands and national education policies (Riehl and Sipple 1996; Louis 1998; Tsui and Cheng 1999). For example, not every teacher will enthusiastically embrace new government policies which create uncertainties, threaten autonomy and agency, and affect the composition or size of their class or what and how they teach. Nor, as Chapter 7 has shown, will every teacher work in a school where leadership, and pupil and staff relationships are uniformly excellent or where values and practices are matched to vision. Our research has also shown that personal life factors, such as family matters, dependants, health or the ageing process, may also have their effects upon energy and enthusiasm. Initial commitment, then, may rise, be sustained or decline depending on teachers' life and work experiences and their management of these.

Sustained commitment is the key expression of the dynamic interplay between teacher identity, agency and context as they affect teachers' perceived effectiveness. It is both socially constructed and a product of personal and professional values. Theories which attempt to locate it in one single perspective, while informative, are unlikely to add to our understanding of its nature and importance in teacher effectiveness, because they are bounded within the limitations of the particularism of the perspective – psychological, socio-cultural, micro-political, social constructivist or therapeutic – which is adopted. In fact, all of these play a part. Teachers' initial and long-term commitment are influenced by life (personal), values and policy contexts (professional) and work (situated) circumstances; and the extent to which teachers are able to manage the positive or negative interactions between these has been explored in Chapters 5 and 6.

The majority of teachers in VITAE appreciated the important role of motivation and commitment in remaining in the job.

Teaching must be the worst job in the world to do if you are not motivated and enthusiastic . . . I have to stop myself working 24 hours a day.

(Hilary, Year 6)

Lack of commitment would prevent me getting the most out of the class.

(Laura, Year 2)

For one young teacher, Elaine,

If I'm not excited or motivated, I find it hard to get the children motivated. Seeing what they gain everyday makes me want to do more.

(Elaine, Year 2)

Pamela's and Christine's experience taught them that:

You've got to believe in what you are doing to get the results over a period.

(Pamela, Year 2)

If teaching is just a job, i.e. just doing the next page in a text book, then that's weak commitment and probably doesn't lead to effective teaching.

(Christine, Year 6)

The establishment and sustaining of relationships with pupils, demands considerable time and emotional as well as intellectual and practical commitment:

Every waking hour through the week I am working to improve what I am doing. It's one of the best jobs, one of the most satisfying you ever have.

(Val, Year 2)

However, comments relating to teachers' professional, situated and personal scenarios, suggested that many teachers work under considerable persistent and negative pressures; and that these are largely connected to deteriorating pupil behaviour and attitudes, lack of parental support, the effects of government policies and, in many cases, a range of personal pressures. For some, these negative pressures are mediated by one or more types of support – internal (values related), situated (in the school and/or department), and external (family, friends).

Overall, the majority of VITAE teachers (74 per cent) were maintaining their sense of commitment. However, a sizeable minority (26 per cent) were not. To put it another way, more than 1 in 4 students were experiencing teaching from teachers who were less committed, and therefore, likely to be less effective than they might be. We have explored the reasons for this in Chapter 7, but it is worth emphasizing that overall poor pupil behaviour was a consistent concern for teachers, and that this was particularly the case for teachers in earlier and later professional life phases.

Chapter 7 identified three broad groupings of committed teachers in the VITAE study, i.e. i) those who sustained commitment, ii) those who sustained commitment despite challenging circumstances, and iii) those whose commitment declined. These groups consisted of teachers from each professional life phase (Chapter 5). However, numbers of committed teachers were not evenly spread between the professional life phases, the different school phases or schools in different socio-economic groupings. The second part of this chapter focuses upon three important influences upon teacher commitment and effectiveness:

1 School phase.
2 Work–life balance.
3 School socio-economic status.

1 School phase

Table 11.1 shows that teachers in primary schools are significantly more likely to sustain (81 per cent versus 65 per cent), and less likely to decline (19 per cent versus 35 per cent), in terms of commitment, than their colleagues in secondary schools.

Primary school teachers in VITAE were more committed than secondary teachers in each professional life phase and over all phases (82 per cent and 64 per cent), and twice as many secondary teachers than primary teachers were less committed over all phases (36 per cent and 18 per cent).

Table 11.1: Teachers' Commitment by School Phase

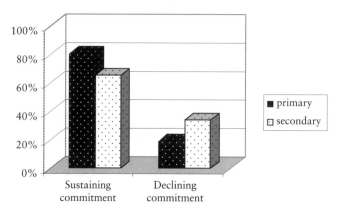

Table 11.2 shows also, that there is a relatively greater decline in commitment among 'late' professional life phase teachers; and that teachers in their early years were, in relative terms, no more or less committed than those in middle or later years.

2 Work–life balance

Work–life balance and life events themselves play a key role in teachers' sense of commitment and effectiveness. Management and leadership responsibilities outside the classroom (79 per cent of all VITAE teachers) increased

Table 11.2: Teachers' Commitment by Professional Life Phase

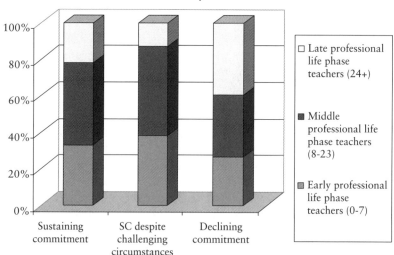

teacher workload and the complexities of work–life management from year 4 of experience onwards; work–life balance emerged as a significant concern in the 8–15 professional life phase; and life events played significant positive and negative roles in teachers' sense of commitment, particularly in the mid to late professional life phases (16–23 and 24–30). For these groups, also, excessive paperwork, policy and heavy workloads were hindrances to their effectiveness.

Here are four examples of teachers from primary and secondary schools, in different socio-economic contexts, whose commitment was being sustained; was at risk of declining; or had declined:

Teacher 1 secondary – committed
Marc taught mathematics in an 11–16 comprehensive school on the outskirts of two adjacent metropolitan boroughs. A broadly average proportion of the pupils were eligible for free school meals, and the school's intake at age 11 was close to average levels of attainment. In January 2002 the school was described by Ofsted as successful with pupils achieving well through a combination of good teaching and very strong and determined leadership and management.

Marc was in his mid-twenties and had been teaching for four years. His father had been happy in teaching for 30 years and his sister was also a teacher. Marc, like these relatives, wanted a job where he could make a difference to children's lives. His first year was spent in a sixth form college before moving to his current post three years ago. Marc enjoyed teaching and was pleased with the progression he had made. He played a lot of sport outside school which, he said, helped get rid of stress.

The headteacher was very 'down to earth' and had the respect of the pupils. The deputy head was also supportive and approachable, but she did not play as big a part in his day-to-day work now that he was not an NQT. Marc described his mathematics department as very close knit – they met together informally at break times and supported each other. He also appreciated the supportive ethos in the whole school. He felt that all staff had good relationships with pupils which produced a good dynamic in classes, and that behaviour throughout the school was good overall.

In the current phase of his professional life, Marc was very career-oriented. He felt that this had had a positive impact on his work because he was spending so much of his time at home preparing lessons. He believed that his professional role would become more important in the next year as he had started thinking about looking for a promotion to second in department.

Teacher 2 primary – committed despite

Daisy was deputy headteacher at an urban primary school with 36 per cent to 50 per cent free school meals and in the lowest group for attainment. She was 43 years old and had taught for 10 years. She came into teaching because she hoped it would fit in with her family commitments. Since then she had moved 'in and out of love' with the job.

She liked change and challenge as they stopped her from becoming stale and bored. She had been appointed to an assistant head post during the project, working with the head to turn around an under-performing school. A little later her school took over a local failing school that was closed and this brought further challenges for her.

The school was on two sites and she was in charge of one of these. While she rose to these challenges, the pressure was relentless and she found it difficult to switch off. She worried about the effect of interruptions on the children she taught, especially those coming from her assistant head's duties. With high motivation, her confidence in behaviour management had also increased – she felt more experienced and in control in this area. She was learning to have fun while working hard, and to be more flexible with the children. She enjoyed being known as a 'nice teacher' who was 'fair'; her children were polite and parents said that they would like their child to be in her class.

However, her life–work balance was 'completely skewed'. Daisy had a significant role in her family with two school-age children at home and others at university. Her husband worked away from home. It now looked as though her marriage might be over. Her way of coping was to throw herself into work and develop her own career. She had no support outside school. It came more from her role in school. The difficult situation outside school was, if anything, making her stronger. She switched off in class and was very pleased that she was still doing 'bloody good lessons', even when she was 'in pieces'.

Teacher 3 primary – commitment at risk

Natalie had taught for 11 years and in this school for three years. She was in charge of mathematics and had an SLT role early in the project, but one year later she moved to teaching Year 5 and stepped down from the SLT.

The majority of pupils at her school came from local authority housing with some in short-term accommodation. Mobility was very high. There was a very high ethnic mix with 23 per cent asylum seekers. Fifty-eight per cent had English as an additional language and 31 per cent of all pupils were still in the early stages of learning English. Forty-seven per cent of the pupils had free school meals and 40 per cent had special educational needs.

The lack of interest, and lack of praise, from the headteacher in this school was 'a downer on morale'. Natalie said, 'When I came here, because I wasn't recognized or praised I just lost interest.' She felt isolated at school. Since joining the SLT she felt cut off from her fellow teachers. She was not pleased with her performance in her leadership role. She also found the atmosphere in the school difficult with staff who were 'bitchy' and 'cliquey' and with low morale. Nevertheless, she enjoyed her good relationships with the pupils.

She still liked teaching – 'my beliefs, attitudes and philosophies I have in life, I share with the children' – but she saw herself at odds with the surrounding educational culture. Her own class rules were completely different from the rest of the school. For her, the most important thing was that the children left 'happy, confident and with a thirst for learning'. However, her personal worries and commitments, the strains of a staff team with low morale and having to teach to exams, had negatively impacted on her work. Having to teach what was required and to the test had 'destroyed' her class and 'destroyed' her own teaching methods. Natalie's parents' deteriorating health had had a negative impact on her. This, coupled with her recent pregnancy, led to her decision of giving up membership of SLT.

Teacher 4 secondary – declining commitment

Jo had taught for 19 years. She was head of English and had entered teaching because of her love of the subject and the rewards of teaching this to others. However, she began to feel strongly that her personal life was greatly affected and compromised by her job. There were 'too many policies' and 'too much paperwork!' She felt guilty about her contributions at home, particularly concerning the time spent with her young child.

She worked in a voluntary aided school, which became a technology college in the mid-1990s. It served a widespread and diverse community drawing its students from 60 primary schools and from homes spread across inner city, suburban and semi-rural locations. Its students were from Christian, other world faiths and secular backgrounds; their parents' occupations were 60 per cent manual, 25 per cent professional and 15 per cent clerical. Thirty-three per cent of pupils were from ethnic minorities, 14 per cent had English as a second language and 25 per cent were eligible for free school meals. There was a wide range of attainment – while 21 per cent of pupils were classified as having special educational needs, a similar proportion had particularly high attainment levels. The school was popular with parents and was oversubscribed.

Jo saw her school as 'very inclusive', with 'a big emphasis on celebrating and rewarding positive achievement'. She described her line manager as 'brilliant'. She had given her support as she struggled with the stress of management issues and helped her prioritize her work. This help was crucially important to her and made her want to try harder. However, she felt less positive about the SLT. Because of the growth of the school, she found that the management became very remote.

For various reasons, many English teachers were leaving in the same year. For Jo, this felt like 'starting over again' as a head of department. She was very pleased when she 'had two fantastic experienced appointments ... which has balanced the department'. She described the overall behaviour of pupils as challenging, but admitted that only a minority were 'naughty ... [but they] respond well if they know you, see you as a person'.

Jo had an ongoing health problem and this had caused difficulties in mobility. When managerial aspects of the job let her down, she returned to her core 'moral' set of values about teaching and remembered the buzz she derived from interacting with pupils. She still liked teaching, but felt that her role as head of department had made her become 'more cynical' about the value of different initiatives she had been asked to implement. She had decided to look for another job at the end of the next academic year, commenting: 'I'm tired. You're always dealing with three or four things at a time.'

> I'm approaching my 40th year. Thinking of carrying on what I'm doing now for the next 20 years fills me with horror. I would like to ease back.

In the past two years her school began to support a local school that was moving toward closure as part of the Government's Transforming Secondary Schools initiative. This had made Jo uncertain about her future role as her school expanded and took on redeployed staff.

3 School socio-economic status: the influence of social disadvantage

There were not only differences between primary and secondary teachers' commitment, but also differences between those in schools in different socio-economic contexts (see Chapter 7 for a detailed discussion of these issues). The socio-economic status (SES) of the school affected teachers' lives and perceptions of effectiveness. Teachers in high SES schools had more positive views of pupil behaviour; those in low SES schools, less positive views.

Meeting what teachers regarded as excessive government targets was challenging, particularly in contexts which were perceived to include a mix of pupils who did not value education and who misbehaved in class regularly. This seemed to be more frequent and more disruptive in secondary than primary schools. In some of these schools, again mostly secondary, parental support was poor also. Secondary teachers spoke in detail of a range of social and policy challenges to their perceived ability to maintain their effectiveness.

These contexts must be of concern in terms of the focus upon raising quality in teaching, learning and achievement and the broader school improvement agenda. More important are their effects upon teacher motivation, commitment, job satisfaction and health. While it is clear that the majority of primary and secondary teachers continued to hold firm to the values and purposes for becoming teachers, it is equally clear that many were under considerable personal stress, whether this related to physical illness or stress in their home life.

These findings suggest that there is a difference in the range and intensity of pupil, parental and government originated challenges which teachers experience according to the relative level of socio-economically deprived contexts in which secondary teachers work; and that teachers in secondary schools experience these more keenly than those in primary schools. Teachers in these schools – particularly secondary teachers – seem to face not one or two but a combination of challenges each day of their working lives. It is the extent to which the combination is able to be ameliorated by other intrinsic and extrinsic support that determines whether teachers are able to survive and – even within difficult circumstances – flourish. In other words, teacher commitment and effectiveness must be understood in the context of the interaction between and the relative influence of these policy, pupil, personal and practice factors.

It is important that the use of performance indicators recognizes the impact of context on attainment. Contextual value added measures provide fairer comparisons that do not penalize those who work in high disadvantage contexts, in the same ways that our league tables of attainment results do.

Conclusions: teacher effectiveness and pupil progress and attainment

One important consequence of the VITAE research, was that not only did we find that differences in the characteristics of pupils do not fully account for the differences in levels of pupil attainment or progress between classes and teaching groups but we found also, that there were statistically significant associations between teachers' commitment and pupils' progress and levels of pupils' performance in value added attainments in national tests at age 7 (Key Stage 1), 11 (Key Stage 2) and 14 (English and mathematics, Key Stage 3).

We believe that this is the first time that research has found associations between these (Table 11.3). Pupils of teachers in each professional life phase who were sustaining or continuing to build their commitment (74 per cent) were more likely to attain results at or above the level expected, regardless of school context. Pupils of the minority of teachers who were not sustaining their commitment and resilience (26 per cent) were more likely to attain results below the level expected, regardless of school context.

Table 11.3: Associations between Commitment and Effectiveness.

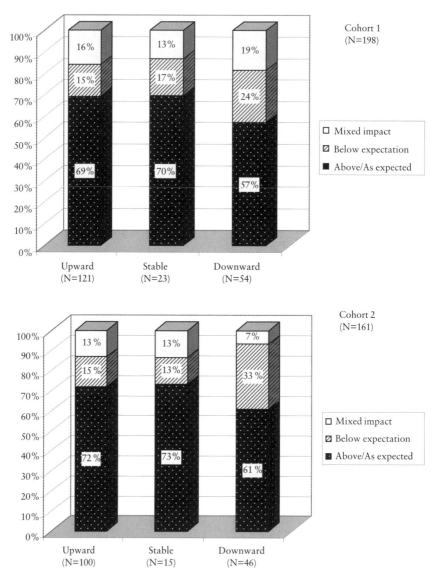

There is much previous research which suggests, like VITAE, that teacher commitment is important because it is a significant factor in teaching quality, teachers' capacities to adapt successfully to change, retention and student attitudes and learning outcomes. At present, in England, we may be witnessing the first signs of a sea of change, in the way policy-makers think about change. While the reform bandwagon shows little sign of slowing, it does seem as though teachers are being invited to adapt to working in a less prescriptively imitative environment than has been the case over the last 20 years. It may be that once again, they have the chance to learn about students' learning, about real pedagogy and to have opportunities to apply such learning albeit within the framework of continuing restricted, and perhaps restrictive, definitions of what counts as effectiveness.

For some, already battered by many years of difficult imposed adaptation and perhaps now cynical about the benefits of more change, it may be too late. However, for many who remain committed to their students, their school, their profession and their own learning, it is not. As the importance of student engagement in learning is being once again acknowledged, and as personalized learning (the worth of individually oriented teaching and learning) is once again emphasized in policy documents, so it is clear that, to be successful, teachers themselves must be passionately motivated and committed. It may be, then, that for the first time in many years, the needs and concerns of policy-makers and classroom teachers are coinciding.

However, as we have seen, for commitment to flourish and for teachers to be resilient and effective, they need a strong and enduring sense of efficacy – the ability to handle new situations confidently, believing that they will make a difference – and they need to work in external and internal environments which are less bureaucratically managerial, less reliant on crude measures of performativity. We know from countless studies that this saps rather than builds morale. They need to work in schools in which leadership is supportive, clear, strong and passionately committed to sustaining the quality of their commitment.

These findings have particularly important implications for headteachers since they suggest that the conditions in which teachers work throughout their lives play a significant part in commitment. We must look more closely, then, at the system itself and the leadership within the system for answers to issues of recruitment and retention, in order to discover what are the most optimum moderating and mediating variables which contribute to sustaining high levels of commitment as a means to raising standards.

Teachers in all countries need support for their commitment, energy and skill over their careers if they are to grapple with the immense emotional, intellectual and social demands, as they work towards building the internal and external relationships demanded by ongoing government reforms and social movements. The picture of teachers in English schools, involved in the VITAE project, gives cause for concern and hope – concern because it is clear that the variations in perceived effectiveness which relate to life events, age, experience, phase of schools and their socio-economic status, do not yet seem to be acknowledged in the school effectiveness, improvement and CPD agendas of policy-makers and school leaders; concern because of the high levels of professional stress which, for many, are having negative effects upon their personal lives; concern, also, as to whether such levels can be sustained without the physical loss of some of the best teachers or loss of their energy, commitment and sense of purpose. Yet there is hope, too, because of the high levels of commitment and agency, often against the odds, which many teachers' accounts reveal, regardless of experience, phase or context.

Research on teacher retention tends to focus on factors affecting teachers' decisions to leave the profession. This research provides a new perspective, focusing upon retention in terms of teacher quality and effectiveness. It suggests that what is required is a better understanding of the factors which enable teachers, not simply to remain in teaching, but more importantly, to sustain their commitment, resilience and, therefore, effectiveness over the whole of their careers.

Key messages

Message 1   There are statistically significant associations between levels of teachers' commitment in all professional life phases and levels of pupil attainment.

Message 2   Teachers who work in challenging socio-economic circumstances are more likely, than others, to experience greater challenges to sustaining their commitment and effectiveness.

Message 3   It is the extent to which these challenges may be ameliorated by intrinsic and extrinsic support, which will determine whether teachers are able to maintain their commitment and effectiveness. The capacity of teachers to exercise agency, commitment and resilience, must be understood in the context of these policy, pupil, personal and practice factors.

Message 4   There are associations between teachers' abilities to manage their professional life phase and identify scenarios successfully, and the extent to which they are able to build capacity to sustain commitment and effectiveness.

Message 5   School phase has a significant influence on teachers' commitment, particularly in their mid-career professional life phases.

Message 6   Teachers in primary schools are more likely to sustain their commitment and perceived effectiveness than their secondary school colleagues, and this is more likely to be the result of positive relationships with colleagues, school leaders and pupils.

Message 7   Commitment (motivation, belief, aspiration) is a necessary but insufficient condition for effectiveness. Resilience (the ability of an individual to withstand or recover quickly from difficult conditions) is a necessary condition for sustaining commitment.

Message 8   Commitment and resilience influence, are influenced by professional life phase and identity. These are mediated positively and negatively by personal, situated and professional influences.

Message 9   Commitment and resilience are key factors in retaining teachers quality, i.e. sustaining their capacities to be effective. National agencies, associations and school leaders need to nurture teachers' commitment and resilience as being a necessary condition for teacher effectiveness and school improvement.

Message 10   Learning and development programmes should differentiate between the needs of: i) teachers in primary and secondary schools; ii) teachers in schools of different SES; iii) less and more experienced teachers; iv) teachers different professional life phases; and v) teachers who are experiencing different 'scenarios'.

Future proofing school reform and renewal: why teachers matter most

This book has been about the work, lives and effectiveness of teachers in English schools. However, the issues raised apply internationally. Teachers' work in all countries, as the range of research literature cited in this book demonstrates, is complex, emotional and intensive. Professional life phases and sense of identity influence all teachers. Wherever they are, teachers' levels of commitment and their capacities for resilience will be mediated by factors in their workplace, personal lives and by the kinds of direction and pace of national and local interventions in the curriculum, and governance of schools which they will need to accommodate. Issues of teacher quality, standards, recruitment and retention are central, as we have seen, to the political agendas in all countries. For some developing countries, recruitment is paramount (Day and Sachs 2004), for others it is retention (Moore Johnson 2004). Although programmes of reform and renewal vary in their scope and intensity from country to country, from culture to culture and even from school to school, they must all take into account the needs, concerns and well-being of the teachers who are expected to implement them, if they are to meet with success. Teachers who are not committed and resilient are unlikely to be effective. Without teachers who are effective, systemic reform and renewal cannot be sustained. It is teachers who matter most in this respect.

There are five core messages emerging from the research on which this book is based. The first is that to achieve and sustain an effective teaching force, in order to raise standards, requires more than structural reform of organizations, or governance of school and classroom conditions, curricula and assessment; and that while system-wide and organizational reculturing is necessary as a means of supporting teachers' capacities to be effective, it too is an insufficient condition. The second is that teachers' well-being and positive professional identity are fundamental to their capacities to become and remain effective. The third is that patterns in teachers' professional life phases and identities can be identified and related to their sense of commitment, resilience and effectiveness. Teachers' effectiveness within these, at least in part, is the consequence of their management of a combination of personal, professional and situated (work-based) influences. The last two are able to be predicted and altered, whereas the first is not. These influences and their relative impact upon teachers' effectiveness are likely to vary over the length of a career. There is a relationship between the ways these influences interact and teachers' sense of professional identity. Without an understanding of these, a close knowledge of their origins and effects and provision of appropriate support and development strategies, it is unlikely that future reform and renewal efforts within and without schools will be any more successful than those of the past. The fourth message is that sustaining commitment, resilience and capacities for effectiveness is likely to be more difficult for teachers in the later years of their professional lives and those in schools serving more disadvantaged communities. The fifth message is that teachers with strong commitment and resilience are likely to be more effective than others; and that sustaining and enhancing commitment and resilience is a key quality and retention issue.

These messages, and their implications, are reproduced below.

Key findings

1 Teachers do not necessarily become more effective over time. A higher proportion of teachers in later years, though still a minority, are at greater risk of becoming less effective.
2 Teacher' sense of positive professional identity is associated with well-being and is a key contributory factor in their effectiveness.
3 Attainments by pupils of teachers who are committed and resilient are likely to exceed those of teachers, who are not.
4 The commitment and resilience of teachers in schools serving more disadvantaged communities are more persistently challenged than others.
5 Sustaining and enhancing teachers' commitment and resilience is a key quality and retention issue.

Major implications

1 National organizations and schools need to target strategies for professional learning and development to support teachers in their later years of experiences.

2 Policy-makers, national organizations and headteachers concerned with raising standards in schools, need to address the associations between teachers' well-being, and their commitment, resilience and effectiveness, by providing more robust comprehensive personnel support structures.
3 Strategies for sustaining commitment in initial and continuing professional development programmes should differentiate between the needs of teachers in different phases of their professional lives.
4 Schools, especially those which serve disadvantaged communities, need to ensure that their CPD provision is relevant to the commitment, resilience and health needs of teachers.
5 Efforts to support and enhance teacher quality should focus upon building, sustaining and retaining their commitment and resilience, as well as on more usual aspects, such as curriculum-related, teaching and role matters.

Figure 12.1 brings together the influences and their effects, and illustrates the complexities of achieving change and sustaining effectiveness revealed by VITAE.

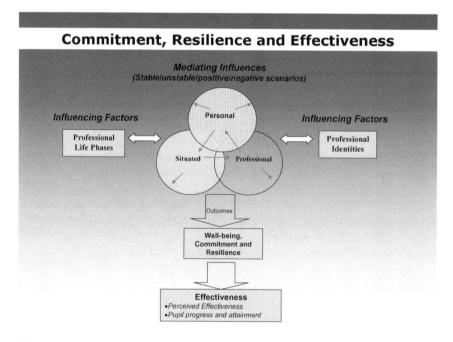

Figure 12.1 Commitment, resilience and effectiveness

Policy, standards and professionalism

> The possibilities (for professionals) of getting it wrong have multiplied
> as both the public and service organization try to manage each other in
> more uncertain times.
>
> (Clarke and Newman 2005: 9)

National policy context

Teachers in the research were influenced not only by short-term policy developments over the three years of the research, but also by the changing policy contexts prior to the VITAE research over the course of their teaching career. This perspective is particularly relevant in England because successive governments have laid strong emphasis on education reform during nearly two decades from 1988 onwards.

In Chapter 1 we gave a brief overview of education policy developments that can be referred to as examples of 'Standards Based Reforms' in England from 1988 onwards, with a particular focus on more recent changes during the course of the VITAE research. We noted criticisms of nearly two decades of policy reform and the resultant intensification of teachers' work. In addition, we summarized the growing evidence of improved standards in England, in terms of national tests as measured by increases in key benchmark indicators of pupils' academic outcomes through national assessments at different Key Stages and public examination results. This internal English evidence of improvement in pupil outcomes is supported by findings from external indicators of levels of attainment in literacy, mathematics and science from international surveys (PIRLS, PISA, TIMSS). It is right to note, however, that evidence of improvement in this and across a range of national policy implementation contexts is not universally accepted. For example, in recent research, Gorard (2006) reported that improvements in secondary school national examination scores were likely to be the results of changes in student intake or the exclusion of problem students prior to examination. He noted that the biggest increase in examination improvements at age 16 took place prior to the introduction of national targets.

The adequacy of the means used to measure progress in attainment over time has also been criticized. Tymms' research (Tymms 2004) suggests that while standards in mathematics and English in primary schools rose between 1995 and 2000, results became 'abruptly flat' between 2000 and 2003, contrary to government claims of further improvement. Smith *et al.* (2004) found that traditional patterns of whole class interaction had not been 'dramatically transformed' by the introduction of National Literacy and Numeracy strategies. Research by Cribb *et al.* (2005) concluded that the much lauded Education Action Zone (EAZ) initiatives were 'not enough to develop (as they were intended to do) meaningful forms of engagement between parents and schools or the wider education system', and Lupton's (2005) research on schools in high poverty contexts concluded that while these, understandably, 'exert downward pressures on quality . . . consistently high levels of quality in schools in the poorest neighbourhoods need to be assured by policy measures that alter their context or, through greater funding, improve their organizational capacity to respond' . . . rather than 'managerialist policies that seek to improve schools by addressing the performance of managers and staff, without a recognition of the context in which this performance takes place'.

We also described the evidence from professional inspection judgements of improvement in the quality of education in relation to the national framework criteria (effectiveness, improvement, leadership and quality of teaching and learning) and the extent of improvement of schools placed in special measures. It has been argued that such improvements have benefited disadvantaged pupils because they are found to be over-represented in schools judged to require special measures or in serious weaknesses (Sammons *et al.* 2004, 2006; Matthews and Sammons 2005). Changes to the inspection framework from 2000 onwards have sought to reduce paperwork and demands on schools, and recently there has been a particular change with an emphasis on light touch, shorter inspections conducted at short notice to reduce the pressures on schools. There is also an emphasis on self-evaluation and review with inspection seen as a means to validate schools' own review processes. The impact of this new regime cannot be gauged through VITAE, however, as it post-dated the research study. Such evidence from Ofsted of improved standards, has been, and continues to be the subject of challenge on the grounds of both effect and efficiency and democratic values. Shaw *et al.* (2003) who analyzed the examination results of over 3000 secondary schools which had been inspected by Ofsted between 1992 and 1997, found that only in schools where achievement 'was already much higher or lower than the average was this associated with slight improvements' (2003: 63); and Fielding (2001) provided a swingeing critical commentary on its philosophical and intellectual underpinnings.

VITAE teachers with more than three years experience consistently rated Ofsted as having the most negative impact on their work. The impact of preparation and the inspection process left some of those involved feeling very demoralized, even when the outcomes had been positive. This was particularly the case for more experienced teachers, one of whom commented, 'It [Ofsted] was quite difficult and there were times when I felt this pressure was unnecessary and I wanted to jack it all in'.

Limits of the new professionalism

At first glance, the rhetoric of a new professionalism appears to present schools and teachers with more autonomy. However, we found minimal evidence of Michael Barber's claim that policy is moving from an era of informed prescription to one of informed professionalism (Barber 2001). His idea of earned autonomy seems to be questionable, given that teachers still see themselves as constrained by central directives, with little sense of what is earned after compliance with them: 'I feel my professionalism is being called into question when I'm being told how to teach all the time' (Year 6 teacher). The exhortations in *Excellence and Enjoyment* (DfES 2003) to teach a broader and more imaginative curriculum were, for our Year 2 and Year 6 teachers, undermined by government and school targets in the national tests in English, mathematics and science. Even in Year 9, where the test results are less crucial since GCSE results in Year 11 are the critical indicators, there was still a considerable emphasis on scores; and teachers reported more pressure to produce results and therefore, more teaching to the test.

In the VITAE survey, over 90 per cent of teachers were satisfied that they could make a difference to their pupils' learning and raise their attainments. However, a third of primary and 29 per cent of secondary teachers reported that they were dissatisfied with the extent to which 'I can be creative in my classroom'. 'Informed professionalism', then, is able to be exercised only within policy-makers' conceptions of what counts as educational success. Thus, in relation, for example, to the much heralded 'personalized learning' agenda in English schools, professionals' decisions about what to do, how to do it and how to assess it are still bound by what Evetts (2005) calls 'organizational professionalism':

> A discourse of control used increasingly by managers in work organizations ... [which] ... involves the increased standardization of work procedures and practices and managerialist controls. It relies on externalized forms of regulation and accountability measures such as target-setting and performance review.

Evetts distinguishes between this and 'occupational professionalism' which:

> ... involves relations of practitioner trust from both employers and clients. It is based on autonomy and professional judgement and assessment by practitioners in complex cases ...
>
> (Evetts 2005)

The point here is not that the former exists at the expense of the latter – teachers should not been seen as passive or compliant in implementing others' agendas if, in their view, this will not be in the interest of their students. As Friedson (2001) has suggested, there is a 'struggle for the soul of professionalism' going on. Many VITAE teachers resented policies which specified what they should teach and how they should be teaching. Such struggles require energy which may distract and detract from the energy needed by teachers to be at their best in the classroom. It is another example of the 'background noise' of policy and social changes with which teachers must live.

Such background noise and the accompanying increases in bureaucratic tasks are associated with increases in forms of managerial and contractual accountability and fewer opportunities to reflect on their teaching, for a significant minority of teachers. They engender, as our research shows, feelings of vulnerability, frustration, anger exacerbated by tiredness, stress and the persistence of misbehaviour by small minorities of students, anxiety because of the complexity of the job; and guilt, sadness, blame and shame at not being able to achieve ideals or targets imposed by others. This is likely to be the case particularly for teachers in the middle and later phases of professional lives. While the majority will manage to sustain their motivation, commitment, emotional resilience and effectiveness, either because of the strength of their own values, supportive home and organizational cultures or combinations of these, more than one in four do not, or are at risk of losing them. This must be a cause for concern to parents, students and those responsible for policies intended to raise standards. It is as well to remind ourselves that 'standards-based and largely cognitive-driven reforms do not capture all of what matters most in developing really good teachers' (Roberts 2005, citing Hargreaves 1995, 2001).

The key messages, in relation to policy led reform, which emerge from our research are as much concerned with volume and rapidity of policy initiatives as with the particulars of the policies. The widespread perception of teachers is that there is too much centrally driven policy and that the rate at which policies are introduced, and then modified, is counter-productive. This is particularly the case for more experienced teachers, the bulk of the current teaching force, many of whom may be progressively alienated by this steady stream of initiatives – which they may interpret as excessive interference in their professional lives. Policy to improve pupils' learning has to be mediated through teachers in the classroom. Thus policy intent is unlikely to be realized if teachers are not 'on-side'.

The perception of VITAE teachers was that policy, particularly in relation to curriculum, assessment and classroom teaching, is still largely handed down rather than negotiated with those who implement it. While the development of the National Workforce Agreement offers a possible means for this negotiated (and necessarily slower) reform process, its success is by no means guaranteed. Our interviews with teachers provided strong evidence that the accountability demands and emphasis on both inspection and assessment were seen as stressful and burdensome by many teachers, particularly those in later professional life phases and in stressful work–life scenarios who were identified as being more vulnerable. This legacy of negativity needs to be managed. There are tensions between legitimate policy concerns to improve pupil outcomes, especially at the lower end, for disadvantaged groups of pupils which thus seek to reduce the equity gap; and the concern to improve the retention and retain the commitment of teachers and promote a positive sense of professional identity.

Teachers' well-being and effectiveness

> Working conditions further detract from the appeal of teaching . . .
> Critics often belittle teachers for their secure salaries, short workdays,
> and long summer vacations, but anyone familiar with schools knows
> that stories about the easy job of teaching are sheer fiction. Good
> teaching is demanding and exhausting work, even in the best of work-
> places . . . Even the most experienced teacher simply cannot rely on
> acquired expertise or dare to teach on automatic pilot, because each
> round of students presents unique instructional dilemmas and
> opportunities.
>
> (Moore Johnson 2004: 10)

To be effective, teachers need to be able to manage successfully the cognitive and emotional challenges of working in different, sometimes difficult scenarios. Their capacities to do so, as we have seen, will vary according to life experiences and events, the strength and conviction of educational ideals, sense of efficacy and agency and the support of leaders and colleagues. All of these contribute, positively and negatively, to their commitment, resilience and effectiveness, both perceived and in terms of measures of pupils' progress and attainment.

Managing the emotional arenas of classroom life is fundamental to effective teaching. A sense of positive professional identity is dependent upon this. The investment of emotional energy in the workplace is not an optional extra for teachers. They cannot, as those in most other professions, 'take a break', or 'reschedule' their work. They are faced each day with thirty or more students some of whom, but by no means all, will be eager to learn; some of whom will have different learning needs; some of whom will not wish to learn; and not all of whom will have stable, secure lives outside school. Evidence suggests that changes in society are making children's and young peoples' lives outside school more fragmented and stressful with resultant behaviour and mental health problems. Effective teachers will strive to engage with all of their students and this requires that they are able to bring reserves of emotional energy to their work. The more such emotional energy is depleted – through adverse effects of personal, workplace or policy experiences – the less will be their capacities for sustaining effectiveness. This is why reformers from outside the school and those who seek to improve from within need to acknowledge the connection between attending to the well-being of the students and attending to the well-being, also, of the adults in the school. Moreover, teachers' sense of well-being is deeply connected with how they define themselves as professionals, and how they see their professionalism being defined by others. Where there are differences, there are likely to be tensions.

Work–life management

The analysis of teachers' professional identities highlighted certain elements of work and life, and the balance between the two, that contributed, positively and negatively, to the ongoing process of identity construction.

> Self-identity is not something that is just given, as a result of the continuities of the individual's action-system, but something that has to be routinely created and sustained in the reflexive activities of the individual . . . A person's identity is not to be found in behaviour, nor – important though this is – in the reactions of others, but in the capacity to keep a particular narrative going. The individual's biography . . . must continually integrate events which occur in the external world, and sort them into the ongoing 'story' about the self.
> (Giddens (1991) cited in Chappell 2005: 206)

The elements that, for a teacher, must be 'continually integrated' during this process include their professional knowledge, their personal experience, the 'micro-politics' of the school setting, and wider socio-cultural contexts, and these can give rise to the development of different positive or negative, stable or unstable identities. Interplay between these different elements is clearly evident from the analyses illustrating how individual teachers draw on a variety of professional, situated and personal factors in constructing their identities. While, in some respects, these are integrated into a coherent sense of identity, this is unlikely to happen where there is imbalance between work and life commitments which impact upon teachers' well-being.

The balance that teachers have to achieve is between the pressures at work and those in their personal life. It may well be that personal and home lives are more complex than in previous decades with increases in dual career families, one parent families and later starts to families. More of those in mid-career may be caring for both young children and elderly relatives.

The majority of teachers in the project, however, were able to manage these. Interestingly, the analysis of teachers' professional identities indicated that feelings of well-being were not connected to the particular scenario the teacher was experiencing or to professional life phase, school phase, school context (FSM) or level of commitment. There was no single, simple cause and effect relationship. However, for some teachers in the VITAE sample, pressures had resulted in high blood pressure, depression, chronic fatigue syndrome and other health related problems.

Stress itself is an inevitable part of work and life. However, there is a point at which everyday stress turns into an unhealthy pressure which has adverse emotional, mental and/or physical effects. Knowledge of causes, levels and impact of stress among teachers is now extensive (Mearns and MacBeath 1983; Kyriacou 1987; Travers and Cooper 1996; Troman and Woods 2001). Goss reports:

> It is now generally accepted that the effects of chronic excess stress include both increased sickness absence and ill health retirements, in addition to increased rates of staff turnover, decreased morale and decreased numbers of applicants for vacant posts. It is also likely that chronic high levels of stress will adversely affect other priority areas including teacher performance and thus, pupil attainment.
>
> (Goss 2005: 6)

Teachers' well-being can be positively and negatively affected by a number of issues, such as the management of the school, the school ethos, the level of morale among staff and the opportunities presented to staff to under-take professional development. It has been suggested that the way to ensure that we have 'healthy teachers' is to provide them with training, support and development opportunities throughout their careers, which take into account specific needs of the individual, including age, experience and phase of professional life. By doing this, teachers are more likely to achieve their personal and professional aims, increase self-esteem, agency and motivation, and sustain their levels of commitment and resilience (Day 1996). These characteristics, described by Goleman (1995) as key to 'emotional intelligence', are fundamental to teachers' ability to manage changes that occur (both at work and home) at particular stages of life, and as demands on their professional and personal time increase.

In a speech given to the London Well-being Conference (April 2005), the Chief Executive of the National Teacher Support Network stated that:

> . . . work life balance isn't just about time . . . It's about head space, it's about relief from worry or anxiety, it's about knowing that someone understands and supports you in the challenges you face, it's about knowing that the school is focused on your development and your

support and that of the whole team. And then it's about being able to have time to yourself, time with your partner, family and friends where the concerns of school are not constantly on your mind.

(Nash 2005: 2)

Human resource support structures

The threat of work–life conflict to teacher well-being has implications, not only for those who must cope with stress and illness, but also for their organizations, government and society as a whole. From the employer's perspective, the inability to balance work and family demands has been linked to reduced work performance and poor morale (Duxbury *et al.* 1994). Other potential impacts of poor teacher well-being on the school are absenteeism, which is estimated to cost approximately £819.20 per year per FTE post (Goss 2005), as well as a decline in energy, commitment, effectiveness and, ultimately, high staff turnover. For the profession it can result in loss of teachers.

Currently within schools, and among school staff, the notion of pastoral care for adults which exists in other small and medium enterprises (SMEs) employing a variety of staff in a number of roles, in the form of 'human resources' (HR) is lacking. In an ideal situation, this concept, within a school setting, would comprise a designated professional who would be responsible for staff well-being, support and development. This role, completely detached from line management duties and individual performance review processes, would take the responsibility away from members of the senior leadership team (SLT) who already have oversight of many specific organizational functions. The benefit of this approach would be the ability to anticipate and support colleagues who are potentially vulnerable or 'at risk' of leaving the school or profession, prior to them experiencing a downward trajectory in terms of loss of agency, commitment and, potentially, effectiveness. This type of preventative strategy in schools could also pre-empt, in some cases, the need for intervention by occupational health or other external professionals.

A strategy of this kind would need to be closely linked with appropriate training and development opportunities. This would not only include provision for school leaders in order that they could effectively facilitate the strategy, but also necessitate responsive professional and/or personal support from the school management in order to encourage teachers' sense of vocation, agency and effectiveness and promote positive career trajectories, particularly for teachers in their middle and final professional life phases.

The VITAE research indicates there is a need to develop school contexts in which teachers can make connections between dimensions of their professional identity, levels of motivation, commitment, job satisfaction and self-efficacy, and their sense of agency and well-being which are crucial to their effectiveness and which, in turn, will aid in the retention of new and experienced teachers.

Building environments for professional growth

The quality of teaching is determined not just by the 'quality' of the teachers – although that is clearly critical – but also by the environment in which they work. Able teachers are not necessarily going to reach their potential in settings that do not provide appropriate support or sufficient challenge and reward. Policies aimed at attracting and retaining effective teachers need both to recruit competent people into the profession, and also to provide support and incentives for professional development and ongoing performance at high levels.

(OECD 2005: 19)

Through VITAE we were able to explore the additional pressures on the teaching profession associated with the rapid pace of change. Coping with multiple initiatives and increased accountability leads many teachers to complain of high levels of stress, increased workloads, time on paperwork and administration and an overemphasis on test results and public examinations that affect their perceived professionalism and effectiveness. Older teachers in later professional life phases, in particular, find the pressures associated with policy changes especially difficult: either because they were trained under a different system and have managed different expectations and experiences in their earlier professional life phases; because resilience has been eroded over the years by a combination of life events and by changes in the demands of teaching, out of classroom responsibilities; or as a consequence of the processes of ageing in a job in which, to be at one's best, demands large intensive amounts of emotional, intellectual and physical energy.

Teachers' professional life phases

Teachers in later professional life phases tend to have additional responsibilities in schools that add to their workload, and they are more likely to have responsibilities for 'delivering' improvements in standards. The commonsense view that teachers necessarily become more effective over the course of their careers is not supported by the evidence. Thus, it cannot be assumed that more experienced teachers are better able to cope and require less support than new entrants. In many ways they are subject to greater pressures and tensions in achieving a work–life balance.

Teachers' effectiveness, then, is not simply a consequence of age or experience. It is influenced by: i) their professional life phases; ii) their sense of professional identity, something which is neither intrinsically stable nor unstable, but which can be affected positively or negatively by different degrees of tension experienced between educational ideals and aspirations, personal life experiences, the leadership and cultures in their schools, pupils' behaviour and relationships and the impact of external policies on their work; and iii) their commitment and resilience, qualities which are dependent on their capacities to manage interactions between personal, work and professional factors, which mediate their professional lives and identities positively or negatively.

Continuing development: keeping the fire alight

Teachers' effectiveness is mediated, also, by continuing professional development, which has a consistently positive influence on teachers across all professional life phases, though needs and concerns vary in relation to these; the extent to which teachers sustain their sense of positive professional identity; the quality of leadership, both at school and department level, relationships with colleagues, and personal support. These are all key influencing factors on teachers' motivation, self-efficacy, commitment and quality retention.

In part, government has recognized teachers' needs for time to engage in learning through the Workforce Remodelling agenda (Chapter 1); and there has been increasing central support for CPD over the past ten years through, for example, the establishment in England of a National College of School Leadership (NCSL), General Teaching Council for England (GTCE) and Teacher Development Agency (TDA). Each of these has a remit for increasing support for teacher learning and development. However, much of the funding for such development has been funnelled into 'professional development activities that match government or institutional development plan priorities or that can be demonstrated to contribute directly and immediately to improvement on students' learning (measured by test scores)' (Gewirtz *et al.* 2006). In this model:

> The sense of learning as personal growth and self-actualization, is lost.
> Learning can no longer be seen as 'lighting fires'.
> (Hodkinson and Hodkinson 2005: 119)

Yet, this is precisely the learning that VITAE teachers across all professional life phases whose fires were in danger of being extinguished, said that they needed; and it is such learning which nurtures commitment, resilience and effectiveness. It is this balance of activities which address the policy, organizational and classroom immediate needs, together with those which support teachers' professional well-being, sense of efficacy and motivation which is needed. There was no suggestion by the overwhelming majority of VITAE teachers that the current reform agenda should be rolled back, that their work should not be monitored or that they should not be accountable. Rather, there was a sense that they wanted the complexity and intensity of their work, and its emotional as well as technical demands, to be acknowledged and appreciated – for more trust to be exercised in their abilities to make teaching and learning judgements and for personalized, differentiated learning support opportunities to be available to them (Hendry 2005; Wallace 2005).

Our findings support arguments for creating more expansive environments for the professional learning of teachers which would be characterized by:

- Close collaborative working
- Colleagues (being) mutually supportive in enhancing teacher learning
- Supported opportunities for personal development that go beyond school or government priorities
- Out of school educational opportunities including time to stand back, reflect and think differently
- Opportunities to integrate off the job learning into everyday practice
- Opportunities to extend professional identity through boundary crossing into other departments, school activities, schools and beyond.

(Hodkinson and Hodkinson 2005: 124)

Of course, the provision, impact and effects of these and other more instrumentally oriented professional learning opportunities will vary, as we have seen, from school to school, department to department and teacher to teacher. Not all schools are fully developed 'professional learning communities' (McLaughlin and Talbert 2006), not all headteachers are committed to professional learning of these kinds as a key means to raising or maintaining teacher commitment, resilience and effectiveness; and not all teachers are enthusiastic to learn. However, if the conditions for learning by adults as well as students in schools are not in place, then teachers' capacities to be effective are likely to be diminished.

Professional learning communities

Achieving effectiveness, raising standards, making schools richer places for children, young people and adults to learn, grow and achieve do not only require that external initiatives are able to connect to efforts to improve schools from within. We know from a range of research internationally that school leaders – particularly the headteacher – may create conditions for individual and organizational effectiveness (Day 2000). We know, also, the importance of building and sustaining 'professional learning communities'. Drawing together two decades of research across multiple national initiatives in America carried out by Stanford's Centre for Research on the Context of Teaching (CRC), Milbrey McLaughlin and Joan Talbert (2006) highlight pressures on teachers to change and improve schools, not unlike those experienced by teachers in England: the need to reconceptualize the learning and teaching relationship, to work successfully with a broader range of students from diverse cultural, ethnic and economic backgrounds and with a greater range of learning needs (2006: 1). The 'hallmark' of the new professionalism, they suggest, will be 'a commitment to lifelong professional learning and collective responsibility for improved student learning' (2006: 2). To achieve the new learning environments and student outcomes demanded by society, however:

> Teachers must make more than technical changes in their practices . . . [embrace] . . . new norms and expectations for students' learning'.
> (McLaughlin and Talbert 2006: 2)

They argue, from a range of analyses grounded in years of research on effectiveness and improvement in schools, for the development of school-based learning communities in which teachers are able to work collaboratively 'to reflect on their practice, examine evidence about the relationship between practice and student outcomes, and make changes that improve teaching and learning for the particular students in their classes' (2006: 4).

It is not our intention here to interrogate, as McLaughlin and Talbert do with the authority of their extensive databases, the anatomy of professional learning communities. Rather, we wish to place the conditions which they – and others – have identified as necessary for the most effective teaching, learning and achievement in the context of the lives, work, effectiveness and future effectiveness of teachers like those 300 who participated in VITAE. What our research has shown clearly is that while aspirations for professional learning communities to be developed are to be applauded, and while there is now a growing body of qualitative and statistical research data which supports the claim that such communities improve teaching, learning and student learning gains, they are likely to remain a small minority, if the means proposed to achieve them remain limited only to an understanding of the importance of strategies which will influence organizational structures and cultures. A corresponding focus upon the broader spectrum of influences upon teachers' capacities to become and remain effective is needed.

Much research acknowledges the importance of nurturing and sustaining trust, providing time, building collegiality and having the right kind of leadership in building commitment. However, it does not focus upon the ways in which such influences interact positively and negatively with teachers' work and lives and professional identities, nor how these affect their capacities to be effective. Their general focus, like much school effectiveness and improvement published research, is almost exclusively on the organizational conditions necessary for effective teachers rather than on how teachers themselves sustain their commitment and maintain their resilience in the context, not only of their organization, but also their work and lives.

It is clear that teachers' values and beliefs, professional life phases and identities are dynamic and subject to a number of key positive and negative influences. Variations in these affect teachers' capacities to be relative and relationally effective over the course of their work lives. As personal lives, curricula and school conditions, and pupils change, it is the extent to which teachers are able to exercise agency in managing the tensions that they may cause which determines whether they are able to sustain and, where appropriate, increase their commitment, resilience and effectiveness. The good news is that most do. However, the effectiveness of a significant number, as we have seen, will be at risk. It is essential, then, that they themselves, and those responsible for their leadership, acknowledge the complexities of the cognitive and sometimes turbulent emotional, social and professional contexts in which they work, and the associations between these and their commitment, well-being, resilience and effectiveness; that they address the statistically significant association illustrated in the previous chapter between the levels of pupils' progress and attainment at Key Stage 1, 2 and 3 (English and mathematics) and the extent to which teachers sustain their commitment.

Supporting experienced teachers and those who work in schools which serve disadvantaged communities

> The challenge is to ensure that all students in all schools have strong and dedicated teachers, for currently the teacher shortage disproportionately affects schools serving students from low income communities.
>
> (Moore Johnson 2004: 8)

Teachers' long-term effectiveness may be at risk for teachers in the later years of their professional lives and those who work in secondary schools. Teachers in primary schools are more likely to sustain their commitment over a career than secondary teachers; teachers who work in schools in more challenging socio-economic contexts are more likely to experience greater challenges to their health, well-being, and thus resilience, than those who work in relatively more advantaged schools.

Our VITAE research indeed confirms that teaching is more stressful in high challenge contexts and indicates that teachers in FSM3 and 4 schools can be seen as more vulnerable in terms of maintaining commitment and likelihood of suffering ill health. Ways of rewarding, supporting and encouraging professionals working in such schools, have received some attention in recent years, and there is evidence that the provision of extra resources in education have particularly targeted schools in areas of high disadvantage. Nonetheless, our research indicates that more recognition of the potential impact on teachers of working in such areas is required.

We have seen throughout the book how central pupils are to teachers' feelings of effectiveness, commitment and satisfaction. Most came into teaching with a desire to make a difference to their pupils' development and they overwhelmingly reported good relationships with their pupils. We have also seen that the pupils themselves are generally positive about their schools and teachers – though this declines with age and varies between schools. However, for many teachers the impact of pupil behaviour is less positive. Teachers in every professional life phase reported behaviour as having a negative impact on their work. They also reported school policies on pupil behaviour as the most important in terms of impact on their classroom teaching.

It is in this context that government policies on inclusion were singled out by many teachers as impacting negatively on their work. The implementation of the inclusive ideas of *Excellence for All* (DfEE 1998) left many of the VITAE teachers believing that they had children with special needs in their classes who needed more specialist help than they could give. As these pupils may have attendant behaviour problems, this also may have involved a level of classroom disruption which affected their teaching. In our interviews at the end of each school year, it was not uncommon for a teacher to single out several pupils with particular special educational needs who had made the teacher feel less effective that year than with previous classes.

The provision of greater support and resources for schools, increases in the numbers of teachers and classroom assistants, and an emphasis on improving the attainments of disadvantaged groups, with specific initiatives in inner city/disadvantaged areas, while retaining a clear focus on accountability mechanisms, has been a focus of policy since 1997. Evaluations of the national strategies suggest they have played an important role in both raising overall attainment levels in English and mathematics and, have helped to narrow the gap between schools at the top and bottom of the achievement distribution. Although standards have risen at the secondary level, there is less evidence of a narrowing of the gap between high and low performing schools. The picture for primary schools is shown in Table 12.1 where it can be seen that there has been particular improvement for pupils in high disadvantage schools. These significant achievements in schools in challenging contexts require greater celebration and are a tribute to the work and commitment of teachers, such as those in our VITAE sample.

Table 12.1: The improvement of KS2 Results in Primary Schools by Level of Social Disadvantage

School FSM Band	Key Stage 2 English % Pupils attaining Level 4		
	1996	2001	2004
8% or less	74	87	88
8+ to 20%	64	78	81
20+ to 35%	51	69	73
35+ to 50%	41	61	67
Above 50%	34	57	63
Total	60	78	81

Source DfES datasets

The experience in England over the past two decades of education reforms, indicates that the hope remains among policy-makers that system-wide change can have long-term effects if sustained, and if policies are complementary and aligned, focusing directly on improving the teaching and learning processes and associated with a commitment to and resources for developing professional practice, with clear monitoring and evaluation. However, our research suggests that there is a need to combine pressure with much greater support, especially for teachers in schools in challenging circumstances, including additional resources, and to recognize the difficulties facing practitioners. The recruitment and retention of teachers, particularly experienced teachers in schools facing challenging circumstances, remains problematic.

The retention of quality: sustaining teachers' commitment and resilience

> The teaching pool keeps losing water because no one is paying attention to the leak. That is, we're misjudging the problem as 'recruitment' when it's really retention.
>
> (Merrow 1999: 38)

The VITAE research shows that maintaining teacher commitment and motivation is important both for retention and for better academic outcomes for pupils. The quality of teachers is at the heart of the success of any educational reforms aimed at raising standards.

We have coined the term, quality retention, to emphasize that sustaining the quality of teachers' commitment and resilience is a key retention issue. In contrast to previous research on teacher retention, which tends to focus on factors affecting teachers' decisions to leave the profession, this research provides a new perspective, focusing on teacher retention in terms of building and sustaining teacher quality and effectiveness over the whole of their careers. It suggests that in comparison to teachers' physical continuation in the role, it is the retention of quality that has major implications for their effectiveness. It is the retention of teachers' hearts and minds, enthusiasm and morale. This form of retention is less easily observed but more closely related to teachers' sense of purpose, self-efficacy, levels of commitment and effectiveness.

The closest definition of teacher quality to that of our VITAE research was stated over two decades ago in the White Paper *Teaching Quality* (1983), presented to Parliament in March 1983.

> Qualifications and training alone do not make a teacher. Personality, character and commitment are as important as the specific knowledge and skills that are used in the day-to-day tasks of teaching.

Teacher quality over teacher quantity

The new and continuing challenges to teacher retention have raised major concerns about retaining effective teachers in schools, with a greater emphasis on teacher quality over teacher quantity (OECD 2005).

> There is now substantial research indicating that the quality of teachers and their teaching are the most important factors in student outcomes that are open to policy influence. There is also substantial evidence that teachers vary markedly in their effectiveness. Differences in student performance are often greater within schools than between schools. Teaching is a demanding job, and it is not possible for everyone to be an effective practitioner and to sustain that over the long-term. However, the general approach to teacher selection and employment has tended to regard teachers as largely interchangeable and to focus on the numbers of teachers rather than on the qualities that they have or could develop.
>
> (OECD 2005: 12)

UNESCO's recent report, *Teachers and Educational Quality* (2006), calls for attention to the need of balancing teacher quantity and quality to improve learning outcomes. In England, a range of continuing efforts to address the difficulties of teacher shortages in the 1990s, including restructuring teachers' pay, providing differentiated career progression routes and more promotion opportunities, has led to an encouraging increase in teacher numbers. The statistical evidence from DfES shows that teacher recruitment and retention has been moving in a positive direction: the vacancy rate in January 2005 was 0.7 per cent, down from 1.4 per cent in 2001 (School Teachers' Review

Body 2005). However, the National Union of Teachers (NUT) warned that half of the increase between 1997 and 2004 comprised teachers who were not qualified regular teachers because of the substantial problems in recruitment and retention in the preceding few years (cited in School Teachers' Review Body 2005). Another less encouraging factor in discussions of teacher retention is that an ageing teaching force might eventually lead to shortages as large numbers of teachers move towards retirement age (Education and Skills Committee 2004; OECD 2005; School Teachers' Review Body 2005).

Teacher quality versus qualified teachers

Previous research on teacher quality and student achievement has established an association between levels of teacher qualifications and students' outcomes. For example, Darling-Hammond (2000) found that measures of teacher preparation and certification were the strongest correlates of student achievement in reading and mathematics. The National Partnership for Teaching in At-Risk Schools (2005) in America, pointed to the negative impact of inexperienced and generally less qualified teachers on the lower quality of education in at-risk schools. The difference in qualification between these teachers and more qualified teachers in successful schools contributed to achievement gaps. In England the DfES stressed the relationship between retaining high quality teachers and pupil achievement – 'Schools which are unable to retain high calibre teachers find it harder to achieve high standards for their pupils' (cited in Education and Skills Committee 2004: 12).

The notion of teacher quality, however, is fundamentally different from the concept of qualified teachers. As UNESCO asserts, 'it is clear that qualifications alone do not make an effective teacher' (2006: 79). Similarly, Tedesco (1997) argues that professionalization alone is insufficient to offset the effects of other social, personal and emotional variables in promoting the quality of education:

> . . . education is an activity where full professionalization is neither possible nor desirable. Attributing excessive value to the systematic use of a theoretical model in a profession whose objective is to bring about changes in individuals is of little benefit in the end to the individuals themselves . . . rather than discussing whether there is a need for greater professionalization in general, it seems preferable to try to identify the main characteristics of teaching work in the context of the new educational challenges.
>
> (Tedesco 1997: 99–100)

A strong conclusion from the 2005 OECD project *Teachers Matter: Attracting, Developing and Retaining Effective Teachers* is the positive effects of teacher motivation and sense of vocation on the quality of teaching. The project report also emphasizes the significance of in-school support in meeting teachers' needs and concerns in pursuit of high quality performance and this message has been reinforced through the VITAE project data.

> Key ingredients in a teacher quality agenda include more attention to the criteria for selection both into initial teacher education and teaching employment, ongoing evaluation throughout the teaching career to identify areas for improvement, recognizing and rewarding effective teaching, and ensuring that teachers have the resources and support they need to meet high expectations. A strong conclusion from the project is that teachers are highly motivated by the intrinsic benefits of teaching – working with children and young people, helping them to develop, and making a contribution to society – and that system structures and school workplaces need to ensure that teachers are able to focus on these tasks.
>
> (OECD 2005: 12)

In VITAE we explored and analysed not only what constituted the essential qualities of an effective teacher, but more importantly, how and why one teacher's effectiveness varies in relation to another's, and how and why teachers' sense of their own effectiveness varies over the course of their individual professional working lives. We found, for example, that teachers do not necessarily become more effective as they grow older. Our research shows that teachers in their early professional life phases (0–3 and 4–7) are more likely to be effective than their counterparts in the middle and later professional life phases. This finding has a profound implication for teacher retention. Previous research shows that teachers are more likely to leave the profession in their first five years of teaching. A large proportion of these teachers, however, as our study suggests, are likely to be effective teachers as indicated by their pupils' progress and attainment. Retaining effective teachers in teaching will thus have a significant impact on the quality of the teaching force, and consequently the quality of educational experience and the achievements.

In common with our findings, in American research on teachers in their early careers, Moore Johnson (2004) urges that efforts to address teacher recruitment and retention must pay careful attention to the school conditions that teachers find upon entry:

> Schools that support teachers over time succeed not only in hiring new teachers, but also in retaining and developing them. These schools are

finders *and* keepers. They leave little to chance and do not assume that good teaching inevitably flows from innate talent, best nurtured in privacy and isolation. Rather, they purposefully engage new teachers in the culture and practices of the school, beginning with their first encounter. In such schools, hiring is the first step of the induction process, a time when both prospective teachers and their future colleagues can exchange rich information about what each has to offer and expects from the other.

(Moore Johnson 2004: 255)

Effective teaching is physically and emotionally demanding. What is required by policy-makers, LAs and school leaders in particular, is a better understanding of how teachers manage the complex interaction of a range of professional, personal and situated mediating factors and other influencing factors (i.e. teachers' professional life phases and identities) to sustain their commitment, resilience and effectiveness over time. The data from 300 VITAE teachers repeatedly points to the positive and/or negative influence of school contexts and culture on their morale and levels of commitment, particularly on the professional outlook of teachers in their early and later years of experience. This observation places responsive in-school support at the centre of the teacher retention agenda. What matters in teacher supply is teacher retention. What counts most in teacher retention is sustaining the quality of teachers' commitment and resilience and, through these, their effectiveness. Teachers matter.

Notes

1 In fact, parents are only entitled to express a preference for a school of their choice. Research indicates that more advantaged parents are more likely to seek to exercise choice. In some areas distance and transport effectively curtail any real choice of school.

2 Local education authorities are now known as local authorities (LAs) and this term will be used throughout the book.

3 Many of the areas relevant to VITAE related to teachers' personal lives. For example, career, emotions, identity and commitment, are explored in later Chapters, therefore not included here.

4 One limitation of the VITAE research design was the absence of classroom observation data (a component of the original proposal that was not funded) for the 300 teachers in the case study sample. The effect of this was that data on different aspects of teachers' classroom practice – including teacher–pupil interactions, etc. – were not collected. Thus, we could not explore variations between teachers in specific aspects of their classroom teaching and pupils' responses in this research study. As a consequence, our quantitative analyses could not measure and test a number of potentially important features of effective teaching behaviours identified in the school and teacher effectiveness literature nor investigate the extent to which they were empirically confirmed for the VITAE sample.

5 The '+' or (–) in combination with the number refers to the teachers who have demonstrated upward or downward professional life phase trajectories.

6 The distribution of late entrants and career-break teachers in the 4–7 professional life phase is: 'growing' group: 6 late entrants; 'coping/managing' group: 7 late entrants, 2 career-break teachers; 'vulnerable/declining' group: 5 late entrants, 1 career-break teacher.

7 Four teachers had very little data and therefore could not be categorized into any sub-groups.

8 Two teachers had little data.

9 Eighteen of the teachers involved in the study did not have enough data to allow a detailed analysis of teacher identity.

10 Because teachers had been involved in more than one type of CPD, the total frequency of responses adds to more than the total of 285 teachers who reponsed.

11 The National Professional Qualification for Headship (NPQH) is one of a number of national programmes for school leaders at all levels provided through a commissioning process by the National College for School Leadership.

12 No prior attainment baseline data were collected at the beginning of the school year for teachers of Year 2 classes, so value added measures of pupil progress could not be calculated.

13 For further discussion of value added measures, see McPherson 1992; Goldstein 1995; Sammons *et al.* 1997a.

14 The baseline assessments were part of the NFER-Nelson 'progress 5–14' series (NFER assessments Progress in English/mathematics 10 and Progress in English/mathematics 13). They provide raw and age standardized scores that adjust pupils' performance according to their age, and provide comparisons with a nationally representative sample.

References

Achinstein, B. (in press) *The Ties That Blind: Community, Diversity and Conflict Among Schoolteachers.* New York: Teachers College Press.

Acker, S. (1999) *The Realities of Teachers' Work: Never a Dull Moment.* London: Cassell.

Alexander, R. (2004) *Excellence, Enjoyment and Personalized Learning: A True Foundation for Choice?* Edited Version of Keynote Address to the National Union of Teachers National Education Conference, 3 July.

Ancess, J. (1997) *Urban Dreamcatchers: Launching and Leading New Small Schools.* New York, NY: National Center for Restructuring Education, Schools, and Teaching (NCREST), Teachers College Press, Columbia University.

Andrews, M. (1983) 'Evaluation: an essential process'. *Journal of Extension* (September–October): 8–13.

Archer, J. (1996) 'Sex differences in social behaviour: Are the social role and evolutionary explanations compatible?' *American Psychologies*, 51: 909–17.

Armor, D., Conroy-Oseguera, P., Cox, M., King, N., McDonnell, L., Pascal, A., Pauly, E. and Zellman, G. (1976) 'Analysis of the school preferred reading programs in selected Los Angeles minority schools', REPORT NO. R-2007-LAUSD. Santa Monica, CA: Rand Corporation (ERIC Document Reproduction Service No. 130 243).

Ashton, P.T. and Webb, R.B. (1986) *Making a Difference. Teachers' Sense of Efficacy and Student Achievement.* New York, NY: Longman.

Askew, M., Brown, M., Rhodes, V., William, D. and Johnson, D. (1997) *Effective Teachers of Numeracy.* London: Kings' College, for the Teacher Training Agency.

Aspinwall, L.G. (1998) 'Rethinking the role of positive affect in self-regulation'. *Motivation and Emotion*, 22: 1–32.

Aspinwall, L.G. (2001) 'Dealing with adversity: self-regulation, coping, adaptation, and health' in A. Tesser, and N. Schwarz (eds) *The Blackwell Handbook of Social Psychology*, Vol. 1, pp. 591–614. Malden, MA: Blackwell.

Ball, S. (2001) 'Labour, learning and the economy: a "policy sociology" perspective' in M. Fielding (ed.) *Taking Education Really Seriously, Four Years Hard Labour*, pp. 45–56. London: Routledge Falmer.

Ball, S.J. and Goodson, I. (1985) *Teachers' Lives and Careers*. Lewes: Falmer Press.

Ballet, K. (2001) Doctoratsproject: Leerkracht zijn in tijden van intensficatie (Being teacher in times of intensification) Unpublished Doctoral dissertation Katholieke Univesiteit, Leuven, Belgium. Cited in R. Van den Berg (2002) 'Teachers' meanings regarding educational practice'. *Review of Educational Research*, 72 (4): 577–625.

Bandura, A. (1986) *Social Foundations of Thought and Action: A Social Cognitive Theory*. Englewood Cliffs, NJ: Prentice-Hall.

Bandura, A. (1989) 'Human agency in social cognitive theory'. *American Psychologist*, 44 (9): 1175–84.

Bandura, A. (2000) 'Cultivate self-efficacy for personal and organizational effectiveness' in E.A. Locke (ed.) *Handbook of Principles of Organization Behaviour*. Oxford: Blackwell.

Barbalet, J. (2002) 'Introduction: Why emotions are crucial' in J. Barbalet (ed.) *Emotional Sociology*, pp. 1–9. London: Blackwell Publishing.

Barber, B.R. (2001) The 'Engaged University' in a Disengaged Society: Realistic Goal or Bad Joke? www.diversityweb.org/Digest/Sm01/engaged.html (accessed 1 Oct 2003).

Barber, M. (2001) Large-scale Education Reform in England: A Work in Progress. Paper presented at the Managing Education Reform Conference, Moscow 29–30 October.

Bartlett, L. (2004) 'Expanding teacher work roles: resource for retention or recipe for overwork?' *Journal of Education Policy*, 19 (5): 565–82.

Belchetz, D. and Leithwood, K. (2006) 'Successful leadership: Does context matter? And if so, how?' in C. Day and K. Leithwood (eds) *Successful School Leadership: International Perspectives*. Dordrecht: Springer.

Bell, L., Bolam, R. and Cubillo, L. (2003) *A Systematic Review of the Impact of School Leadership and Management on Student Outcomes*. London: EPPI–Centre, Institute of Education, University of London.

Benard, B. (1991) *Fostering Resiliency in Kids: Protective Factors in the Family, School and Community*. San Francisco, CA: Western Regional Educational Laboratory.

Benard, B. (1995) 'Fostering resilience in children'. *ERIC/EECE Digest*, EDO-PS-99.

Benner, P.E. (1984) *From Novice to Expert: Excellence and Power in Clinical Nursing Practice*. Menlo Park, CA: Addison Wensley.

Berman, P. and McLaughlin, M. (1977) *Federal Programs Supporting Educational Change, Vol. VII. Factors Affecting Implementation and Continuation*. Santa Monica, CA: RAND.

Berman, P., McLaughlin, M., Bass, G., Pauley, E. and Zellman, G. (1977) *Federal Programs Supporting Educational Change: Vol. VII. Factors Affecting Implementation and Continuation* (Rep. No. R-1589/7-HEW). Santa Monica, CA: RAND. (ERIC Document Reproduction Service No. 140 432).

Bernstein, B. (1996) *Pedagogy, Symbolic Control and Identity*. London: Taylor and Francis.

Blasé, J.J. (1986) 'A qualitative analysis of sources of teacher stress: consequences for performance'. *American Educational Research Journal*, 23 (1): 13–40.

Blasé, J. and Blasé, J. (1999) 'Principals' instructional leadership and teacher development: teachers' perspectives'. *Educational Administration Quarterly*, 35 (3): 349–78.

Block, J.H. and Block, J. (1980) 'The role of ego-control and ego resiliency in the organization of behaviour' in W.A. Collins (ed.) *Minnesota Symposium on Child Psychology*, Vol. 13, pp. 39–101. Hillsdale, NJ: Erlbaum.

Bloom, B.S. (1976) *Human Characteristics and School Learning*. New York, NY: McGraw-Hill.

Bogler, R. (2002) 'Two profiles of schoolteachers: a discriminant analysis of job satisfaction'. *Teaching and Teacher Education*, 18 (6): 665–73.

Bolam, R. (1990) 'Recent developments in England and Wales' in B. Joyce (ed.) *Changing School Culture through Staff Development*, The 1990 ASCD Yearbook, pp. 147–67. Alexandria, VA: Association for Supervision and Curriculum Development (ASCD).

Borich, G. (1996) *Effective Teaching Methods*, 3rd edn. New York, NY: Macmillan.

Bottery, M. (2005) 'The Individualization of Consumption: A Trojan Horse in the Destruction of the Public Sector?' *Educational Management, Administration and Leadership*, 33 (3): 267–88.

Boyle, M. and Woods, P. (1995) The composite head: coping with changes in the primary headteacher's role. Paper presented at the European Conference on Educational Research, Bath, September.

Brandt, R. (1996) *Powerful Learning*. Alexandria, VA: ASCD.

Brennan, M. (1996) *Multiple Professionalisms for Australian Teachers in an Important Age*. New York, NY: American Educational Research Association.

Brophy, J. and Good, T. (1986) 'Teacher behavior and student achievement' in M. Wittrock (ed.) *Handbook of Research on Teaching*, pp. 340–70). New York, NY: Macmillan.

Bryk, A.S., Lee, V.E. and Holland, P.B. (1993) *Catholic Schools and the Common Good*. Cambridge, MA: Harvard University Press.

Bryman, A. (1988) *Quality and Quantity in Social Research*. London: Allen and Unwin.

Buhler, C. and Marschak, M. (1968) 'Basic tendencies of human life' in C. Buhler and F. Massarik (eds) *The Course of Human Life: A Study of Goals in the Humanistic Perspective*, pp. 92–102. New York, NY: Springer.

Bullough, R.V. and Baughman, K. (1997) *'First-Year Teacher', Eight Years Later*. New York, NY: Teachers College Press.

Burke, R.J. and Greenglass, E. (1993) 'Work stress, role conflict, social support and psychological burnout among teachers'. *Psychological Reports*, 73: 371–80.

Burke, R.J. and Greenglass, E. (1995) 'A longitudinal study of psychological burnout in teachers'. *Human Relations*, 48: 187–202.

Bush, T. and Middleton, D. (2005) *Leading and Managing People in Education*. London: 101 Productions.

Bushnell, M. (2003) 'Teachers in the Schoolhouse Panopticon'. *Education and Urban Society*, 35 (3): 251–72.

Butt, R. (1984) 'Arguments for using biography in understanding teachers' thinking' in R. Halkes and J.K. Olson (eds) *Teacher Thinking: A New Perspective on Persisting Problems in Education*, pp. 95–102. Lisse: Swets and Zeitlinger.

Butt, R. and Raymond, D. (1989) 'Studying the nature and development of teachers' knowledge using collaborative autobiography'. *International Journal of Educational Research*, 13 (4): 403–19.

Calderhead, J. (1986) A Cognitive Perspective on Teaching Skills. Paper presented at the British Psychological Society Education Section Annual Conference, Nottingham.

Campbell, R.J. (2003) 'Differential teacher effectiveness: towards a model for research and teacher appraisal'. *Oxford Review of Education*, 29 (3): 347–62.

Campbell, R.J. and St.J. Neill, S.R. (1994) *Primary Teachers at Work*. London: Routledge.

Campbell, R.J., Evans, L., St. J. Neill, S.R. and Packwood, A. (1991) *Workloads, Achievements and Stress: Two Follow-up Studies of Teacher Time in Key Stage 1*. Warwick: Policy Analysis Unit, Department of Education, University of Warwick.

Castells, M. (1997) *Power of Identity: The Information Age: Economy, Society and Culture*. Cambridge, MA: Blackwell.

Chapman, C. and Harris, A. (2004) 'Improving schools in difficult and challenging circumstances'. *Educational Research*, 46 (3): 219–28.

Chapman, D.W. (1982) A model of the influences on teacher attrition. *Journal of Teacher Education*, 34: 43–49.

Chappell, T. (2005) *The Inescapable Self: An Introduction to Western Philosophy*. London: Orion Publishing.

Chitty, C. (2004) *Education Policy in Britain*. Basingstoke: Palgrave Macmillan.

Clark, C.M. and Peterson, P.L. (1986) 'Teachers' thought processes' in M.C. Wittrock (ed.) *Handbook of Research on Teaching*, 3rd edn, pp. 255–96. New York, NY: Macmillan.

Clarke, J. and Newman, J. (2005) The rise of the citizen-consumer: implications for public service professionalism. Paper for Changing Teacher Roles, Identities and Professionalism Seminar, King's College London, 19 October 2005.

Cooper, K. and Olson, M. (1996) 'The multiple I's of teacher identity' in M. Kompf, R.T. Buak, W.R. Bond and D.H. Dwuret (eds) *Changing Research and Practice: Teachers' Professionalism, Identities and Knowledge*. London: Falmer Press.

Cooper, P. and McIntyre, D. (1996) *Effective Teaching and Learning: Teachers' and Students' Perspectives*. Buckingham: Open University Press.

Cresswell, J.W. (2003) *Research Design: Qualitative, Quantitative and Mixed Methods Approaches*. Thousand Oaks, CA: Sage Publications.

Cribb, A., Gewirtz, S., Hextall, I. and Mahony, P. (2005) Connecting teachers' lives to teachers' professional practice. A paper for discussion at the TLRP conference, November 2005, Warwick.

Crosswell, L. (2006) Understanding teacher commitment in times of change. Unpublished EdD thesis submitted to Queensland University of Technology, Brisbane, Australia.

Dainton, S. (2005) 'Reclaiming teachers' voices'. *Forum*, 47 (2,3): 159–67.

Darling-Hammond, L. (2000) 'Teacher quality and student achievement: a review of state policy evidence'. *Education Policy Analysis Archives*, 8 (1). http://epaa.asu.edu/epaa/v8n1 (accessed 17 July 2006).

Datnow, A. (2000) 'Implementing an externally developed school restructuring design: enablers, constraints and tensions'. *Teaching and Change*, 7(2): 147–71.

Datnow, A., Hubbard, L. and Mehen, H. (2002) *Educational Reform Implementation: A Constructed Process*. London: Routledge.

Day, C. (1993) 'The importance of learning biography in supporting teacher development: an empirical study' in C. Day, J. Calderhead and P. Denicolo (eds) *Research on Teacher Thinking: Understanding Professional Development*. London: Falmer Press.

Day, C. (1996) 'The good life: healthy teachers, healthy learners and the importance of schooling in lifelong learning' in P. Maxted (ed.) *For Life: A Vision for Learning in the Twenty-First Century*. London: RSA.

Day, C. (1999) *Developing Teachers: The Challenges of Lifelong Learning*. London: Falmer Press.

Day, C. (2000) 'Teachers in the twenty-first century: time to renew the vision'. *Teachers and Teaching: Theory and Practice*, 6 (1): 101–15.

Day, C. (2002) 'The challenge to be the best: reckless curiosity and mischievous motivation'. *Teachers and Teaching: Theory and Practice*, 8 (3/4): 421–34.

Day, C. (2004) *A Passion for Teaching*. London and New York: Routledge Falmer.

Day, C. and Hadfield, M. (1996) 'Metaphors for movement: accounts of professional development' in M. Kompf, R.T. Boak, W.R. Bond and D.H. Dworek (eds) *Changing Research and Practice: Teachers' Professionalism, Identities and Knowledge*, pp. 149–66. London: Falmer Press.

Day, C. and Leithwood, K. (2007). 'Building and sustaining successful principalship: key themes' in C. Day and K. Leithwood (eds) *Successful Principal Leadership: An International Perspective*. Dordrecht, The Netherlands: Springer.

Day, C. and Sachs, J. (eds) (2004) *International Handbook on the Continuing Professional Development of Teachers*. Maidenhead: Open University Press.

Day, C., Harris, A., Hadfield, M., Tolley, H. and Beresford, J. (2000) *Leading Schools in Times of Change*. Buckingham: Open University Press.

Day, C.W., Elliot, B. and Kington, A. (2005) 'Reforms, standards and teacher identity: challenges of sustaining commitment'. *Teaching and Teacher Education*, 21: 563–77.

Day, C.W., Kington, A., Stobart, G. and Sammons, P. (2006a) 'The personal and professional selves of teachers: stable and unstable identities'. *British Educational Research Journal*, 32 (4): 601–16.

Day, C., Sammons, P., Stobart, G. and Kington, A. (2006b) 'Variations in the work and lives of teachers: relative and relationship effectiveness'. *Teachers and Teaching: Theory and Practice*, 12 (2): 169–92.

Day, C., Stobart, G., Sammons, P., Kington, A., Gu, Q., Smees, R. and Mujtaba, T. (2006c) *Variation in Teachers' Work, Lives and Effectiveness*. London: DfES.

De Fraine, B., Van Damme, J. and Onghena, P. (2002) 'Accountability of schools and teachers: What should be taken into account?' *European Education Research Journal*, 1 (3): 403–28.

Denicolo, P. and Pope, M. (1990) 'Adults learning – teachers thinking' in C. Day, M. Pope and P. Denicolo (eds) *Insights into Teachers' Thinking and Practice*. London: Falmer Press.

Denzin, N.K. (1984) *On Understanding Emotion*. San Francisco, CA: Jossey-Bass.

Department for Education and Employment (1997) *Excellence for all Children: Meeting Special Educational Needs*. London: DfEE.

Department for Education and Employment (1998) *Teachers Meeting the Challenge*. London: The Stationery Office.

Department for Education and Skills (1999) Tender No: 4/RP/173/99. London: DfES.

Department for Education and Skills (2002) *Time for Standards: Reforming the School Workforce*. London: DfES.

Department for Education and Skills (2003) *Excellence and Enjoyment: A Strategy for Primary Schools*. London: DfES.

Department for Education and Skills (2005) *Professional Development for Teachers Early in their Careers: An Evaluation of the Early Professional Development Pilot Scheme*. London: DfES.

Dinham, S. and Scott, C. (1996) *The Teacher 2000 Project: A Study of Teacher Satisfaction, Motivation and Health*. Sydney: University of Western Sydney, Nepean.

Dinham, S. and Scott, C. (2000). 'Moving into the third, outer domain of teacher satisfaction'. *Journal of Educational Administration*, 38 (4): 379–96.

Docking, J. (ed.) (1999) *National School Policy Major Issues in Education Policy for Schools in England and Wales 1979 onwards*. London: David Fulton Publishers in association with Roehampton Institute London.

Docking, J. (ed.) (2000) *New Labour's Policies for Schools Raising the Standard?* London: David Fulton Publishers.

Dreyfus, H.L. and Dreyfus, S.E. (1986) *Mind Over Machine: The Power of Human Intuition and Expertise in the Era of the Computer*. New York, NY: The Free Press.

Duncombe, R. and Armour, K.M. (2004) 'Collaborative professional learning: from theory to practice'. *Journal of In-Service Education*, 30 (1): 141–66.

Duxbury, L., Higgings, C. and Lee, C. (1994) 'Work–family conflict: a comparison by gender, family type and perceived control'. *Journal of Family Issues*, 15: 449–66.

Earl, L., Levin, B., Leithwood, K., Fullan, M., Watson, N. with Torrance, N., Jantzi, D. and Blair, M. (2001) *OISE/UT Evaluation of the Implementation of the National Literacy and Numeracy Strategies*. Toronto: Ontario Institute for Studies in Education, University of Toronto.

Earl, L., Watson, N., Levin, B., Leithwood, K., Fullan, M. and Torrance, N. (2003) *Watching and Learning 3*. OISE/UT Evaluation of England's National Literacy and Numeracy Strategies, Third and Final Report. Ontario: Ontario Institute for Studies in Education, University of Toronto.

Earl, W.L. (1987) 'Creativity and self-trust: a field study'. *Adolescence*, 22: 419–32.

Easterlin, R.A. (2003) 'Building a better theory of well-being' in L. Bruni and P.L. Porta (eds) *Building a Better Theory of Well-Being*, pp. 29–64. Oxford: Oxford University Press.

Ebmeier, H. and Nicklaus, J. (1999) 'The impact of peer and principal collaborative supervison on teachers' trust, commitment, desire for collaboration and efficacy. *Journal of Curriculum and Supervision*, 14 (4): 351–78.

Education and Skills Committee (2004) *Secondary Education: Teacher Retention and Recruitment, Fifth Report of Session 2003–2004*, Vol. 1. London: The Stationery Office.

Elkins, T. and Elliott, J. (2004) 'Competition and control: the impact of government regulation on teaching and learning in English schools'. *Research Papers in Education*, 19 (1): 15–30.

Elliott, B. and Crosswell, L. (2001) Commitment to Teaching: Australian perspectives on the interplays of the professional and the personal in teachers' lives. Paper presented at the International Symposium on Teacher Commitment at the European Conference on Educational Research, Lille, France.

Elliott, J. (2004). 'Making teachers more accountable: models, methods and processes'. *Research Papers in Education*, 19 (1): 7–14.

Elmore, R.F. (2006) Leadership as the Practice of Improvement. Paper presented at the International Conference on Perspectives on Leadership for Systematic Improvement, sponsored by OECD, 6 July, London, UK.

Emmet, D. (1958) *Function, Purpose and Powers*. London: Macmillan.

Englund, T. (1996) 'The public and the text'. *Journal of Curriculum Studies*, 28 (1): 1–36.

Eraut, M. (1994) *Developing Professional Knowledge and Competence*. London: Falmer Press.

Erikson, E. (1959) 'Identity and life cycle'. *Psychological Issues*, 1: 1–171.

Evans, L. (1998) *Teacher Morale, Job Satisfaction and Motivation*. London: Paul Chapman Publishing.

Evans, L. (2001) Delving deeper into morale, job satisfaction and motivation among education professionals, in *Educational Management, Administration and Leadership*, 29 (3): 291–306.

Evans, L., Packwood, A., St. J. Neill, S. R. and Campbell, R.J. (1994) *The Meaning of Infant Teachers' Work*. London: Routledge.

Evans, R.N. (1992) 'The state of the union in industrial, technical and technology teacher education'. *Journal of Industrial Teacher Education*, 29 (2): 7–14.

Evetts, J. (2005) The Management of Professionalism: A contemporary paradox. Paper presented to ESRC Seminar Series, Changing Teacher Roles, Identities and Professionalism, Kings College, London.

Farber, B.A. (1991) *Crisis in Education: Stress and Burnout in the American Teacher*. San Francisco, CA: Jossey-Bass.

Feiman-Nemser, S. (1990) 'Teacher preparation: structural and conceptual alternatives' in W.R. Houston (ed.) *Handbook of Research on Teacher Education*. New York, NY: Macmillan.

Fessler, R. and Christensen, J. (1992) *The Teacher Career Cycle: Understanding and Guiding the Professional Development of Teachers*. Boston, MA: Allyn and Bacon.

Fielding, M. (2001) 'Ofsted, inspection and the betrayal of democracy'. *Journal of Philosophy of Education*, 35 (4): 695–709.

Fielding, M. (2006) Contexts, communities, networks: mobilizing learners' resources and relationships in different domains. Paper presented at ESRC Teaching and

Learning Research Programme (TLRP) Thematic Seminar Series, University of Exeter, Seminar Four, 22 February 2006.

Firestone, W.A. (1996) 'Images of teaching and proposals for reform: a comparison of ideas from cognitive and organizational research'. *Education Administration Quarterly*, 32 (2): 209–35.

Firestone, W.A. and Pennell, J.R. (1993) 'Teacher commitment, working conditions and differential incentive policies'. *Review of Educational Research*, 63: 489–526.

Flammer, A. (1990) *Erfahrung der eignen Wirksamkeit* (Experiencing Self-efficacy). Bern, Switzerland: Huber.

Fraser, B.J. (1989) 'Research syntheses on school and instructional effectiveness' in B.P.M. Creemers and J. Scheerens (eds) *International Journal of Educational Research*, 13 (7): 707–19.

Fraser, B.J. (1991) *Educational Leadership*, 4 (197): 46.

Fraser, H., Draper, J. and Taylor, W. (1998) 'The quality of teachers' professional lives: teachers and job satisfaction'. *Evaluation and Reserach in Education*, 12 (2): 61–71.

Fredrickson, B.L. (2001) 'The role of positive emotions in positive psychology: the broaden-and-build theory of positive emotions'. *American Psychologist*, 56 (3): 218–26.

Fredrickson, B.L. (2004) 'The broaden-and-build theory of positive emotions'. *The Royal Society*, 359: 1367–77.

Fredrickson, B.L. and Joiner, T. (2002) 'Positive emotions trigger upward spirals toward emotional well-being'. *Psychological Science*, 13: 172–5.

Freeman, A. (1987) 'Pastoral care and teacher stress'. *Pastoral Care in Education*, 5 (1): 22–8.

Fried, R. (2001) *The Passionate Teacher: A Practical Guide*, 2nd edn. Boston, MA: Beacon Press.

Friedson, E. (2001) *Professionalism: The Third Logic*. Cambridge: Polity Press.

Frone, M.R., Yardley, J.K. and Markel, K.S. (1997) 'Developing and testing an integrative model of the work–family interface'. *Journal of Vocational Behaviour*, 50: 145–67.

Fukuyama, F. (1999) *The Great Disruption: Human Nature and the Reconstitution of Social Order*. London: Profile Books.

Fullan, M. (1993) *Change Forces Probing the Depths of Educational Reform*. London: Falmer Press.

Fullan, M. and Hargreaves, A. (1996) *What's Worth Fighting for? Working Together for your School*. Toronto and New York, NY: Elementary Teachers Federation of Ontario and Teachers College Press.

Gage, N.L. (1978) *The Scientific Basis of the Art of Teaching*. Columbia: Teachers' College Press.

Galloway, D., Pankhurst, F., Boswell, K., Boswell, C. and Green, K. (1982) 'Sources of stress for class teachers'. *National Education*, 64: 166–9.

Galton, M. and Hargreaves, L. (1996). ' "Today I felt I was actually teaching": the effects of class size on teachers' classroom behaviour'. *Education Review*, 10 (2): 26–33.

Galton, M. and McBeath, J. with Page, C. and Steward, S. (2002) *A Life in Teaching? The Impact of Change on Primary Teachers' Working Lives*. A report commissioned by the NUT. Cambridge: University of Cambridge, Faculty of Education.

Gannaway, H. (1976) 'Making sense of school' in M. Stubbs and S. Delamont (eds) *Explorations in Classroom Observation*. London: Wiley and Sons.

Garmezy, N. (1990) A closing note: Reflections on the future, in J. Rolf, A. Master, D. Cicchetti, K. Neuchterlein and S. Weintraub (eds). *Risk and Protective Factors in the Development of Psychopathology*, pp 527–34. New York, NY: Cambridge University Press.

Gergen, K. (1987) 'Toward self as a relationship' in K. Yardley and T. Honness (eds) *Self and Identity: Psychological Perspectives*. New York, NY: John Wiley.

Gewirtz, S., Ball, S.J. and Bowe, R. (1995) *Markets, Choice and Equity*. Buckingham: Open University Press.

Gewirtz, S., Cribb, A., Mahony, P. and Hextall, I. (2006) Changing Teacher Roles, Identities and Professionalism: A Review of Key Themes from the Seminar Papers. Paper for discussion at Seminar 9 at the Changing Teacher Roles, Identities and Professionalism seminar series, King's College London 26 June 2006.

Ghaith, G. and Shaaban, K. (1999) 'The relationship between perceptions of teaching concerns, teacher efficacy and selected teacher characteristics'. *Teaching and Teacher Education*, 15: 487–96.

Gibson, S. and Dembo, M. (1984) 'Teacher efficacy: a construct validation'. *Journal of Educational Psychology*, 76: 569–82.

Giddens, A. (1986) *Constitution of Society*. Berkeley, CA: University of California Press.

Giddens, A. (1991) *Modernity and Self-Identity*. Stanford: Stanford University Press.

Glass, G.V. (1977) 'Integrated findings: the meta-analysis of research'. *Review of Research in Education*, 5: 351–79.

Glickman, C.D. and Tamashiro, R.T. (1982) 'A comparison of first year, fifth year and former teachers as efficacy, ego development and problem solving'. *Psychology in the Schools*, 19 (4): 558–62.

Golby, M. (1996) 'Teachers' emotions: an illustrated discussion'. *Cambridge Journal of Education*, 26: 423–34.

Goldstein, H. (1995). *Multilevel Statistical Models*. London: Edward Arnold.

Goldstein, L. (1997) *Teaching with Love: A Feminist Approach to Early Childhood*. New York, NY: Peter Lang.

Goleman, D. (1995) *Emotional Intelligence*. New York, NY: Bantam Books.

Goodlad, J. (1990) *Teachers for our Nation's Schools*. San Francisco, CA: Jossey-Bass.

Goodson, I. (2003) *Professional Knowledge, Professional Lives: Studies in Education and Change*. Maidenhead: Open University Press.

Goodson, I. and Hargreaves, A. (eds) (1996) *Teachers' Professional Lives*. London: Falmer Press.

Goodson, I.F. and Numan, U. (2002) Teacher's life worlds, agency and policy contexts. *Teachers and Teaching: Theory and Practice*, 8 (3/4): 269–77.

Goodson, I., Moore, S. and Hargreaves, A. (2006) 'Teacher nostalgia and the sustainability of reform: the generation and degeneration of teachers' missions, memory, and meaning'. *Educational Administration Quarterly*, 42 (1): 42–61.

Googins, B. (1991) *Work/Family Conflicts: Private Lives, Public Responses.* New York, NY: Auburn House.

Gorard, S. (2006) 'Value added is of little value'. *Journal of Educational Policy,* 21 (2): 233–41.

Gordon, K.A. (1995) 'The self-concept and motivational patterns of resilient African American high school students'. *Journal of Black Psychology,* 21: 239–55.

Gordon, K.A., Longo, M. and Trickett, M. (2000) 'Fostering resilience in children'. *The Ohio State University Bulletin,* 875–99: http://ohioline.osu.edu/b875.

Goss, S. (2005). *Counselling: A Quiet Revolution.* London: Teacher Support Network.

Grant-Vallone, E.J. and Donaldson, S. (2001) 'Consequences of work–family conflict on employee well-being over time'. *Work and Stress,* 15 (3): 214–26.

Greene, J.C., Caracelli, V.J. and Graham, W.F. (1989) 'Toward a conceptual framework for mixed-method evaluation designs'. *Educational Evaluation and Policy Analysis,* 11: 255–74.

Gronn, P. (2000) 'Distributed properties: a new architecture for leadership'. *Educational Management and Administration,* 28 (3): 317–38.

Gronn, P. (2002) 'Distributed leadership' in K. Leithwood and P. Hallinger (eds) *Second International Handbook of Educational Leadership and Administration,* pp. 653–96. Dordrecht: Kluwer.

Grossman, P., Wineburg, S. and Wollworth, S. (2000) In Pursuit of Teacher Community. Paper presented at the annual meeting of the American Educational Research Association, New Orleans.

Grundy, S. and Robinson, J. (2004) 'Teacher professional development: themes and trends in the recent Australian experience' in C. Day and J. Sachs (eds) *International Handbook on the Continuing Professional Development of Teachers.* Maidenhead: Open University Press.

Grzywacz, J.G. (2000) 'Work–family spill-over and health during midlife: is managing conflict everything?' *American Journal of Health Promotion,* 14 (4): 236–43.

Grzywacz, J. and Marks, N. (2000) 'Family, work, work-family spillover, and problem drinking during midlife'. *Journal of Marriage and Family,* 62 (2): 336–48.

Guardian (2003) *Workload Hits Teacher Morale.* (Report on GTC/Guardian/Mori Teacher Survey). 7 January: 8.

Guskey, T. and Huberman, A.M. (1995) *Professional Development in Education: New Paradigms and Practices.* New York, NY: Teachers College Press.

Haigh, G. (1995) 'To be handled with care'. *Times Educational Supplement,* February 10: 3–4.

Hall, B.W., Pearson, L.C. and Carroll, D. (1992) 'Teachers' long-range teaching plans: a discriminant analysis'. *Journal of Educational Research,* 85: 221–5.

Hallam, S. (2002) *Ability Grouping Practices and Consequences, NSIN Research Matters No. 16, Spring 2002.* London: National School Improvement Network, Institute of Education, University of London.

Hammersley, M. (1996) 'Post mortem or post modern? Some reflections on British sociology of education'. *British Journal of Educational Studies,* 44.

Hammersley, M. and Atkinson, P. (1983) *Ethnography: Principles in Practice.* London: Tavistock.

Hansen, D.T. (1995) *The Call to Teach*. New York, NY: Teachers College Press.

Hargreaves, A. (1993) 'Individualism and individuality: reinterpreting the teacher culture' in J.W. Little and M.W. McLaughlin (eds) *Teachers' Work: Individuals, colleagues, and contexts*, pp. 51–76. New York, NY: Teachers College Press.

Hargreaves, A. (1994) *Changing Teachers, Changing Times – Teachers' Work and Culture in the Postmodern Age*. London: Cassell.

Hargreaves, A. (1995) 'Realities of teaching' in L.W. Anderson (ed.) *International Encyclopaedia of Teaching and Teacher Education*, 2nd edn, pp. 80–7. Oxford: Pergamon.

Hargreaves, A. (1996) 'Revisiting voice'. *Educational Researcher*, (January/February): 1–8.

Hargreaves, A. (1997) 'Rethinking educational change' in A. Hargreaves (ed.) *Rethinking Educational Change with Heart and Mind*, The 1997 ASCD Yearbook. Alexandria, VA: Association for Supervision and Curriculum Development.

Hargreaves, A. (1998) 'The emotional practice of teaching'. *Teaching and Teacher Education*, 14 (8): 835–54.

Hargreaves, A. (1999) 'Series editor's forward' in S. Acker (ed.) *The Realities of Teachers' Work: Never a Dull Moment*. London: Cassell.

Hargreaves, A. (2000) 'Mixed emotions: teachers' perceptions of their interactions with students'. *Teaching and Teacher Education*, 16: 811–26.

Hargreaves, A. (2001) 'The emotional geographies of teaching'. *Teachers' College Record*, 103: 1056–80.

Hargreaves, A. (2003) *Teaching in the Knowledge Society: Education in the Age of Insecurity*. New York, NY: Teachers College Press.

Hargreaves, A. (2005) 'Educational change takes ages: life, career and generational factors in teachers' emotional responses to educational change'. *Teaching and Teacher Education*, 21: 967–83.

Hargreaves, A. and Fink, D. (2006) *Sustainable Leadership*. San Francisco, CA: Jossey-Bass.

Hargreaves, A. and Fullan, M. (eds) (1992) *Understanding Teacher Development*. London: Cassell.

Hargreaves, D.H. (1994) 'The new professionalism: the synthesis of professional and institutional development'. *Teaching and Teacher Education*, 10 (4): 423–38.

Harris, A. (2004) 'Distributed leadership and school improvement: leading or misleading?' *Educational Management and Administration*, 32 (1): 11–24.

Harris, A. (2005) 'Leading or misleading: distributed leadership and school improvement'. *Journal of Curriculum Studies*, 27 (3): 255–67.

Harris, A.L., Jamieson, I. and Russ, J. (1996) *School Effectiveness and School Improvement: A Practical Guide*. London: Pitman Publishing.

Hay McBer (2000) *Research into Teacher Effectiveness: A Model of Teacher Effectiveness*. London: DfEE.

Helsby, G. (1996) 'Defining and developing professionalism in English secondary schools'. *Journal of Education for Teaching: International Research and Pedagogy*, 22 (2): 135–48.

Helsby, G. (1999) *Changing Teachers' Work: The Reform of Secondary Schooling*. Milton Keynes: Open University Press.

Helsby, G., Knight, P., McCulloch, G., Saunders, M. and Warburton, T. (1997) Professionalism in Crisis. A report to participants on the professional cultures of teachers research project, Lancaster University, January.

Henderson, M. and Milstein, M. (2003) *Resiliency in Schools: Making it Happen for Students and Educators*. Thousand Oaks, CA: Corwin Press.

Hendry, R. (2005) Workplace remodeling in the public services: a union perspective. Paper presented at C-TRIP Seminar 6: What can be learnt from other professions? 19 October.

Higgins, C.A., Duxbury, L.E., and Irving, R.H. (1992) 'Work–family conflict in the dual-career family'. *Organizational Behavior and Human Decision Processes*, 51: 51–75.

Higgins, C., Duxbury, L. and Lee, C. (1994) 'Impact of life-cycle stage and gender on the ability to balance work and family responsibilities'. *Family Relations*, 43 (2): 144–50.

Hill, P.W. and Rowe, K.J. (1996) 'Multilevel modeling in school effectiveness research'. *School Effectiveness and School Improvement*, 7 (1): 1–34.

Hochschild, A. (1983) *The Managed Heart: Commercialisation of Human Feeling*. London: University of California Press.

Hodkinson, H. and Hodkinson, P. (2005) 'improving schooteachers' workplace learning'. *Research Papers in Education*, 20 (2): 109–31.

Howard, S., Dryden, J. and Johnson, B. (1999) 'Childhood resilience: review and critique of literature'. *Oxford Review of Education*, 25 (3): 307–23.

Hoy, A.W. and Spero, R.B. (2005) 'Changes in teacher efficacy during the early years of teaching: a comparison of four measures'. *Teaching and Teacher Education*, 21: 343–56.

Hoyle, E. (1974) 'Professionalility, professionalism and control in teaching'. *London Educational Review*, 3 (2): 15–7.

Huberman, M. (1989) 'The professional life cycle of teachers'. *Teachers College Record*, 91 (1): 31–57.

Huberman, M. (1993) *The Lives of Teachers*. London: Cassell.

Huberman, M. (1995) 'Networks that alter teaching'. *Teachers and Teaching: Theory and Practice*, 1 (2): 193–221.

Huberman, M. with Marie-Madeleine Grounauer and Jürg Marti (1993) *The Lives of Teachers*. London: Cassell.

Hughes, E.C. (1952) 'The sociological study of work: an editorial introduction'. *American Journal of Sociology*, 57: 423–6.

Huppert, F. and Bayliss, N. (2004) 'Well-Being: Towards and integration of psychology, neuro-biology and social science'. *Philosophical Transactions of the Royal Society B: Biological Sciences*, online 11 August.

Hutchinson, G.E. and Johnson, B. (1993) 'Teaching as a career: examining high school students' perspectives'. *Action In Teacher Education*, 15: 61–7.

Ingersoll, R.M. (2003) *Who Controls Teachers' Work?* Cambridge MA: Harvard University Press.

Ingvarson, L. and Greenway, P.A. (1984) 'Portrayals of teacher development'. *Australian Journal of Education*, 28 (1): 45–65.

Isen, A.M. (1990) 'The influence of positive and negative affect on cognitive organization: some implications for development' in N. Stein, B. Leventhal and

T. Trabasso (eds) *Psychological and Biological Approaches to Emotion*, pp.75–94. Hillsdale, NJ: Erlbaum.

Jackson, P.W., Boostrom R.E. and Hansen, D. (1993) *The Moral Life of the Schools*. San Francisco, CA: Jossey-Bass.

James, C., Connolly, M., Dunning, G. and Elliott, T. (2006) *How Very Effective Primary Schools Work*. London: Paul Chapman.

James-Wilson, S. (2001) The Influence of Ethnocultural Identity on Emotions and Teaching. Paper presented at the Annual Meeting of the American Educational Research Association, New Orleans, April 2000.

Jantzen, J.M. (1981) 'Why college students choose to teach: a longitudinal study'. *Journal of Teacher Education*, 32 (2): 45–7.

Jeffrey, B. and Woods, P. (1996) 'Feeling deprofessionalised'. *Cambridge Journal of Education*, 26 (3): 325–43.

Joyce, B. and Showers, B. (1991) *Information Processing Models of Teaching*. Aptos, CA: Booksend Laboratories.

Kelchtermans, G. (1996) 'Teacher vulnerability: understanding its moral and political roots'. *Cambridge Journal of Education*, 26 (3): 307–24.

Kelchtermans, G. (2005) 'Teachers' emotions in educational reforms: self-understanding, vulnerable commitment and micropolitical literacy'. *Teaching and Teacher Education*, 21 (8): 995–1006.

King, M.B. Newmann, F.M. (1999) 'School capacity as a goal for professional development: mapping the terrain in low income schools', annual meeting of AERA, Montreal.

Korthagen, F.A.J. and Wubbels, T. (1995) 'Characteristics of reflective practitioners: towards an operationalization of the concept'. *Teachers and Teaching: Theory and Practice*, 1 (1): 51–72.

Kushman, J.W. (1992) 'the organisational dynamics of teacher workplace commitment: a study of urban elementary and middle schools'. *Educational Administration Quarterly*, 28 (1): 5–42.

Kyriacou, C. (1987) 'Teacher stress and burnout: an international review'. *Educational Research*, 29: 146–52.

Kyriacou, C. (2000) *Stress Busting for Teachers*. Cheltenham: Stanley Thornes.

Kyriacou, C. and Roe, H. (1988) 'Teachers' perceptions of pupils' behaviour problems at a comprehensive school'. *British Educational Research Journal*, 14 (2): 167–73.

Kyriacou, C. and Sutcliffe, J. (1978) 'Teacher stress: prevalence, sources and symptoms'. *British Journal of Educational Psychology*, 48: 159–67.

Kyriakides, L. (2004) 'Differential school effectiveness in relation to sex and social class: some implications for policy evaluation'. *Educational Research and Evaluation*, 10 (2): 141–61.

Lasch, C. (1991) *True and Only Heaven: Progress and Its Critics*. New York, NY: Norton.

Lasky, S. (2000) 'The cultural and emotional politics of teacher–parent interactions'. *Teaching and Teacher Education*, 16: 843–60.

Lasky, S. (2004) Teacher professional vulnerability in a context of large-scale government mandated secondary school reform. Unpublished doctoral dissertation, Ontario Institute for Studies in Education, University of Toronto, Ontario.

Lasky, S. (2005) 'A sociocultural approach to understanding teacher identity, agency and professional vulnerability in a context of secondary school reform'. *Teaching and Teacher Education*, 21 (8): 899–916.

Lawlor, S. (ed.) (2004) *Comparing Standards: Teaching the Teachers*. Report of the Politeia Educational Commission. London: Politeia.

Lawton, D. (2005) *Education and Labour Party Ideologies 1900–2001 and Beyond*. Abingdon: Routledge Farmer.

LeCompte, M.D. and Dworkin, A.G. (1991) *Giving Up on School: Student Dropouts and Teacher Burnouts*. Newbury Park, CA: Corwin Press.

Leithwood, K. and Jantzi, D. (2005) A review of transformational school literature research 1996–2005. Paper presented at the annual meeting of the American Educational Research Association, Montreal, QC.

Leithwood, K. and Levin, B. (2004) *Approaches to the Evaluation of Leadership Programmes* and *Leadership Effects*. London: DfES.

Leithwood, K., Jantzi, D. and Mascall, B. (1999) *Large-scale Reform What Works?* First annual report: External evaluation of the UK national literacy and national numeracy strategy. Toronto: University of Toronto, OISE.

Leithwood, K., Day, C., Sammons, P., Harris, A. and Hopkins, D. (2006) *Successful School Leadership: What it is and how it influences pupil learning*. London: DfES.

Leithwood, K. and Riehl, C. (2005) 'What we know about successful school leadership' in W. Firestone and C. Riehl (eds) *A New Agenda: Directions for Research on Educational Leadership*. New York, NY: Teachers College Press.

Lieberman, A. (1996) 'Practices that support teacher development: transforming conceptions of professional learning' in M.W. McLaughlin and I. Oberman (eds) *Teacher Learning: New Policies, New Practices*. New York, NY: Teachers College Press.

Light, R.J. and Smith, P.V. (1971) 'Accumulating evidence and procedures for resolving contradictions among difference research studies'. *Harvard Educational Review*, 41: 429–71.

Lightfoot, S.L. (1983) 'The lives of teachers' in L.S. Shulman and G. Sykes (eds) *Handbook of Teaching and Policy*, pp. 241–60. New York, NY: Longman.

Little, J.W. (1986) 'Seductive images and organizational realities on professional development' in A. Lieberman (ed.) *Rethinking school improvement*. New York, NY: Teachers College Press.

Lortie, D. (1975) *School Teacher: A Sociological Study*. Chicago, IL: University of Chicago Press.

Louis, K.S. (1998) 'Effects of teacher quality worklife in secondary schools on commitment and sense of efficacy'. *School Effectiveness and School Improvement*, 9 (1): 1–27.

Louis, K. and Kruse, S. (1995) *Professionalism and Community: Perspectives from Urban Schools*. Thousand Oaks, CA: Corwin Press.

Louis, K. and Miles, M. (1991) 'Managing reform: lessons from urban high schools'. *School Effectiveness and School Improvement*, 2 (2): 75–96.

Lupton, R. (2005) 'Social justice and school improvement: improving the quality of schooling in the poorest neighbourhoods'. *British Educational Research Journal*, 31 (5): 589–604.

Luthar, S. (1996) Resilience: A construct of value? Paper presented at the 104th Annual Convention of the American Psychological Association, Toronto.

Luthar, S., Cicchetti, D. and Becker, B. (2000) 'The construct of resilience: a critical evaluation and guidelines for future work'. *Child Development*, 71 (3): 543–62.

Luyten, H. (1995) 'Teacher change and instability across grades'. *Educational Research and Evaluation*, 1 (1): 67–89.

Luyten, H. and Snijders, T. (1996) 'School effects and teacher effects in Dutch elementary education'. *Educational Research and Evaluation*, 2 (1): 1–24.

MacBeath, J. and Galton, M. with Susan Steward, Charlotte Page and Janet Edwards (2004) *A Life in Secondary Teaching: Finding Time for Learning*. Report for National Union of Teachers. Cambridge: Cambridge Printing.

Maclean, R. (1992) *Teachers' Careers and Promotional Patterns: A Sociological Analysis*. London: Falmer Press.

MacLure, M. (1993) 'Arguing for your self: identity as an organising principle in teachers' jobs and lives'. *British Educational Research Journal*, 19 (4): 311–22.

Marks, M.B. and Louis, K.S. (1999) 'Teacher empowerment and the capacity for organizational learning'. *Educational Administration Quarterly*, 35 (special issue): 707–50.

Matthews, P. and Sammons, P. (2004) *Improvement Through Inspection: An Evaluation of the Impact of Ofsted's Work*. London: Ofsted, Institute of Education, London. http://www.oftsed.gov.uk/publications/index.cfm?fuseaction=pubs. displayfil eandid =3696andtype=pdf.

Matthews, P. and Sammons, P. (2005) 'Survival of the weakest: the differential improvement of schools causing concern in England'. *London Review of Education*, 3 (2): 159–76.

McAdams, P. (1993) *The Stories We Live By: Personal Myths and the Making of the Self*. New York, NY: Guildford Press.

McKinney, M., Sexton, T. and Meyerson, M.J. (1999) 'Validating the efficacy-based change model'. *Teaching and Teacher Education*, 15 (5): 471–85.

McLaughlin, M. (2001) 'Sites and sources of teacher learning' in C. Sugrue and C. Day (eds) *Developing Teachers and Teaching: International Research Perspectives*. London: Falmer Press.

McLaughlin, M. and Talbert. J.E. (2006) *Professional Communities and the Work of High School Teaching*. Chicago, IL: University of Chicago Press.

McLaughlin, M.W. and Talbert, J.E. (2006) *Building School-Based Teacher Learning Communities: Professional Strategies to Improve Student Achievement*. New York, NY: Teachers College Press.

McNess, E., Broadfoot, P. and Osborn, M. (2003) 'Is the effective compromising the affective?' *British Educational Research Journal*, 29 (2): 243–57.

McPherson, A. (1992) Measuring value added in schools: National commission on education, briefing 1, February. London: National Commission on Education.

Mearns, D. and MacBeath, J. (1983) 'More stress: less escape'. *Times Educational Supplement Scotland*, April 1.

Meijer, C. and Foster, S. (1988) 'The effect of teacher self-efficacy on referral chance'. *Journal of Special Education*, 22: 378–85.

Merrow, J. (1999) 'The teacher shortage: wrong diagnosis, phony cures'. *Education Week*, 38: 64.

Miller, L. (1999) 'Reframing teacher burnout in the context of school reform and teacher development in the United States' in R. Vandenberghe and A.M. Huberman (eds) *Understanding and Preventing Teacher Burnout a Sourcebook of International Research and Practice*. Cambridge: Cambridge University Press.

Moore, W. and Esselman, M. (1992) Teacher efficacy, power, school climate and achievement: a desegregating district's experience, paper presented at American Educational Research Association conference, San Francisco, April.

Moore Johnson, S. (2004) *Finders Keepers: Helping New Teachers Survive and Thrive in our Schools*. San Francisco, CA: Jossey-Bass.

Mortimore, P. and Watkins, C. (1999) *Understanding Pedagogy and its Impact on Learning*. London: Paul Chapman Publishing.

Mortimore, P., Sammons, P., Stoll, L., Lewis, D. and Ecob, R. (1988) *School Matters: The Junior Years*. Somerset: Open Books Publishing.

Muijs, D. and Reynolds, D. (2005) *Effective Teaching: Evidence and Practice*. London: Sage.

Muijs, D., Harris, A., Chapman, C., Stoll, L. and Russ, J. (2004) 'Improving schools in socio-economically disadvantaged areas: an overview of research'. *School Effectiveness and School Improvement*, 15 (2): 149–75.

Mujtaba, T. (2005) Questionnaire analyses: initial survey and VITAE teachers. Unpublished VITAE report.

Mulford, W., Silins, H. and Leithwood, K. (2005) *Educational Leadership for Organisational Learning and Improved Student Outcomes*. Dordrecht: Kluwer Academic Publishers.

Munroe, N. (1997) 'Radical Surgery'. *Times Educational Supplement for Scotland*, 3 October: 5–14.

Murname, R.J., Singer, J.D., Willett, J.B., Kemple, J.J. and Olsen, R.J. (1991) *Who Will Teach?* Cambridge, MA: Harvard University Press.

Myers, J. (2004) 'Using technology tools to support learning in the English language arts'. *Contemporary Issues in Technology and Teacher Education* (Online serial), 3 (4): http://www.citejournal.org/vol3/iss4/general/article2.cfm.

Nash, P. (2005) Change and challenge. Speech to London Well-Being Conference, British Library, April 21: http://www.teachersupport.info/upload/Teacher-Support/documents/Speechtowellbeingconference_210405.pdf (accessed July 15 2006).

NASUWT (2002) Measures to improve pupils, a response to the Secretary of State, 12 December. Birmingham.

National Partnership for Excellence and Accountability in Teaching (NPEAT) (1998). *Improving Professional Development: 8 Research-based Principles*. Washington, DC: Author.

National Partnership for Teaching in At-Risk Schools (2005) *Qualified Teachers for At-Risk Schools: A National Imperative*. Washington, DC: National Partnership for Teaching in At Risk Schools.

National Union of Teachers (2001) *Unacceptable Pupil Behaviour*. London: NUT.

Neugarten, B.L. (1973) 'Personality change in late life: A developmental perspective' in C. Eisdorfer and M.P. Lawton (eds) *The Psychology of Adult Development and Aging*, pp. 311–35. Washington DC: American Psychological Association.

Nias, J. (1981) 'Commitment and motivation in primary school teachers'. *Educational Review*, 33 (3): 181–90.

Nias, J. (1989) *Primary Teachers Talking: A Study of Teaching as Work*. London: Routledge.

Nias, J. (1996) 'Thinking about feeling: the emotions in teaching'. *Cambridge Journal of Education*, 26 (3): 293–306.

Nias, J. (1998) 'Why teachers need their colleagues: a developmental perspective' in A. Hargreaves, A. Leiberman, M. Fullan and D. Hopkins (eds) *International Handbook of Educational Change*, pp. 1257–71. Dordrecht: Kluwer.

Nias, J. (1999) 'Teachers' moral purposes: stress, vulnerability, and strength' in R. Vandenberghe and A.M. Huberman (eds) *Understanding and Preventing Teacher Burnout: A Sourcebook of International Research and Practice*, pp. 223–37. Cambridge: Cambridge University Press.

Nieto, S. (2003) *What Keeps Teachers Going?* New York, NY: Teachers College Press.

Nieto, S. (2005) 'Qualities of caring and committed teachers' in S. Nieto (ed.) *Why We Teach*, pp. 203–20. New York, NY: Teachers College Press.

OECD (2004) *Learning for Tomorrow's World: First results from PISA 2003*. Paris: OECD.

OECD (2005) *Teachers Matter: Attracting, Developing and Retaining Effective Teachers*. Paris: OECD.

Ofsted (2004) *Standard and Quality 2002/03*, annual report of Her Majesty's Chief Inspector of Schools. London: Ofsted.

Osborn, M. (1995) Not a seamless robe: a tale of two teachers' responses to policy change. Paper presented at the European Conference on Educational Research, Bath, September.

Osborn, M. (1996) Book review, *The Highs and Lows of Teaching: 60 Years of Research Revisited. Cambridge Journal of Education*, 26: 455–61.

Osborn, M. and Broadfoot, P. (1992) 'The impact of current changes in english primary schools on teacher professionalism'. *Teachers' College Record*, 94 (1): 138–51.

Osborn, M., Abbot, D., Broadfoot, P., Croll, P. and Pollard, A. (1996) 'Teachers' professional perspectives: continuity and change' in R. Chawla-Duggan and C.J. Pole (eds) *Reshaping Education in the 1990s: Perspectives on Primary Schooling*. London: Falmer Press.

Oswald, M., Johnson, B. and Howard, S. (2003) 'Quantifying and evaluating resilience-promoting factors – teachers' beliefs and perceived roles'. *Research in Education*, 70: 50–64.

Ozga, J. (1995) 'Deskilling a profession: professionalism, deprofessionalization and the new managerialism' in H. Busher and R. Saran (eds) *Managing Teachers as Professionals in Schools*. London: Kogan Page.

Palmer, P.J. (1998) *The Courage To Teach: Exploring the Inner Landscapes of a Teacher's Life*. San Francisco, CA: Jossey Bass.

Parkay, F.W., Greenwood, G., Olejnik, S. and Proller, N. (1988) 'A study of the relationship among teacher efficacy, locus of control, and stress'. *Journal of Research and Development in Education*, 21 (4): 13–22.

Parsons, C. (1996) *Education, Exclusion and Citizenship*. London: Routledge.

Parsons, S. and Bynner, J. (1998) *Influences on Adult Basic Skills Factors Affecting the Development of Literacy and Numeracy from Birth to 37*. London: The Basic Skills Unit.

Pavalko, R.M. (1971) *Sociology of Occupations and Professions*. Itasia, IL: F.E. Peacock.

Pence, A.R. (ed.) (1998) *Ecological Research with Children and Families: From Concepts to Methodology*. New York, NY: Teachers' College Press.

Perrott, E. (1982) *Effective Teaching*. London: Longman.

Pollard, A. (1985) *The Social World of the Primary School*. London: Holt, Reinhart and Winston.

Pollard, A. (ed.) (1994) *Look Before You Leap? Research Evidence for the Curriculum at Key Stage 2*. London: Tyrell Press.

Pollard, A., Broadfoot, P., Croll, P., Osborn, M. and Abbott, D. (1994) *Changing English Primary Schools? The Impact of the Education Reform Act at Key Stage One*. London: Cassell.

PriceWaterhouseCoopers (2001) *Teacher Workload Study*. London: DfES.

Prick, L. (1986) *Career Development and Satisfaction Among Secondary School Teachers*. Amsterdam: Vrije Universiteit, Amsterdam.

Prick, L. (1989) 'Satisfaction and stress among teachers'. *International Journal of Educational Research*, 13: 363–77.

Pulkkinen, M-L. and Aaltonen, J. (2003) 'Sense of agency in narrative processes of repeateadly convicted drunk drivers'. *Counselling Psychology Quarterly*, 16 (2): 145–59.

Reid, I., Brain, K. and Boyes, L.C. (2004) 'Teachers or learning leaders? Where have all the teachers gone? Gone to be leaders, everyone'. *Educational Studies*, 30 (3): 251–64.

Revell, P. (2005) *The Professionals: Better Teachers, Better Schools*. Stoke on Trent: Trentham Books.

Reyes, P. (1990) 'Organisational commitment of teachers' in P. Reyes (ed.) *Teachers and Their Workplace*, pp. 143–63. Newbury Park, CA: Sage.

Reynolds, A. (1995) 'The knowledge base for beginning teachers: education professionals' expectation versus research findings on learning to teach'. *Elementary School Journal*, 95 (3): 199–221.

Rich, Y. (1993) 'Stability and change in teacher expertise' *Teaching and Teacher Education*, 9 (2): 137–46.

Richardson, G.E., Neiger, B.L., Jenson, S. and Kumpfer, K.L. (1990) 'The resiliency model'. *Health Education*, 21 (6): 33–9.

Riehl, C. and Sipple, J.W. (1996) 'Making the most of time taken and talent. Secondary school organisational climates, teaching tasks environments, and teacher commitment'. *American Educational Research Journal*, 33 (4): 873–901.

Rippon, J.H. (2005) 'Re-defining careers in education'. *Career Development International*, 10 (4): 275–92.

Ritzer, G. (1972) *Man and His Work: Conflict and Change*. New York, NY: Appleton-Century-Crofts.

Roberts, L. (2005) Racialized identities in Initial Teacher Training. Paper presented at C-TRIP Seminar 2: Professional identities and teacher careers, 15 March.

Rogers, C. (1969) *Freedom to Learn*. Columbus, OH: Charles E. Merrill Publishing Company.

Rosenholtz, S.J. (1989) *Teachers Workplace. The Social Organization of Schools.* New York, NY: Longman.

Ross, J.A. (1992) 'Teacher efficacy and the effect of coaching on student achievement'. *Canadian Journal of Education*, 17 (1): 51–65.

Rudduck, J., Day, J. and Wallace, G. (1997) 'Students' perspectives on school improvement' in A. Hargreaves (ed.) *Rethinking Educational Change with Heart and Mind*, 1997 ASCD Yearbook, pp. 73–91. Alexandria, Virginia: ASCD.

Rudow, B. (1999) 'Stress and burnout in the teaching professional: European studies, issues, and research perspectives' in R. Vandenberge and A.M. Huberman (eds) *Understanding and preventing teacher burnout: A sourcebook of international research and practice*, pp. 38–58. New York, NY: Cambridge University Press.

Russell, J. (1996) *Agency – Its Role in Mental Development*. Hove: Erlbaum (UK) Taylor and Francis.

Rutter, M. (1990) 'Psychosocial resilience and protective mechanisms' in J. Rolf, A. Masten, D. Cicchetti, K. Neuchterlein and S. Weintraub (eds) *Risk and Protective Factors in the Development of Psychopathology*. New York, NY: Cambridge University Press.

Rutter, M., Maughan, B., Mortimer, P. and Ousten, J. (1979) *Fifteen-thousand Hours: Secondary Schools and their Effects on Children*. Cambridge, MA: Harvard University Press.

Sachs, J. (2003) 'The activist professional'. *Journal of Educational Change*, 1: 77–95.

Sammons, P. (1996) 'Complexities in the judgement of school effectiveness'. *Educational Research and Evaluation*, 2: 113–49.

Sammons, P. (1998) Applying value added methods to investigate children's attainment and development over four years. Paper presented at the International Congress for School Effectiveness and Improvement. University of Manchester, UK, January.

Sammons, P. and Smees, R. (1998) 'Measuring pupil progress at Key Stage 1: using baseline assessment to investigate value added'. *School Leadership and Management*, 18 (3): 389–407.

Sammons, P., Thomas, S. and Mortimore, P. (1997a) *Forging Links: Effective Schools and Effective Departments*. London: Paul Chapman.

Sammons, P., West, A. and Hind, A. (1997b) 'Accounting for variations in pupil attainment at the end of Key Stage 1'. *British Educational Research Journal*, 23: 489–511.

Sammons, P., Elliot, K., Welcomme, W., Taggart, B. and Levacic, R. (2004) 'England a country report' in H. Dobert, K. Eckhard and W. Sroka (eds) *Conditions of School Performance in Seven Countries: A Quest for Understanding the International Variation of PISA Results*. Munster: Waxmann.

Sammons, P., Siraj-Blatchford, I., Sylva, K., Melhuish, E., Taggart, B. and Elliot, K. (2005) 'Investigating the effects of pre-school provision: using mixed methods in the EPPE research'. *International Journal of Social Research Methodology*, 8 (3): 207–24.

Sammons, P., Matthews, P., Day, C. and Gu, Q. (2006) 'Exploring the impact of aspects of the London Leadership Strategy'. *Journal of Education for Students Placed at Risk*, forthcoming.

Sandholtz, J. (2000) 'Interdisciplinary team teaching as a form of professional development'. *Teacher Education Quarterly*, 27 (3): 39–54.

Schneewind, K.A. (1995) 'Impact of family processes on control beliefs' in A. Bandura (ed.) *Self-Efficacy in Changing Societies*. Cambridge: Cambridge University Press.

Schön, D. (1987) *Educating the Reflective Practitioner*. San Francisco, CA: Jossey-Bass.

School Teachers' Review Body (2005) Fifteenth Report – 2005. Presented to Parliament by the Prime Minister and the Secretary of State For Education and Skills by Command of Her Majesty, November.

Schools Health Education Unit (2004) *Young People in 2004*. Exeter: author.

Seligman, M. (2002) *Authentic Happiness*. New York, NY: Free Press.

Sharp, S. and Croxford, L. (2003) 'Literacy in the first year of schooling: a multilevel analysis'. *School Effectiveness and School Improvement*, 14 (2): 213–31.

Shaw, I., Newton, D.P., Aitkin, M. and Darnell, R. (2003) 'Do Ofsted inspections of secondary schools make a difference to GCSE results?' *British Educational Research Journal*, 29 (1): 63–75.

Shulman, L.S. (1986) 'Those who understand: knowledge growth in teaching'. *Educational Researcher*, 15 (2): 4–14.

Sikes, P., Measor, L. and Woods, P. (1985) *Teacher Careers: Crises and Continuities*. London: Falmer Press.

Sleegers, P. and Kelchtermans, G. (1999) 'Inleiding op het themanummer: professionele identiteit van leraren (Professional identity of teachers)'. *Pedagogish Tijdschrift*, 24: 369–74.

Smith, F., Hardman, F., Wall, K. and Mroz, M. (2004) 'Interactive whole class teaching in the National Literacy and Numeracy Strategies'. *British Educational Research Journal*, 39 (3): 395–411.

Smithers, A. and Robinson, P. (2003) *Factors Affecting Teachers' Decisions to Leave the Profession*. Research Report, RR430. London: DfES.

Smithers, A. and Robinson, P. (2005) *Teacher Turnover, Wastage and Movements between Schools*. Research Report No. 640. London: DfES.

Smylie, M. (1999) 'Teacher stress in a time of reform' in R. Vandenberghe and A.M. Huberman (eds) *Understanding and Preventing Teacher Burnout a Sourcebook of International Research and Practice*. Cambridge: Cambridge University Press.

Smylie, M.A. (1988) 'The enhancement function of staff development: organizational and psychological antecedents to individual teacher change'. *American Educational Research Journal*, 25 (1): 1–30.

Sockett, H. (1993) *The Moral Base for Teacher Professionalism*. New York, NY: Columbia University, Teachers College Press.

Spillane, J.P. (2006) *Distributed Leadership*. San Francisco, CA: Jossey-Bass.

Spillane, J., Halverson, R. and Diamond, J. (2001) Towards a theory of leadership practice: a distributed perspective. Northwestern University, Institute for Policy Research Working Article.

Sternberg, R.J. and Horvath, J.A. (1995) 'A prototype view of expert teaching'. *Educational Researcher*, 24: 9–17.

Stobart, G. and Stoll, L. (2005) The Key Stage 3 Strategy: what kind of reform is this? *Cambridge Journal of Education*, 35 (2): 225–38.

Stokes, L. (2001) 'Lessons from an inquiring School: forms of inquiry and conditions for teacher learning' in A. Lieberman (ed.) *Teachers Caught in the Action: Professional Development that Matters*. New York, NY: Teachers College Press.

Stoll, L. and Fink, D. (1996) *Changing Our Schools: Linking School Effectiveness and School Improvement*. Buckingham: Open University Press.

Stoll, L., Fink, D. and Earl, L. (2003). *It's About Learning (And It's about Time): What's in it for Schools?* London: Routledge Falmer.

Strand, S. (1997) 'Pupil progress during Key Stage 1: a value added analysis of school effects'. *British Education Research Journal*, 23: 471–87.

Strand, S. (1999) 'Pupil background and baseline assessment results at age 4'. *Journal of Research in Reading*, 22: 14–26.

Strand, S. (2000) Pupil mobility, attainment and progress during key stage 1: a case study in caution. Paper presented at the British Educational Research Association Annual Conference, Cardiff University, September 7–10 (available on www.leedsac.uk/educol/documents/00001484.htm).

Strand, S. (2002) 'Pupil mobility, attainment and progress during Key Stage 1: a study in cautious interpretation'. *British Educational Research Journal*, 28 (1): 63–78.

Strauss, A. and Corbin, J. (1998) *Basics of Qualitative Research, Techniques and Procedures for Developing Grounded Theory*, 2nd edn. Thousand Oaks, CA: Sage.

Sturman, L. (2002) *Contented and Committed? A Survey of Quality of Working Life Amongst Teachers*. Slough: NFER.

Sugrue, C. (1997) *Complexities of Teaching: Child-centred Perspectives*. London: Falmer Press.

Suh, E., Diener, E. and Fujita, F. (1996) 'Events and subjective well-being: only recent events matter'. *Journal of Personality and Social Psychology*, 70 (5): 1091–102.

Sukhanandan, L. and Lee, B. (1998) *Streaming, Setting and Grouping by Ability: A Review of the Literature*. www.nfer.ac.uk/pubs/streaming2/html.

Sumsion, J. (2002) 'Becoming, being and unbecoming an early childhood educator: a phenomenological case study of teacher attrition'. *Teaching and Teacher Education*, 18: 869–85.

Talbert, J. (1995) 'Boundaries of teachers' professional communities in US high schools: power and precariousness of the subject department' in L. Siskin and J. Warren-Little (eds) *The Subjects Question: Departmental Organization in the High School*. New York, NY: Teachers College Press.

Talbert, J.E. and McLaughlin, M.W. (1996) 'Teacher professionalism in local school contexts' in I.F. Goodson and A. Hargreaves (eds) *Teachers' Professional Lives*. Washington, DC: Falmer Press.

Tashakkori, A. and Teddlie, C. (1998) *Mixed Methodology: Combining Qualitative and Quantitative Approaches*. Thousand Oaks, CA: Sage.

Tashakkori, A. and Teddlie, C. (eds) (2003) *Handbook of Mixed Methods in Social and Behavioral Research*. Thousand Oaks, CA: Sage.

Teddlie, C. (1994) 'integrating classroom and school data in school effectiveness research' in D. Reynolds, B. Creemers, P. Nesselrodt, E. Schaffer, S. Stringfield and C. Teddlie, *Advances in School Effectiveness Research Practice*. Oxford: Pergamon.

Teddlie, C. and Stringfield, S. (1993) *Schools Make a Difference: Lessons Learned from a 10 year Study of School Effects*. New York, NY: Teachers College Press.

Tedesco, J.C. (1997) *The New Educational Pact: Education, Competitiveness and Citizenship in Modern Society*. Paris: UNESCO

Thrupp, M. (2003) 'The school leadership literature in managerialist times: exploring the problem of textual apologism'. *School Leadership and Management*, 23 (2): 149–72.

Travers, C.J and Cooper, C.L. (1996) *Teachers Under Pressure: Stress in the Teaching Profession*. London: Routledge.

Troman, G. (1996) 'The rise of the new professionals? The restructuring of primary teachers work and professionalism'. *British Journal of Sociology of Education*, 17 (4): 473–87.

Troman, G. and Woods, P. (2001) *Primary Teachers' Stress*. London: Routledge.

Tschannen-Moran, M., Woolfolk Hoy, A. and Hoy, W. K. (1998) 'Teacher efficacy: its meaning and measure'. *Review of Educational Research*, 68: 202–48.

Tsui, K.T. and Cheng, Y.C. (1999) 'School organisational health and teacher commitment: a contingency study with multi-level analysis'. *Educational Research and Evaluation*, 5 (3): 249–65.

Tymms, P. (2004) 'Are standards rising in English primary schools?' *British Educational Research Journal*, 30 (4): 477–94.

Tyree, A.K. (1996) 'Conceptualising and measuring commitment to high school teaching'. *Journal of Educational Research*, 89 (5): 295–304.

UNESCO (2006) *Teachers and Educational Quality: Monitoring Global Needs for 2015*. Paris: UNESCO.

Van Den Berg, R. (2002) 'Teacher's meanings regarding educational practice'. *Review of Educational Research*, 72 (4): 577–625.

Vandenberghe, R. and Huberman, M. (1999) *Understanding and Preventing Teacher Burnout: A Sourcebook of International Research and Practice*. Cambridge: Cambridge University Press.

Walberg, H.J. (1986) 'Synthesis of research on teaching' in M.C. Wittrock (ed.) *Handbook on Research on Teaching*, 3rd edn., pp. 214–29.

Walberg, H.J. (1991) 'Productive teaching and instruction: assessing the knowledge base' in H.C. Waxman H.J. and Walberg (eds) *Effective Teaching: Current Research*. Berkeley, CA: McCutchan.

Walford, G. (2005) 'Introduction: education and the Labour Government'. *Oxford Review of Education*, 31 (1): 3–9.

Wallace, M. (2005) Towards effective management of a reformed teaching profession. Paper presented at C-TRIP Seminar 4: Enactments of professionalism: classrooms and pedagogies, 5 July.

Waller, M. (2001) 'Resilience in ecosystemic context: evolution of the concept'. *American Journal of Orthopsychiatry*, 7(3): 290–7.

Walsh, F. (1998) *Strengthening Family Resilience*. New York, NY: Guildford Press.

Wang, M.C., Haertel, G. and Walberg, H.J. (1993) 'Synthesis of research: what helps students learn?' *Educational Leadership*, 51 (4): 74–9.

Warren-Little, J. (1981) The power of organizational setting: school norms and staff development. Paper presented at the American Educational Research Association, Los Angeles.

Warren-Little, J. (1993) *Teachers Professional Development in a Climate of Reform*, NCREST Reprint Series, New York, NY: Teachers College, Columbia University.

Warren-Little, J. (1999) Teachers' professional development in a context of high school reform: findings from a three year study of restructuring schools. Paper presented at the American Educational Research Association, Montreal, Canada.

Warren-Little, J. (2001) Locating learning in teachers' communities of practice. Keynote lecture presented at the Biennial Conference of the International Study Association of Teachers and Teaching, Lisbon, Portugal, September.

Watts, H. (1981) 'Can you feed a frog on tadpole Food?' *Insight, Journal of the National Conference of Teachers' Centres Leaders*, 4 (2): 32–40.

Weiner, L., Swearingen, J., Pagano, A. and Obi, R. (1993) Choosing teaching as a career. Comparing motivations of Harvard and urban college students. Paper presented to the Conference of the Eastern Education Research Association, Clearwater, Florida.

Welch, K.E. (1987) 'A critique of classical rhetoric: the contemporary appropriation of ancient discourse'. *Rhetoric Review*, 6 (1): 79–86.

Werner, E. (1990) 'Protective factors and individual resilience' in S.J. Meisels and J. Shonkoff (eds) *Handbook of Early Childhood Intervention*, pp. 97–116. New York, NY: Cambridge University Press.

Westheimer, J. (1998) *Among School Teachers: Learning, Meaning and Identity*. Cambridge: Cambridge University Press.

Whitty, G. (2002) *Making Sense of Education Policy*. London: Paul Chapman.

Wittrock, M.C. (ed.) (1986) *Handbook of Research on Teaching*, 3rd edn. New York, NY: Macmillan.

Witziers, B., Sleegers, P. and Imants, J. (1999) 'Departments as teams: functioning, variations and alternatives'. *School Leadership and Management*, 19 (3): 293–304.

Wong, R. (1994) 'Eye on politics: the four ugly lies about immigrants'. *Asian Week* (Stamford, Conn.: Ethnic NewsWatch, SoftLine Information Inc., February 11 1994).

Woods, P. (1978) 'Negotiating the demands of schoolwork'. *Curriculum Studies*, 10 (4): pp. 309–27.

Woods, P. (1993) Adaptation and Self-Determination in English Primary Schools. Paper presented at Symposium on Teaching, Curriculum and Educational Research, St Patrick's College, Dublin, September.

Woods, P. (1995) *Creative Teachers in Primary Schools*. Buckingham: Open University Press.

Woods, P. (1999) 'Intensification and stress in teaching' in R. Vandenberghe and A.M. Huberman (eds) *Understanding and Preventing Teacher Burnout: A Sourcebook of International Research and Practice*, pp. 115–38. Cambridge: Cambridge University Press.

Woods, P. (2001) 'Teaching and learning in the new millennium' in C. Sugrue (ed.) *Developing Teachers and Teaching Practice: International Research Perspectives*. London: Falmer Press.

Woods, P. and Jeffrey, B. (1996) *Teachable Moments: The Art of Teaching in Primary Schools*. Buckingham: Open University Press.

Woods, P., Jeffery, B. and Troman, G. (1997) *Restructuring Schools, Reconstructing Teachers*. Buckingham: Open University Press.

Woolfolk, A.E., Rosoff, B. and Hoy, W.K. (1990) 'Teachers' sense of efficacy and their beliefs about managing students'. *Teaching and Teacher Education*, 6: 137–48.

Wragg, E.C. (1984) 'Conducting and analysing interviews' in J. Bell, T. Bush, A.L. Fox, J. Goodey and S. Goulding (eds) *Conducting Small-Scale Investigations in Educational Management*, pp. 177–9. London: Harper and Row.

Zehm, S. and Kottler, J.A. (1993) *On Being a Teacher: the Human Dimension*. Thousand Oaks, CA: Corwin Press.

Zembylas, M. (2003) 'Emotions and teacher identity: a poststructual perspective' *Teachers and Teaching: Theory and Practice*, 9 (3): 213–38.

Zimpher, N. (1989) 'The RATE project: a profile of teacher education students' *Journal of Teacher Education*, 40 (6): 27–30.

Index

TEACHERS AND ASSISTANTS WORKING TOGETHER

Karen Vincett, Hilary Cremin and Gary Thomas

Essex County Council Special Educational Needs and Psychology Service; University of Leicester, University of Birmingham, UK

> Few areas of education can equal the growth rate of that for teaching assistants over the past seven years, doubling to more than 133,000 in England between 1997 to 2004. TAs are vital in the development of inclusive education, yet their status, pay, conditions, qualifications and their relationship with classroom teachers are all of deep concern in the majority of cases. This excellent, practical book is a welcome and much-needed authoritative study of the allimportant relationship between TA and teacher.
>
> Mark Vaughan OBE, Founder and Co-Director,
Centre for Studies on Inclusive Education

This book is for teachers and teaching assistants seeking to improve the ways in which they work together to meet the needs of children in their classes. It outlines the thinking behind the employment of teaching assistants in the classroom and spells out some of the teamworking opportunities and problems that can arise. Drawing on original research, it explores ways in which teachers and teaching assistants can work together to support children's learning and examines different models of working together.

This unique book provides:

- Highly effective models for working together, tried and tested in schools
- A practical section with activities, hand-outs and resources that teachers can use to develop these models in their own schools

This is a key text for classroom teachers, teaching assistants, trainee teachers and post-graduate education students, and those studying for foundation degrees for teaching assistants. It is also of use to parents, headteachers, educational psychologists, and other support personnel.

Contents

Preface – Acknowledgements – Part 1: Theory, Research and Practice on Teamwork in Classrooms – Introduction – The rise of the teaching assistant – Teacher-TA partnership working – Meeting children's needs – reflective practice, reflective teamwork – Three models of teamwork in classrooms – Action research into the models – phase 1 – Themes from using the models in practice – phase 1 – Action research into the models Phase 2 – 'Working Together' – Part 2: Implementation in Schools – Introduction – Using the models – CPD activities – A Toolkit for classroom research – References – Index

June 2005   192pp   0 335 21695 1 (Paperback)   0 335 21696 X (Hardback)